CW00391983

BALTHAS
A GUIDE FOR THE

BALTHASAR:
A GUIDE FOR THE PERPLEXED

RODNEY A. HOWSARE

t&t clark

Published by T&T Clark International
A Continuum Imprint

The Tower Building   80 Maiden Lane
11 York Road   Suite 704
London   New York
SE1 7NX   NY 10038

www.continuumbooks.com

British Library Cataloguing-in-Publication Data
A catalogue record for this book is available from the British Library

ISBN: 978-0-567-03198-3 (Hardback)
        978-0-567-03199-0 (Paperback)

Typeset by Newgen Imaging Systems Pvt Ltd, Chennai, India
Printed and bound in Great Britain by CPI Antony Rowe, Chippenham,
Wiltshire

CONTENTS

ACKNOWLEDGMENTS

No book is possible without the collaboration, friendship and work of a lot of people. While not blaming them for any of the shortcomings in what follows, I would like to thank the following people. First, I wish to thank my wife Kelly, the English teacher, for reading the manuscript and making numerous points about style, grammar, grace and clarity. I also want to thank her for putting up with the work schedule that this book required, especially over the summer of 2008, when I would normally have been offering more help around the house. I wish also to thank DeSales University for the sabbatical granted during the spring of 2008. A great deal of the work for this book was accomplished during that semester. I would also, then, like to thank my colleagues in the philosophy and theology department at DeSales, especially Maura Hearden for reading the manuscript and correcting all sorts of problems, and Larry Chapp for his theological collaboration over all these years. He is largely responsible for the section on traditional Thomism in the last chapter. Finally, I would like to thank the folk at T&T Clark, especially Thomas Kraft, first, for suggesting the project to me and, then, for his patience during the writing of it. I would like to dedicate this book to my parents, for first introducing me to the God who is love.

ABBREVIATIONS

WORKS BY HANS URS VON BALTHASAR

ET (I–IV)	*Explorations in Theology*, vols I–IV
GL (I–VII)	*The Glory of the Lord: A Theological Aesthetics*, vols I–VII
KB	*The Theology of Karl Barth*
MW	*My Work in Retrospect*
TD (I–V)	*Theo-Drama: Theological Dramatic Theory*, vols I–V
TL (I–III)	*Theologic*, vols I–III

INTRODUCTION

Perhaps no thinker is more suited to a "Guide for the Perplexed" than Hans Urs von Balthasar, for a number of reasons. First, he makes enormous demands on his reader, both in terms of the density of his arguments and in terms of what he expects them already to know. Next, he is in so many ways out of keeping with the standard theology found in universities these days that it is hard for the reader to know where to situate his thought. He certainly cannot be fitted into the worn out categories of "conservative" or "liberal," but he doesn't even fit easily into the standard "schools" that one hears so much about these days: "postliberalism," "postmetaphysical," "Radical Orthodoxy", etc. Finally, he wrote a lot. Without even going into the literally hundreds of articles and books, the student who sits before his masterwork, the famous trilogy of theological aesthetics, dramatics and logic, must feel a bit overwhelmed. "Where do I even begin?!"

In what follows, then, I have tried to address, at least in part, all three of these perplexing aspects of Balthasar's thought. Rather than try to offer a systematic overview of his theology, I have, instead, tried to get to the heart of his theological approach. The book has essentially two parts: the first three chapters introduce the reader to the man and his method. The next three chapters introduce the reader to central aspects of Balthasar's theology proper, with a nod to each part of the trilogy. A final chapter, then, offers a conclusion and suggestions about Balthasar's role in theology today. In short, there is no way to understand Balthasar without getting to the knotty center of his thought, especially in terms of the analogy of being, Christology and the doctrine of the Trinity. By focusing on those elements, I hope this book will aid the reader who has been daunted by the perplexing nature of this giant of twentieth-century theology.

CHAPTER ONE

BALTHASAR: THE MAN AND HIS PLACE IN TWENTIETH-CENTURY THOUGHT

And then the first Spiritual Exercises with him were a great experience for me, because a man was speaking here who disappeared behind the Gospel. At first I thought: My God, one might as well set up a record player there, that's how much his personality stood in the background.[1]

Biographical Sketch: The Early Years

Balthasar's repeated insistence that the ideal human person is one in whom person and mission coincide should serve as a cautionary note against any undue interest in his life "behind" his work. He rarely says anything about, for instance, his childhood beyond the fact that his Catholic faith was always an unproblematic one, and that his mother was very devout. Nevertheless, Balthasar does give certain hints regarding key turning points in his life, enough at least to shed light on the mission from which his work as a theologian is absolutely inseparable.[2] He was born in Lucerne, Switzerland in 1905 into a fairly aristocratic Catholic family, which included some significant members of Swiss culture and society. His father was a canton builder—responsible, among other things, for the St. Karli-Kirche in Switzerland—and his mother was the first general secretary of the Swiss League of Catholic Women. Of special significance from his childhood was his early immersion in and enormous gift for music, which would later help to account for his love of Mozart and his esteem for the importance of high culture in general. As a child he also spent a significant amount of time with his aunt, in a setting where "cosmopolitan attitudes and trilingualism (German, French, and English) were taken for granted."[3]

Balthasar's penchant for high culture, primarily in the forms of literature and music, marked his studies even in his "High School" (i.e. college) days, where, in contrast to a particularly studious friend, he claims to have spent all his time "on music and Dante and standing on my bed in the dormitory at night trying to get enough light to read *Faust*."[4] But this proclivity also accounts for his decision to enter graduate school in order to pursue "German studies," a program which took him through nine semesters, spent alternately in Vienna, Berlin and Zurich, and which extended far beyond the confines of just *German* studies. During these years he was exposed to a fairly rigorous study of what we would call Western Civilization, except that it included, in Balthasar's case, the study of Sanskrit and Indo-European linguistics.[5] All of this is to say that Balthasar's eventual interest in theology came in a rather roundabout way, namely, through the study of human culture in general, a fact which helps to account, at least in part, for the unconventional nature of his theological style.

There are two further things which this course of studies, eventually leading to his dissertation on eschatological themes in German literature, helps to account for. First, it enabled Balthasar in an absolutely natural fashion to avoid the sort of separation between "secular" and theological studies which had so determined the Catholic theology of his day, distinguishing it from the older tradition of Catholic theology. If Balthasar was later, under the influence of Henri de Lubac, to come to prefer the theology of the Church Fathers to that of neo-scholasticism, it was at least in part because the former engaged in theological work as if it was always and already naturally connected to the perennial human questions. For the Fathers, as for Balthasar, it was only obvious that Christ would have something to say to the philosophical questions of the day, insofar as, in Christ, God's dialogue with humanity was now to occur in the context of human language and culture. Second, Balthasar's training explains the accord between his approach and those in the so-called hermeneutical tradition of contemporary philosophy. For Balthasar, all human thought occurs in the context of a conversation that has been going on for some 3,000 years, a point which enables him to begin his own study of the history of Western metaphysics with the following quote from Goethe:

> Whoever cannot give account
> Of three thousand years,
> Let him remain in darkness, unlearned,
> And live from day to day.[6]

However, pointing out the importance of the fact that Balthasar's doctorate was in German literature rather than theology is not to say that he was uninterested in theological questions; it is rather to say that, in Balthasar's view, theological questions were not separable from human questions. This fact explains his rejection both of the lack of culture in the neo-scholastic approach to theology and the lack of attention to theological themes in the standard approach to art and literature of his day. As he put it in 1929:

> It may seem strange, in an historical investigation, to use philosophy and theology to explain works of art, and *vice versa* . . . without much reference to their aesthetic qualities. The results of this method will be its only justification.[7]

Already at this early phase of his studies, in other words, and long before he would come to take Henri de Lubac's position on the relationship between nature and grace, Balthasar was insisting that human beings are *naturally* theological creatures. The modern period, in other words, was not, for all of its forgetfulness of God, any more theologically neutral than any period before it. It is hard to underestimate the importance of this insight for Balthasar's subsequent theological development, for it would enable him to perceive modernity as not so much post-Christian or anti-Christian, but as something more akin to a Christian heresy.

It was during his doctoral studies that Balthasar went on the 30-day retreat with Fr. Friedrich Kronseder, S.J., which would account for his call to the priesthood. In 1929, upon the completion of his doctorate, he began his journey towards ordination in the south German province of the Society of Jesus, and it was under these auspices that he began his philosophical and theological studies. These studies included, first, philosophy at Pullach—which

Balthasar would later describe famously as languishing in the deserts of neo-scholasticism—and then theology at Fourviere. Although the method in both places was neo-scholastic—an approach that will be addressed at greater length below—there were already influences in both places who would help to guide Balthasar through what must have been a difficult time: they were, at Pullach, Erich Przywara, and at Fourviere, mentors, especially Henri de Lubac, teachers, such as Henri Rondet, and fellow students, such as Jean Danielou and Henri Bouillard. A particularly amusing anecdote from this time period has Balthasar sitting through lectures with his ears stuffed, reading through the works of Augustine.[8]

Upon completion of his theological studies and priestly formation, Balthasar made another retreat, this time in order to discern the precise nature of his priestly vocation. After it, he was given the choice either to become a professor at the Gregorian University in Rome—with three other priests, he was to have established an institute for ecumenical theology—or to remain in Basel as a chaplain. The fact that he chose the latter is but another enormously significant clue to Balthasar's theological development: he was never particularly interested in contributing to the sort of standard, academic theology of his time. This is not to say that he preferred the "devotional" to the "intellectual;" on the contrary, even Balthasar's pastoral work would have all of the characteristics of the high intellectual culture which had marked his studies to this point. It is rather the case that, like Nietzsche before him, Balthasar found the hyper specialization and methodological restrictions of the typical university theology program to be too constricting for his theological approach. Furthermore, he bemoaned the artificial separation of theology and holiness that had marked Catholic theology since the late Middle Ages. At any rate, Balthasar's work as a student chaplain included not only the typical pastoral work—saying masses and hearing confessions—it also involved the initiation of a number of cultural and intellectual enterprises, most notably, The *Studentische Schulengsgemeinschaft* (SG) with a student and friend named Robert Rast. Balthasar not only helped to found this student organization, but he also attended many of its debates and activities, and, above all, organized a number of courses and conferences, inviting the likes of Hugo and Karl Rahner, Henri de Lubac, Gustav Siewerth, Yves Congar, Martin Buber and others.

Besides this organization, Peter Henrici mentions two other important activities which preoccupied Balthasar during his student chaplain days: "first and foremost was his activity as an editor and translator."[9] Since Balthasar and many others perceived fascism to be a thoroughgoing attack upon Europe's cultural heritage, he began, with the help of several friends, a series of books called the Klosterberg collection. The series was to consist of 50 short anthologies, ten to be done by Balthasar himself, among the most important of which were: Goethe, Novalis, Nietzsche, Claudel, Peguy, Bernanos and Mauriac. The second important sphere of activity during these years concerns Balthasar's encounter with Protestantism, especially in the person of Karl Barth, whom he had already addressed in his doctoral work. Since Barth is one of the major influences discussed below, the mention of this encounter will suffice for the present. Furthermore, because Balthasar's biography now becomes inseparable from various friendships and corroborations, I will turn to the most important of his early influences.

BIOGRAPHICAL SKETCH: IMPORTANT EARLY INFLUENCES

Erich Przywara

The first person to be mentioned, in keeping with chronology, is Erich Przywara. Even during Balthasar's years at Pullach, Przywara, although never an official teacher, became one of his chief mentors. While Balthasar, in school, was studying the standard neo-scholastic manuals, with Przywara he was reading Augustine and Aquinas, bringing them into dialogue with modern thinkers such as Hegel, Scheler and Heidegger. This approach, which assumes that thinkers across time can be brought into dialogue over the so-called big questions, was to characterize Balthasar's own approach from this time on. It is not simply that the positions of the moderns could be judged in the light of the thought of the past—something that was already becoming obsolete in the radically historicist approach of the academy—but that the thought of the ancients and medievals could find a new relevance in the light of the new questions of the day. Here, it was not enough to ask what Augustine said about this or that question during the fourth century, but one must push through to what his thought has to say about questions that he could never have foreseen.

This approach to the past amounts to a real retrieval in which it is assumed that the thought of the past is great enough to stand up to new questions and new circumstances. It goes against the approach of the hyper traditionalist, who is only interested in repeating what Augustine *said*, and against the hyper modern, who assumes that ancient thought has been rendered obsolete; Przywara or Balthasar would insist, rather, that past thought can take on a new light in the context of current conversations. One is reminded here of Hans Georg-Gadamer's critique of period-piece reproductions of baroque or classical music. While the impression is given that the period-piece performance shows a higher regard for the music of the past—so much so that it wants to perform the music exactly as it was performed in its day—there is in fact an insinuation that such music is not capable of making the transition to a contemporary musical setting. In a paradoxical way, the music is left incapable of speaking to the contemporary listener, its importance being relegated to the historical rather than the musical.[10]

But Przywara's biggest influence on Balthasar has to do with the issue of the analogy of being, which the former was developing in his dialogue with Karl Barth.[11] The issues here are complex and since they will be dealt with at greater length in what comes later, I will only offer an outline of the main issues at present. Karl Barth had famously rejected the analogy of being—the doctrine which asserts that between the Being of God and the being of the world there exists a likeness—on account of the fact that a human philosophical construction was permitted to establish the relationship between God and the world prior to God's free self-disclosure. That is, the relationship between God and the world was allegedly contained in a human concept, in this case "Being," which included both God and the world. It is likely that Barth's critique is directed at the older, two-tiered approach to this problem as we find it in neo-scholasticism. Here, reason (nature) first establishes the existence of God and his relationship with the world before the appeal is made to God's (supernatural) self-revelation in Scripture. Barth insists that the God that is reached in this prior stage can only be an idol, a god of human making. In Przywara's approach, however, the analogy between God and the world derives from, even as it is intent upon highlighting, the absolute incomprehensibility of God to finite understanding. What separates God from the world and what makes the world similar to God stand in direct proportion to one another. God simply is; the world is only on account of God, or, only *in* God. Therefore, insofar as the world is at all, it must be similar to the God who is: here is the similarity. However, only God simply *is*; the world may not have been: here is the (greater) dissimilarity. Any prior knowledge of God on the part of the creature, prior, that is, to God's explicit self-revelation in Christ or in Scripture, stems from God insofar as human beings only have such knowledge on account of the fact that they are created in God's image. Here Przywara believes that he can do justice to Barth's fear that human beings make the first move in the knowledge of God. Any analogy, in Przywara's view, is based on the fact that God makes the first move towards the creature in the act of creation.

Two further things should be said about Balthasar's encounter with Przywara at this point. First, Balthasar credits Przywara for his first exposure to Aquinas's teaching on the real and fundamental distinction between God and the world, an insight which made Przywara more Thomistic in Balthasar's view than the two-tiered, neo-scholastic Thomists of his seminary training. In this doctrine we have an emphasis on the fact that God is not simply the highest in a chain of beings, a notion that would reduce God to just another being among beings, but that in God alone being (that God is) and essence (who/what God is) perfectly coincide. Another way of saying the same thing is to say that, while all other beings are only potential, being only one instance of a more general phenomenon (i.e. each individual human being is but an example of the category "human being"), God is pure act, being the single and only example of God. Thus, there is a real and fundamental distinction between the God who is, to borrow language from Aquinas, the pure act of to be itself (*ipsum esse subsistens*), and the created order, which has its being only as a gift. Second, this emphasis on the real distinction eventually led Balthasar to two other Catholic philosophers, Gustav Siewerth and Ferdinand Ulrich, who would help him to see that Przywara's approach on this question was overly negative or apophatic.[12] These two philosophers enabled Balthasar to see that Przywara sometimes allowed the "ever greater dissimilarity" between God and the world (Fourth Lateran Council) to eclipse the genuine similarity. By beginning more strenuously than had Przywara with the doctrines of creation and Christology, Balthasar was better able to do justice to the positivity of the created order. In creating the world, God had created something that was not God, something which had a genuine and distinct existence of its own, and had pronounced it "very good." Furthermore, when God became man in the person of Jesus Christ, he did so without in any way violating or destroying the humanity of that person.[13] Here Balthasar insists that even the analogy of being finds its source and completion in a proper understanding of the person of Christ. Nevertheless, Balthasar's friendship with Przywara remained a very important one and Przywara's influence should not be underestimated. Indeed, when in 1946 Przywara was suffering from a "serious nervous disorder," Balthasar went to Germany to bring Przywara back to Basel "where his friend slowly recuperated."[14]

Henri de Lubac

It is almost impossible to address all of the many ways in which de Lubac influenced Balthasar's theology, for he was a constant theological companion from the latter's student years in the 1930s to his death in 1988 (de Lubac died in 1991). In Balthasar's brief account of his theological development prior to 1940, de Lubac's name figures rather heavily,[15] but it is the short book, *The Theology of Henri de Lubac*, which gives the fullest account of this influence.[16] Three areas in particular emerge in this short but weighty book that are worth consideration, for they will help to shed light on the fuller discussion of these issues in the chapters below. They are: the little work *Catholicism*, the relationship between nature and grace, and the retrieval of medieval exegesis.

The first area of impact comes from the important little book *Catholicism*; indeed, it would be hard to overestimate the influence of this book, not only on Balthasar but on an entire generation of theologians, the young Joseph Ratzinger among them. In the book, two important themes emerge, both intent upon calling into question the standard approach to theology that was dominant in the early half of the twentieth century. The first theme concerns the corporeal and communal nature of the Catholic faith against the regnant individualism that was dominant at this time; the second concerns its deeply historical nature against the ahistorical rationalism which marked modern thought. With regard to the former, de Lubac reminds us that the biblical and Patristic approach to the question of salvation was never an individualistic one, that, more specifically, sin had not only damaged the individual's relationship with God, but had also destroyed the intended unity of the human race. God's salvific plan, in short, extends not to isolated individuals or even merely to the Church, but to the entire human family. Of course this involves re-emphasizing the fact that God is both creator and redeemer, and that his actions concern, therefore, humanity as a whole. This emphasis on the universality of God's salvific will enables de Lubac to shed new light on the Church's role in the world. The Church is that community which God has reconciled to himself and to each other through Jesus Christ, and serves, therefore, as a sacrament of salvation *for* the world. In the Church the world sees what it is intended to be, namely, the human family reconciled to God and each other in Christ. Finally, the Eucharist—against any one-sided fixation on the question of Real Presence—is reintegrated as the sacrament of unity: through it the Church becomes what it is consuming, the body of Christ.

The second major theme mentioned above was the historical nature of the Christian faith. Since God's redemption of the human race is not a unilateral one, it occurs in history. It is this fact that accounts for God's long "pedagogy" with Israel, leading up to the coming of Christ. This preparation is necessary insofar as, for human beings, truth is always mediated through history and culture. It is interesting to note that de Lubac also sees an analogous preparation in the great religions, although he does this without downplaying the uniqueness and normativity of God's dealings with Israel. Two further points should be mentioned in this regard. First, de Lubac makes an early case here for the possibility of salvation outside of the structural precincts of the Catholic Church. As Balthasar summarizes de Lubac's position, "As with the Old Covenant, so all the religious efforts of man have contributed in their own way and at their stage of development to provide the basis of the coming consummation."[17] He then goes on to quote de Lubac accordingly:

By an extension of the dogma of the communion of saints, it seems right to think that although [these religions] themselves lack the normal conditions for salvation, they will be able nevertheless to obtain this salvation by virtue of the mysterious bonds that unite them to believers . . . What is insufficient can be sufficient because the "more" exists to supply what is lacking.[18]

What Balthasar finds particularly attractive about de Lubac's approach to this problem is that it at once affirms the universality of

9

salvation without in any way having to downplay the indispensable role of Christ and his Church. Indeed, salvation is universal not in spite of the unique role of Christ and his Church, but because of it. Second, such an approach refuses to work out the relationship between Christianity and the "world" religions on the basis of some prior, theologically neutral vantage point. Implied in de Lubac's treatment is the fact that no such stance in fact exists, for every approach to the problem of religious diversity must bring with it at least an implicit theology of religions.

One final aspect of *Catholicism* should be singled out for its influence on Balthasar's theological development: its doctrine of election. Again, on account of the communal approach of the book, de Lubac is able to deal with the nagging problem of predestination—a problem which haunts the theologies of Augustine, Aquinas, Luther, Calvin, and, then, Jansen—in a much more biblical manner. When Paul speaks of predestination and election, we are shown, he does not speak in terms of individuals but in terms of peoples, specifically Israel and the Church. This gets us around the difficulty of certain biblical texts wherein it seems that God has predestined some individuals for heaven and others for hell. Here Balthasar sees a foreshadowing of Barth's doctrine of the election of all people in Christ, against any Calvinistic notion of a limited atonement. It is important to point out, however, that de Lubac maintains God's universal salvific will without in any way subscribing to the condemned doctrine of apocatastasis: the notion that all individuals will ultimately be saved. The question of who will and who will not be saved is one to which God alone holds the answer.[19]

Throughout this section on de Lubac, the central question has been the place of Christianity in a post-Christian world. How, the question is, does Christianity respond to secularism? The tempting response is simply to reject all that is modern and withdraw into intra-ecclesial concerns. As we have seen, this is not de Lubac's approach. But in order for the Church to respond to this new situation, he insisted, it must get to the roots of modern secularism. This leads us to the second major area of de Lubac's influence. Like Gilson, his friend and confidant, de Lubac traces the origins of modernity back behind the usual suspects—Bacon, Descartes, Newton, et al.—to late medieval nominalism. For it is nominalism, with its notion of a nature devoid of any intrinsic connection to the divine, which paves the way for modernity's mechanistic and atheistic understanding of the cosmos. Specifically, de Lubac found in the neo-scholastic notion that human beings have two separate ends, a natural end—happiness in this world—which can be achieved through their natural powers, and a supernatural end—the face-to-face vision of God—which can only be achieved through superadded grace, the seeds of the modern notion that human beings can address the concerns of this world as if the God question makes no difference. In short, de Lubac locates the origins of modern atheism in the theology of the late Middle Ages, insisting that its doctrine of a "pure nature" devoid of any intrinsic connection to the supernatural paved the way for modern secularism.

Because this problem is so central to de Lubac's contribution to contemporary Catholic theology, and because, furthermore, Balthasar was to follow him closely in this regard, it will be helpful to provide some important, even if necessarily brief, historical background. This background is not only crucial to understanding de Lubac, it also provides a necessary foundation for locating Balthasar's own place in twentieth-century Catholic thought. Once again, the dominant theological approach in Catholic circles both in the late nineteenth century and early twentieth century was neo-scholasticism. Neo-scholasticism was marked by a method which was highly systematic in nature, allotting everything to its proper place in the system. Not only were the various articles of the creed treated in separate treatises, there was also a clear demarcation between the realms of reason (philosophy) and faith (theology), as well as between natural theology, apologetics, and positive theology, and morality. There was also a marked tendency in the neo-scholastic approach towards a rationalism which isolated thinking from the influences of the body, language and history, and which treated art, feeling, mysticism, and the like with something close to disdain. It was precisely this tendency towards rationalism and extreme objectivism on the part of neo-scholasticism which gave rise, in the early part of the twentieth century, to the Catholic modernist movement.[20] If the neo-scholastics were going to emphasize the objectivity of theological knowledge and the propositional nature of truth, the modernists were going to emphasize the importance of subjectivity and experience as the proper categories of religious knowledge.

At issue between the neo-scholastics and their modernist counterparts was the nature of theological knowledge, and at the background of this issue was the philosophical dispute between realism and idealism. To put it succinctly, for the realist, truth is a property in things which actually exists outside of the mind of the knower, and knowledge occurs when there is a correspondence between the mind of the knower and the thing which is known. Knowing occurs, in other words, when the knower knows the thing as it actually is. Idealists, on the other hand, following Kant, were skeptical that the knower ever knows the thing "out there" as it actually is. Or, as Kant would put it, we can never know the "thing in itself," we can only know the appearance of the thing as it now exists, *via* representation, in the mind of the knower. At the one end of this debate we have an insistence that knowledge is "objective," that knowing involves knowing the object as it actually is; at the other end we have the notion that knowledge is "subjective," that knowledge only extends to the subject's reproduction of the thing in the categories of the mind. This modern philosophical debate also had repercussions in the question of theological knowing. The object of theological knowledge is God. According to traditional teaching, God is known sufficiently only through his self-revelation in Scripture, tradition and the Magisterium, the so-called sources of revelation. According to the neo-scholastics, God reveals himself objectively in these sources and this objective knowledge is revealed in a propositional way. The approach of neo-scholasticism, in short, is decidedly "from above." Theological knowledge of God is given to faith, but it is given by God and from God in the propositions of revelation. Theological knowledge occurs when there is a correspondence between the mind of the believer and the propositions of revelation.

Of course the skepticism of the modern period and its scientific method cast a radical doubt upon such an approach. One need only recall Lessing's famous statement that the accidental truths of history (for instance, the bodily resurrection of Christ) cannot provide the basis for the necessary truths of reason. Or, as one of Maurice Blondel's fellow students once asked him, "Why should I be obliged to inquire into and take account of a casual event which occurred 1900 years ago in an obscure corner of the Roman Empire?"[21] This sort of skepticism led modernist Protestants and Catholics to look for another basis for theological knowledge, one which could circumvent Lessing's "ugly ditch" separating the events of history from the truths of reason, and this basis was to be located in the realm of universal human experience. It was to be located, more specifically, in the universal religiosity of humanity. This approach, it was thought, could escape Lessing's skepticism, even as it answered Kant's criticism that the truths of revelation, insofar as they come from God, are "heteronomous" to human beings (i.e. "extrinsic"). This charge of "extrincism," the notion that if God's truth comes to us only from the outside it can never really be ours, was taken very seriously by the Catholic modernists, as the following sentences of George Tyrrell should make clear:

> In other words, the teaching from outside must evoke a revelation in ourselves. The prophet's experience must become experience for us. It is to this evoked revelation that we answered by the act of faith, recognizing it as God's word in us and to us. Were it not already written in the depths of our being, where the spirit is rooted in God, we could not recognize it . . . without personal revelation, there can be no faith, nothing more than theological or historical assent. Revelation cannot be put into us from outside. It can be occasioned, but it cannot be caused, by instruction.[22]

In the face of this debate, between the neo-scholastics and their modernist counterparts, there were several notable theologians and philosophers who found themselves in a sort of no man's land, rejecting what they considered to be both the false objectivism and extrinsicism of the neo-scholastics and the false subjectivism of the modernists. Such individuals were held in suspicion, in turn, by both sides of the debate, but as time has passed they could be counted among the heroes of late nineteenth- and early twentieth-century Catholic theology. They include, from the famous Tubingen School in Germany, Johann Adam Mohler and Johan Sebastian Drey; from England, John Henry Cardinal Newman; and from France, Maurice Blondel and Joseph Marechal. Although there are differences, even significant ones, between these thinkers, they all shared a common refusal to accept the either/or of the conflict outlined above, finding in the theology of the Church Fathers and High Scholasticism an approach to these problems which was neither falsely objectivist nor subjectivist. Typical in this regard is John Henry Newman's distinction, in *An Essay in Aid of a Grammar of Assent*, between "real" and "notional" assent. What is important in Newman's discussion is *both* the fact that a mere notional assent to the external propositions of theology is *insufficient* for genuine religious knowledge, *and* the fact that real assent, the assent, we might say, of the whole person made possible only by the gift of faith, can never dispense with notional assent. Notional assent—the assent to external propositions—is at once insufficient and yet absolutely indispensable to genuine Christian knowledge. It is unfortunate that the Catholicism of the nineteenth and early twentieth centuries was impatient with this sort of thinking and that it therefore cast suspicion over many of the thinkers just mentioned; John Henry Newman, incidentally, was no exception in this regard.

The thinker from this generation who most influenced de Lubac, however, was Maurice Blondel (1861–1949). Through a phenomenological analysis of human action, Blondel believed that he had found the key to overcoming the false separation in modern thought between the subject and the object, between the finite and the infinite, and between the immanent and the transcendent. Although human action begins in the freedom of the relatively autonomous human person, such action is always directed, even if unconsciously, to some end which transcends that individual person. Blondel began his famous work *L'Action* by asking, "Yes or no, has human life any meaning, has man a destiny," and he went on to insist that this problem demands a solution, a solution which receives its answer in the very activity of human life. This is not the place to go into Blondel's rather complex theory of action, but what is important for the present purposes is what his approach does to the problem of nature and grace. Blondel was dissatisfied with the extrinsicist approach of a traditional apologetics, which was intent upon adding Christian truth onto the truncated version of reason which was dominant in modern thought. Instead, Blondel wanted to show that a genuine philosophy—one which he insisted became visible in his treatment of action—opened up quite naturally into questions of a religious and even theological nature. He furthermore insisted that human nature was oriented, by its nature, to that which transcends that nature, namely, the supernatural. If Christians, he insisted, did not set about to heal the impoverished philosophy of modernity, then the Christian faith would be bound to appear "heteronomous" or of only "extrinsic" concern to the natural affairs of human beings.

It was just this approach—Blondel later called it the "method of immanence"—which would attract the young de Lubac. But it would take de Lubac's full genius to take up, clarify, and provide traditional support for Blondel's seemingly novel approach to the problem of nature and grace. And in a series of works beginning in 1946 with

Surnatural: Études historiques and extending to 1965, with the publication of *Le Mystère du surnaturel* and *Augustinisme et théologie moderne*, de Lubac did just that.[23] Specifically, he set out to show that according to the great tradition of Catholic thought, human beings have one single end, namely to see God, and this was in contradistinction to the notion invented, according to de Lubac's account, by Cajetan and others, that human beings have two separate ends.[24] As he proceeded, de Lubac knew that he had to avoid two extremes:

> If one were obliged to affirm that the order of nature and the order of grace were totally alien to each other, the salvation that we experience in Jesus Christ would by necessity be reduced to an optional and insignificant "plus." If, on the contrary, we allowed a more or less explicit immanentism of grace, for which grace would do nothing more than make explicit and complete what is already potentially present in nature, the newness of God's advent would seem to be compromised, if not downright superfluous.[25]

If the former of these extremes was the temptation prior to the Council, the latter has been the temptation ever since. In order to avoid them, de Lubac therefore insisted that we must hold fast to the paradox of a human nature that is *by nature* ordered to an end that it is not equipped *by nature* to attain. It is important to remember that the problem in the background here is that of modern secularism, that the God question has become irrelevant to the work-a-day world. The first of these extremes plays into modern secularism by relegating what is specifically Christian to something extrinsic to the natural order; the second of these, by declaring human activity as already implicitly graced, can give the implication that the Christian specifics are superfluous, even if perhaps desirable. On the one hand, grace becomes extrinsic to nature; on the other hand, grace becomes a property within nature itself.

It should go without saying, then, that de Lubac had enemies on both sides of the above equation: in his early years he suffered at the hands of the neo-scholastic dualists (who had significant influence in the Church's hierarchy), and in his later years he was generally considered passé by the growing number of theological immanentists. The former were worried, as they were with Blondel, that de Lubac's approach made grace a necessity, that if human beings were created in order to be united to God, then God owed them the grace to achieve this union. In response to this de Lubac used a number of analogies in order to illustrate that the natural ordination to God does not undermine the gratuity of grace. In the first place he appealed to the fact that God's entire plan of cosmic evolution, which seems to have human beings as its goal, in no wise implies that human beings arise out of a sort of inner and purely immanent necessity to the evolutionary order. Secondly, he appeals to the relationship between the covenants.

[I]f it is true that the whole history of Israel is ultimately only meaningful through the coming of Jesus Christ, which it had prepared and to which it was wholly ordered, is that any reason to dispute the entirely gratuitous newness of Christ's coming, even in its relationship to Israel.[26]

With regard to the immanentist approach, on the other hand, de Lubac insisted that this natural orientation was precisely that, a *natural* orientation. It is for this reason that he was not in agreement with Karl Rahner's solution to the problem, namely the so-called "supernatural existential."[27] As we will come to see later, this seemingly minor difference will help to account for Balthasar's own misgivings regarding Rahner's approach. Both de Lubac and Balthasar feared that if this orientation were considered already to be "graced" or to be itself "supernatural," it would necessarily, even if unintentionally, mean the downplaying of the newness of Christ, a downplaying, that is, of the necessary caesura between the natural orientation and the subsequent gift. It is precisely this caesura that accounts for the biblical emphasis on conversion and repentance.

Lastly, something should be said about de Lubac's retrieval of medieval exegesis (the third area mentioned above), and this for a few reasons. First, it will assist us better to understand the continued relevance of his treatment of nature and grace as outlined above; second, it will give us a typical example of de Lubac's approach to the past, an approach that is profoundly similar to that of Balthasar; and, finally, it will provide an excellent foundation for the next chapter dealing with Balthasar's own theological method. At the end of his introduction to the 1998 re-issue, in English, of *The Mystery of the Supernatural*, David L. Schindler asks about the continued relevance of the book. On the one hand, he notes, few people today would wish to defend the old, two-tiered approach to nature and grace which de Lubac so adeptly dismantled; on the other, however, "it seems equally clear that a 'softer,' or what may be called 'methodological,' version of the 'pure nature' theory remains widespread."[28] As Schindler goes on to explain, this methodological version consists of an approach to theology which brackets out faith in order to find "common ground" with the critical methods dominant in the academy. Like the old two-tiered approach before it, this one too has apologetic intentions: if Christianity is going to get a hearing in the modern, secularized world, it must be able to show that its methods meet up to the standards expected of the other disciplines. This is a very complex question and I have no intention of trying to solve it here, but it is clear that de Lubac's retrieval of medieval exegesis was a response, in part, to this latter form of nature-grace dualism.

Briefly, while it is certainly the case that there is a great deal of wisdom in this newer approach, a great deal that de Lubac himself would have applauded, the subtle point of his position is that even such a methodological move—for instance, bracketing questions of faith in order to determine whether or not a saying of Jesus contained in a given Gospel may actually be traceable to the historical Jesus—can never imply the *neutrality* of any observer vis-à-vis God's self-revelation in Jesus Christ. The scholar is always, already, in the Christian view of things, related to the God of Jesus Christ, and is either marked by belief or unbelief. As Schindler puts it:

> I am not suggesting, of course, that one cannot legitimately abstract from the order of grace—in the name of common ground, critical method, or reason. The point, and it is fundamental for de Lubac, is that this abstraction must not be taken to imply that the order of grace is to be subsequently (simply) *added* to what has been first abstracted . . . The fact that the "superaddition" occurs now for methodological reasons does not render it any less problematic as a false abstraction hence as wrongly autonomous, relative to the order of grace.[29]

What this has to do with the question of scriptural exegesis should be obvious, and de Lubac's position here is also subtle.[30] While in no way suggesting a simple return to the methods of the Fathers and medievals, de Lubac attempted a retrieval of what was still valid in their approach. He does this by distinguishing between the method as it was practiced—and this is precisely what, he suggests, we should not attempt to repeat in our new historical circumstances[31]—and the underlying insight which prompted it, and which remains as valid as it ever was. This underlying insight can be boiled down to a simple affirmation: that the way one treats any given part of Scripture will be determined by what one thinks of the whole of Scripture. For the Church Fathers, the so-called "spiritual meaning" of a given text— what has been called more disparagingly the "allegorical meaning"—is the meaning of that text in the light of Jesus Christ. Scripture as a whole—the Old and New Testaments as canonized by the early Church—is about Jesus Christ, so that no part can *finally* be understood if it is not at some point read in the light of Jesus Christ.

What does this, then, have to do with what was said above about nature and grace? While it is one thing to bracket the question of faith for methodological purposes, it is a whole other thing to say that such a bracketing approach has the final word. For de Lubac, nature is *intrinsically* open to grace, not *extrinsically*. As applied to Scripture, the literal meaning of the text—the question of what happened, or of what the author of the text originally intended—*intrinsically* opens up to the question of the ongoing *significance* of what happened, or what the text *means*. In such a view, the question of Jesus' identity is not a question that is extrinsic to the study of the Bible. As many have pointed out, the current interest in these texts would not exist if it were not for the significance of the person of Jesus Christ. One could say in this regard that the literal sense, the one which most concerns modern exegetes, concerns the *part* of the text, while the spiritual sense concerns the *whole*. And it is precisely this aspect of the older approach—beyond all of the specifics of its allegorizing—that cannot be put aside. In fact, it is impossible to do so, for as soon as we decide to read the part as if that is all there is, we have in fact said something about the whole that implies a faith stance, even if a negative one. This does not, of course, rule out the historical-critical approach to Scripture. But it does, first, insist that the method allow itself to be open *intrinsically* to the meaning that the text finally has for faith, and, second, that it allow itself to be incorporated into a larger approach to Scripture which includes the meaning of the whole. This does not seem, in the final analysis, to be too far from the so-called "canonical" approach of the late Brevard Childs.

Adrienne von Speyr

We have already seen several reasons why Balthasar's theology does not fit easily into the modern university setting. He refused to engage in the study of philosophy, literature, art or history as if theological questions were irrelevant, just as he rejected a style of theology which went about its business unaware of the larger cultural and intellectual questions of the day. He, furthermore, rejected the pandering of the academy to the methodology of the hard sciences, which had led not only to a false specialization, but also to a condescending attitude towards the past that, even as it studied it, placed itself over, above and outside of its concerns. Finally, he bemoaned the separation of theology from sanctity which was bound to happen in a strictly academic context. Those who would wish to give Balthasar's theology a greater hearing in the modern university are sometimes tempted to downplay these sorts of things, or to try to find some sort of compromise between his approach and a more scientific, academic approach. And yet the greatest single obstacle to Balthasar's reception into the academic theological guild is almost without a doubt his collaboration with Adrienne von Speyr. Here, if Balthasar is going to receive a hearing in the halls of academe, compromise must give way to outright denial. The fact that Balthasar foresaw this temptation, however, and did everything in his power to prevent it should give his interpreters pause. As he put it in the important little work, *Our Task*:

> This book has one chief aim: to prevent any attempt being made after my death to separate my work from that of Adrienne von Speyr. It will show that in no respect is this possible, as regards both theology and the developing community.[32]

Of course this still leaves the rather complex work of determining just how to interpret her influence, and the influence of her intense spiritual experiences, upon his work. Hopefully what follows will shed some light on a topic which will likely never be completely settled.

Balthasar met Adrienne in 1940, the year which she would also be received into the Catholic Church under Balthasar's supervision. When she met him, she was a Protestant and a physician living in Basel. Although she was raised in Protestantism, and was in some ways quite devout, there was always a sense, on her part, that she was missing out on important aspects of the Christian faith. For instance, from the time she was little she longed to confess her sins to someone.

She had also had a strange attraction to Ignatius of Loyola, and even had a vision of him in 1908, when she was still a child. Later on, as a young lady and when she was still a Protestant, she gave a series of talks on Ignatius for the women of her church. Strangest of all, however, was the strong sense that she had through her entire childhood that she had a missing brother, or perhaps even a twin. Later on she came to see all of these things as signs that she was somehow destined someday to meet Balthasar, and that the two of them would cooperate in some sort of mission. And, in fact, after she was received into the Church, she and Balthasar began a close collaboration that would not cease until her death.[33]

The collaboration began, primarily, with Balthasar in the role of spiritual director and confessor. He was immediately struck not only by her keen intelligence and intuitive grasp of the Catholic faith, but also by the intense experiences and visions which she would share with him in their meetings. Before long Balthasar was playing the role of stenographer to Adrienne's visions. Without going into the details of this, two things should be noted in particular. First, from 1940 onwards Adrienne was receiving intense spiritual visions having to do with the formation of a new sort of community within the Catholic Church. From the beginning she was certain that this community, whatever its nature, would be the common work (the "child" as she called it) of her and Balthasar. Second, some of Adrienne's experiences included "dark nights" where she would encounter the torments of sin and even hell. I mention these two things in particular because they were to have the most direct impact on Balthasar's life and thought. As he put it:

> The implications of Adrienne's Holy Saturday and other "hellish" experiences—for theology, mysticism, and ordinary Christian life— are incalculable and will have to be studied slowly and carefully.[34]

With regard to the community, Adrienne had envisioned something that would involve a close and literal following of Christ in the evangelical councils—poverty, obedience and chastity—but which would not, for all of that, involve any sort of withdrawal from the world. In her diary she notes that she knows,

> a number of educated young women who certainly don't belong in a regular monastery but who ought to leave the world for a period

of recollection and spiritual formation and then return to the world at full strength.[35]

For Balthasar's part, who never seems to have doubted the legitimacy of Adrienne's experiences, it was a matter of figuring out how such a community—to which he was sympathetic from the beginning—might fit into ecclesial norms and laws. There was certainly nothing in his personal theological opinion at this time to rule out such a venture. It is furthermore important to note that neither Balthasar nor Adrienne were aware of any inclinations along these lines on the part of others elsewhere in the Church, nor had Pius XII's *Provida Mater* (1947) yet been written, which would give canonical status to such "secular institutes." Finally, in *Our Task*, Balthasar is adamant that the idea and plan for the community first came from Adrienne.[36]

Already, under the influence of de Lubac and those key figures behind his work (Blondel, et al.), Balthasar had come to reject an isolated form of Catholicism that busied itself with internal matters at the expense of its mission to the world. Now, in his collaboration with Adrienne, this notion, that the Church must take the message of Christ right to the heart of the world, came to find a very concrete solution: a secular institute. The only problem was that there was no real canonical status yet for such communities. Due to the enormous influence of Ignatius of Loyola, both on Balthasar and Adrienne, and due also to the fact that Balthasar was already a Jesuit, it was just assumed that, were the two to begin some sort of secular institute, it would be under the auspices of the Jesuit order. In fact, it was at Adrienne's suggestion that Balthasar approach his immediate superiors in order to see if such a thing could be done. The unfortunate response from his superiors led to what Balthasar has repeatedly called the most difficult decision of his life, his departure from the Jesuits. Balthasar is especially insistent in this regard that Adrienne is not to "blamed" for his departure, stating numerous times that, as difficult as it was for him to leave, it was even more difficult for her. At one point she was even tempted to pray for her own death in order to spare Balthasar this decision. "I am mentioning this," Balthasar states, "only to show the heavy responsibility that Adrienne felt for my departure from the Society; it was almost more than she could bear."[37]

Indeed, from 1945 to 1950, when Balthasar actually left the Society of Jesus, he had a series of difficulties. His father died in 1946, as did his friend—mentioned above in connection with the

Schulungsgemeinschaft—Robert Rast, at the young age of 26. It was also in "46 that he first found out that the Society would not oversee his and Adrienne's community, a decision which he was to appeal unsuccessfully on a couple of occasions in Rome before Father General Johann Baptist Janssens. Meanwhile, his friends from Lyons—de Lubac, Bouillard, Fessard and Danielou—were coming under ecclesiastical fire for allegedly engaging in a "new theology." After the failed attempts at appeal, and during a retreat with a Father Donatien Mollat, Balthasar made the difficult decision, with Father Mollat's agreement, that if the Society would not sponsor the secular institute he would leave the Jesuits. He left the order in February of 1950. If the decision was a difficult one, it was one which Balthasar made with a great deal of confidence, a confidence explicable at least in part on account of the "superabundance of charismatic attestation—multiple stigmatization, healings and other miracles, vision upon vision"—coming from Adrienne.[38]

After leaving the Jesuits, Balthasar's life became consumed with a number of ventures, most importantly the founding of the secular institute which he and Adrienne had envisioned, the Community of Saint John. In order to make money, however, he embarked on a number of lecture tours in the 1950s, the basic contents of which we can see in his little book, *The God Question and Modern Man.* Along with the Community of Saint John, mention ought to be made of Johannes Verlag, the publishing company which Balthasar founded, primarily to publish the works of Adrienne, and the International Catholic Review, *Communio,* suggested by Adrienne as early as 1945, but not actually begun—with the German edition—until 1973.

However, the main purpose of this sketch of Balthasar's cooperation with Adrienne is to assess the degree of her influence on his thought (and *vice versa*). On the one hand, many of the themes which Balthasar claims to have gotten from Adrienne are themes which we can already trace to his early encounters with Przywara and de Lubac, and, behind them, thinkers like Blondel and Marechal, and, behind them, the great saints, Doctors and Fathers of the Church. Recognizing this could lead to the extreme view that Adrienne has little to no influence upon Balthasar's *theological* development, or, that the little influence that she had was for the worse.[39] I suspect that people who make such claims are trying to protect Balthasar's place in the academy, a place where stigmatists and visionaries, at least Christian ones, are generally not highly regarded. On the other hand, there are certain themes in Balthasar's thought which, even if they can be seen in seed in his early influences, develop to maturity only after his encounter with Adrienne. Chief among these is surely his theology of Holy Saturday, but her influence can also be seen is his theology of the sexes, marriage, the Evangelical Counsels, Mary, the Church, as well as his Trinitarian theology and Christology. To offer just one specific example, I mention the emphasis on the unity of person and mission in Balthasar's Christology. It is not that the early influences do not help to account for the eventual positions which Balthasar would take on each of these matters, it is rather that the particular features of these positions, the things which make them, one could say, distinctively Balthasarian, cannot be accounted for apart from her experiences, dictations, advice and writings. If nothing else, she kept his theology from becoming merely intellectualistic and abstract, as the following comment from Adrienne might help to clarify,

> May I say something painful, though I mean it kindly? When I read what you have written . . . I sometimes feel you are writing for a totally theoretical person, in other words, for someone who lives only in your mind, a person who has all your presuppositions, who always *a demi* [half] shares your understanding, and this person simply does not exist. So I think it would be good for you to get to know the "normal" man. Somehow you must be brought through him to him . . . You can't just write for the sake of the subject matter. You have to do it for the reader.[40]

In the final analysis, then, I would suggest that Adrienne did have a significant influence upon Balthasar's theological development (a development that cannot be as easily separated from his entire mission as some have suggested), but that he, in turn, helped to bring her experiences into expression within the context of the Church's theological tradition. She said herself that she needed a theologian to help her to sort through and understand her experiences.[41] Neither he nor she would have wanted to initiate anything into Christianity which did not meet with the approval of the Church, and that is why Balthasar was always careful to submit his ideas and her experiences to the proper ecclesial authorities.

Karl Barth

Before closing this chapter on Balthasar's life and early influences, brief mention should be made of his friendship and dialogue with Karl Barth. Here, again, one might be to tempted to suggest that the engagement with Barth added little that was genuinely new to Balthasar's theology, that everything that he gets from Barth was already there in de Lubac and others. Indeed, Balthasar himself supports such a reading in part in the following comment in a letter to de Lubac: "I am finishing my Karl Barth, which is basically a discussion between him and you. I would like to dedicate this book to you, he owes you almost everything."[42] But the "almost" here is likely significant, and I would like to suggest that what Balthasar took from Barth most of all was the latter's dogged Christocentrism. It is not that de Lubac's thought was not already Christocentric, it is more that he often allowed the terminology of his adversaries to tinge the debate concerning nature and grace, faith and reason, and the like in an overly abstract direction. What Barth would eventually demand is that all such debates be worked out in the light of the Chalcedonian doctrine of Jesus Christ: fully God and fully man.

Balthasar had already addressed Barth's thought to some degree in his dissertation, but in the 1940s the two developed a friendship, based partly on common theological interests and partly on a common love for the music of Mozart. It did not hurt that they both lived in Basel. In fact, in the late 1940s Balthasar was invited to partake in Barth's seminar at Basel, and from 1949–1950 Balthasar gave a series of lectures on Barth which the latter himself attended. These prompted a book on Barth's theology which came out in 1951, which Barth enthusiastically welcomed.[43] At the bottom of Balthasar's respect lay Barth's commitment to overcome the extreme subjectivism of modern theology, not with a return to an older, biblical positivism, but with a renewed emphasis on the significance of the person of Jesus Christ. In his own way, Barth was responding to a dualism in Protestant circles which was akin to the Catholic one outlined above, even if the former was along "liberal" or subjectivist lines, and the latter was along "conservative" or objectivist lines. What they had in common was a starting point which excluded Christ until it was too late: the liberal, that is, until Christ could only be understood as the highest expression of human subjectivity; the conservative, until Christ was no longer intrinsically related to human beings *as human beings*. Both de Lubac and Barth, then, saw modern secularism as a result of a failure at the level of Christology.

Balthasar, furthermore, saw Barth's early attack on Catholicism—recall his famous statement that the analogy of being was the invention of the AntiChrist—as similar to those of Blondel and de Lubac. Balthasar's book, then, seems to have had a double purpose. First, to summarize and point out the validity of Barth's critique of a certain style of Catholic thinking, and, second, to demonstrate to Barth that genuine Catholicism is not guilty of the charges that he was making. In fact, this second purpose seems to have included a not so subtle suggestion that Barth's own theological approach, if not taken into a fuller Catholic one, resulted in a "Christological straightjacket." If Balthasar appreciated Barth's attempt to think all human problems in the light of Christ—in keeping with the famous line from *Gaudium et Spes* 22—he worried about Barth's tendency to denigrate the natural in the light of the supernatural. Because in Jesus Christ a full humanity flourishes along with a full divinity—without confusion, without separation—there is no need on the part of the Christian to rob the human (natural) in order to pay the divine (supernatural). Because God both created the natural order and then expropriated it without destroying it in the incarnation, the Christian must be the first to preserve the proper autonomy of that which is natural. A Christocentric approach, far from undermining this, is the only one to properly assure it. Nevertheless, Barth's doctrine of election and his insistence on treating all articles of the creed from a Christological perspective would remain a permanent influence on Balthasar's subsequent theological development.

CONCLUSION: THE LATER YEARS

The purpose in this chapter was rather humble: it was neither to present an exhaustive biography, nor was it even to introduce all of the significant influences upon Balthasar's thought—this would have required discussion of a host of thinkers from Homer to Buber, and would have necessarily included, for instance, Gustav Siewerth and Ferdinand Ulrich, not to mention Heinrich Schleier and Louis Bouyer; it was, rather, to offer enough of a glimpse into Balthasar's life and influences to prepare the way for the more detailed treatment of his thought which follows. In his later years Balthasar continued his work primarily as publisher, lecturer, priest and writer. In June 26, 1988, just days before receiving the Cardinal's hat from John Paul II, Balthasar died as he was preparing to celebrate morning Mass.

CHAPTER TWO

BALTHASAR'S METHOD: BACKGROUND AND HISTORY

It both makes sense from the nature of the case and is a historically proven fact that Neoplatonism and Christian theology were able to travel a good part of the way together. On the other hand, their paths diverged from their very origin. The contrast between the biblical and nonbiblical "concepts" of God already suggests this, and Christian thought came to realize it at the latest by the time of the Council of Nicea. Now, this divergence has left open two possible outcomes: Christians have either fundamentally reinterpreted the theoretical and practical methods of Neoplatonism or else have ignored, or, at least, insufficiently corrected, the divergence itself—a move that has taken a bitter toll in the history of Christian theological theory and spiritual mystical praxis. [1]

Before proceeding to this or that aspect of Balthasar's theology, it is important to have a basic grasp of his understanding of the nature of theology and of theology's relationship to philosophy. In fact, as the next two chapters unfold it will become clear that this is the most perplexing aspect of Balthasar's entire work. Why, the question is, does he do theology the way he does? Why write a trilogy based on the classical "transcendental properties of Being": the Beautiful, the Good and the True? What role, if any, does philosophy play for/in theology? Why begin with beauty? What is "meta-anthropology"? But before we will be in a position to answer any of these questions, it will be helpful to have a basic understanding both of the current state of the question, and of the historical roots of these questions. Any theologian who has opted to do theology in the context of the transcendental properties of Being must owe a great deal to the history of Western thought. Before proceeding, then, to Balthasar's own theological method, I will provide the necessary background in this chapter by, first, looking briefly at the current state of the problem, and, second, by examining Balthasar's reading of the history of Western metaphysics and the impact that this history has had on the nature of theology.

THE PROBLEM OF THEOLOGICAL METHOD

It is axiomatic for Balthasar that the method for any science must be determined by the object of that science.[2] This may sound trite until we consider that one of the crises of modern thought as diagnosed by the philosopher Hans-Georg Gadamer is the captivity of the various intellectual disciplines to the methodology of the hard sciences. Indeed, for Gadamer, modernity can practically be defined by the attempt to conceive all truth on the terms set out by the empirical sciences. Theology has been no exception in this regard, and it will be helpful for the reader to recall the discussion over the nature of theology that was begun in the last chapter in the context of the theology of Henri de Lubac. De Lubac is important for the question of method insofar as he is, historically speaking, a transitional figure. He was born and engaged in his formative theological work in the pre-Vatican II context of neo-scholasticism, and he spent his later years in the post-Vatican II context of theological secularism and historical-criticism. Or, as de Lubac put it himself:

On the one hand, though the dualist—or, perhaps better, separatist—thesis has finished its course, it may be only just beginning to bear its bitterest fruit. As fast as professional theology moves away from it, it becomes so much more widespread in the sphere of practical action. While wishing to protect the supernatural from any contamination, people had in fact exiled it altogether—both from intellectual and from social life—leaving the field free to be taken over by secularism. Today that secularism, following its course, is beginning to enter the minds even of Christians. They too seek to find harmony with all things based upon the idea of nature which might be acceptable to a deist or atheist: everything that comes from Christ, everything that should lead to him, is pushed so far into the background as to look like disappearing for good.[3]

It is important to notice the connection between the dualism of the neo-scholastic approach and the secularism of the post-conciliar approach insofar as both of them result from a failure to integrate properly the realms of nature and grace or reason and revelation. It was the older dualism that had allowed questions of a specifically theological nature to be pushed into the background, or at least to arrive very late on the scene, creating a vacuum that had to be filled by some other way of looking at the world. De Lubac refers to this new outlook as "secularist," meaning an approach to intra-mundane problems which involves a bracketing of the God-question, a reduction of philosophy to the empirical realm, and a radical postponement of the theological. It means, in short, a purely rational account—and rational here is defined by the scientific method—of human affairs. In such a context, the fate of theology—and, therefore, of theological method—is pre-determined. Either it will have to be relegated to the realm of the private and subjective (fideism), or it will have to establish itself as being also scientific and meet up to secularist criteria (rationalism). And it is precisely this either/or that sets the context for the contemporary debate over theological method.

It will likely prove helpful, in the context of the problem just outlined, to compare Balthasar's theological approach to that of two other giants of twentieth-century theology, Karl Barth and Karl Rahner, a tactic that is supported by Balthasar himself.[4] This will also be beneficial because the schools associated with these men, the post-critical school on the one hand and the Transcendental Thomist or the mediating school on the other, still exert a fair amount of influence in the current discussion of theological method. As David Tracy states in his foreword to Jean-Luc Marion's *God Without Being*:

> Christian theology today is marked by a great divide. The traditional historical divides within Christianity—Protestant, Catholic, Orthodox—remain intact but have become far less significant than they have been historically. Rather, a peculiarly modern conflict now crosses all the major Christian theological traditions, whether Catholic, Protestant or Orthodox. Since Schleiermacher and Hegel, Christian theology has been in intense internal conflict over its proper response to modernity (and more recently, as in Marion, to post-modernity). There are many ways to describe this pervasive modern theological conflict. For present purposes, we may

name it a conflict between two basic theological strategies on the proper Christian response to modernity . . . One classic modern strategy wants to correlate the claims of reason and the disclosures of revelation. The other strategy believes that reason functions best in theology by developing rigorous concepts and categories to clarify theology's sole foundation in revelation. On this second view, since revelation alone is theology's foundation, any attempt at correlation is at best a category mistake—at worst, an attempt to domesticate the reality of God by means of reason and Being.[5]

If we follow Tracy's lead here in delineating modern theological method in terms of a mediating school and a revelocentric school, then surely Karl Rahner must be considered one of the main sources of the former, while Karl Barth stands at the origins of the latter. We have already offered some of the historical background to Rahner's approach in the previous chapter while discussing de Lubac's treatment of the relationship between nature and grace. Like de Lubac, Rahner accepted the so-called method of immanence of Blondel and Marechal. He understood that if revelation were only of extrinsic interest to human beings *qua* human beings, then it would be impossible to answer the objections of a Kant that revelation is simply "heteronomous" to human concerns. There must be something, in this view, in the very structure of human nature and human knowing which opens up *as human* to that which transcends the human, so that human beings can hear and respond to the Word of God when it comes. Or, as Rahner puts it, human beings are finite creatures, situated in a particular place and a particular time who are, nevertheless, open to that which transcends place and time. They are, to use the title of one of Rahner's works, "hearers of the word," and are ready, as such, to hear a word from that which transcends the finite and time-bound, namely, God. As Christians, of course, it is axiomatic that God's final word comes to us in the person of Jesus Christ. And yet Rahner wants to caution against the notion that this word comes to us from nowhere. Recall the question in the last chapter posed to Blondel: "Why should I be obliged to inquire into and take account of a casual event which occurred 1900 years ago in an obscure corner of the Roman Empire?" Accordingly, Rahner presents Jesus, not as a "word from nowhere," but as the archetypical hearer of the word. In his earthly form, Jesus exemplifies what it means to be open to transcendence, to be a hearer of the word, and as such becomes the most fully human person who ever lived. If Rahner's starting point is therefore anthropological—he begins with human beings and their search for a meaning which transcends the moment—his end point is God's self-revelation in Jesus Christ, and the path from one to the other is evolutionary and ascending in nature.[6]

For Karl Barth, the approach just outlined cannot help but reduce the God of Jesus Christ to the level of the highest aspirations of humanity, and cannot, therefore, escape either the charge of a Feuerbach, that God is just "man writ large," or Heidegger's famous critique of "onto-theology." If Rahner's starting point is anthropology, Barth's is Jesus Christ, specifically, the Jesus Christ who, far from coming as the highpoint of all human philosophical, moral and religious endeavors, comes as the final word of judgment upon them. For Barth, in short, Jesus Christ is the end (and not in the sense of goal) of all religion, precisely because religion is the history of humanity's search for God, while Jesus Christ is the personification of God's search for humanity. Barth's approach forces us to remember that it was precisely one of the most advanced and cultured societies in human history that put Jesus to death on a cross, and that it was the most religiously advanced people in history who cooperated in this decision. We must also recall Barth's own experience in the early part of the twentieth century when the high, democratic culture of Western Europe instigated two of the worst wars in human history. What worries Barth, therefore, about human nature is not so much its capacity for atheism as its capacity for idolatry, not so much its disbelief as its over-belief in its own ability to transcend history in the direction of some ultimate meaning or kingdom. God's self-revelation in Jesus Christ, especially in Christ crucified and forgiving his enemies, marks God's answer *from above* to the human desire to storm heaven *from below*. If in Rahner's view *eros* seems naturally to culminate in *agape*, in Barth's view *agape* is God's judgment on human *eros*.

And so we are back to the two alternatives outlined in the David Tracy quote above: either a mediating theology which emphasizes the continuity between the human search for God and God's self-revelation in Jesus Christ, or a revelocentric approach that emphasizes the uniqueness and singularity of Jesus Christ in the midst of the various human attempts to reach transcendence. It would seem that we are stuck with a theological method that salvages universality or relevance at the cost of specific content, or one that salvages specificity and content at the cost of universality. But it should be noted that both Rahner and Barth work very hard to eschew this either/or. After all, Rahner's entire transcendental approach culminates quite specifically in Jesus Christ, and not in some vague "God of the philosophers." And Karl Barth precisely sees Jesus Christ as the only and therefore *universal* answer to the catastrophic consequences of humanity's attempt to construct a god in its own image. It must be remembered that Barth sees the human tendency towards idolatry as itself being universal. If Rahner's universal anthropology culminates in the one and only Jesus Christ, Barth's Jesus Christ becomes the universal and necessary antidote for human idolatry.

And yet the dangers in both methods are apparent as soon as one looks at the other side. Rahner's approach really does make it difficult to account for the cross and the radical nature of New Testament conversion. If Jesus is just the highest example of humanity transcending itself towards God, why should he have been so offensive to the most philosophically astute (the Romans) and to the most religiously astute (the officials of the Judaism of Jesus' day)? Barth's view, on the other hand, makes it difficult to account for the fact that anybody should be attracted to Jesus' message at all. If what Jesus reveals about God simply goes against everything that human nature is oriented towards, why would human beings respond to it? Why would it be good news? Why, most importantly, would the incarnation of Jesus Christ not have resulted in the destruction of human nature, rather than in the healing thereof? After all, Jesus is not only fully God, he is also fully human.

Understanding this conflict between these two giants of twentieth-century theology and the alternative methods that their theologies have produced will go a long way in helping us to understand Balthasar's distinct contribution to the question of theological method. But before we can proceed to this contribution, it is important to see where Balthasar places his approach into the overall history of Christian thought. This is important, for Balthasar was intent upon not allowing modernity alone to set the tone of the discussion. Sometimes the way forward requires a look back, and Balthasar had learned from de Lubac that a return to the wellsprings can often provide the best water for the journey ahead. Fortunately for our present purposes, Balthasar himself wrote a number of essays and books which provide the historical context for his own theological endeavor.

BALTHASAR'S READING OF THE HISTORY OF THEOLOGY: THE FATHERS, THE SCHOLASTICS AND OURSELVES

The purpose of this section is simply to place Balthasar's thought—since he insists upon doing so himself—in a context larger than the one just outlined. In order to do so in the space allotted, this will obviously have to be little more than a sketch. But a sketch can often be beneficial in spite of its shortcomings. In a number of places, but most importantly in his programmatic little book *Love Alone is Credible*, Balthasar places his unique approach to theology—an approach he refers to as the "third way of love alone"—in the context of the three periods of church history: the ancient, the medieval and the modern (sometimes collapsing the first two into one). It is likely the case that when most people try to situate Balthasar into a theological school or camp, the first one that comes to mind is the so-called *ressourcement* school, associated with de Lubac, Danielou, Chenu, Bouillard, et al. But in a much neglected talk given at the Catholic University of America Balthasar made his own attempt to locate his thought, and while it is certainly not false that Balthasar was deeply associated with the *ressourcement* movement mentioned above, it is not without significance that Balthasar did not simply situate himself in this school. After highlighting the characteristics of two schools, the "transcendental approach" (associated with Rahner) and then the school deriving from de Lubac's *Catholicism* (discussed above in Chapter One), Balthasar places himself in the school of those who are "overwhelmed by the Word of God in the way the beloved is overwhelmed by the declaration of the lover."[7] Besides himself, Balthasar mentions three other twentieth-century thinkers: Heinz Schürmann, a German biblical theologian who refused to kowtow to the rationalism of so much modern biblical scholarship, Louis Bouyer and Heinrich Schlier, both converts, the latter being also a biblical scholar.

Surprising as this placement is, it helps to account for Balthasar's complex relationship with the Church Fathers and what he calls their "cosmocentric" theological method, a relationship complex enough to warrant seemingly contradictory assessments in the secondary literature, and even in Balthasar himself.[8] In one breath, for instance, Balthasar can call Dionysius the Aeropagite the most aesthetic of theologians, only to turn around in the next to accuse him of never even mentioning the cross (i.e. of neglecting the historical and particular in the light of the cosmic and universal). In what follows, I will offer a brief presentation of Balthasar's critique of the cosmocentric and anthropocentric methods so that we might be in a better position to understand Balthasar's alternative. I will break this section up into three sub-sections, dealing, respectively, with the cosmocentric approach, the role of Thomas Aquinas, and the anthropocentric approach. But before doing so, a brief comment about historical method is in order.

For Balthasar, because theology must always make use the of the linguistic and cultural "vestments" of its time and place, retrieval of past Christian thought will always involve a process of discerning between that which is authentically Christian in any historical figure, and that which is merely the product of the thought-forms which are being used. This is precisely an act of discernment because there is no scientific or dialectical method that makes the task an easy or straightforward one. Too often, for instance, Protestant thinkers have made too neat and clean a distinction between the "pure Gospel" and its human expression in order to enact a return to some fictitious, purely evangelical way of thinking, only to fail to realize that the New Testament itself was written in Greek and made use of the very thought forms that are being rejected. In other words, in their rush to divest the Gospel of all foreign vestments they have not only failed to appreciate the fact that God's grace is universally active, they have also ended up throwing out things which are actually an integral part of the Christian faith. Balthasar once quipped that Barth's theology sometimes tried to be more biblical than the Bible. At the other end sits the hyper-traditionalist Catholic who thinks that anything less than a slavish repetition of everything that Aquinas taught amounts to a betrayal of the tradition. While Balthasar's method of discernment does not subscribe to the Protestant myth of some pre-linguistic, purely evangelical way of thinking—after all, God is the God of reason and language as well as faith, the God of creation as well as redemption—it does endeavor to make sure that the distinctively Christian is being allowed to transform the thought form which is being appropriated. In the great Christian thinkers of the past, this generally means allowing their better moments—when Christ truly does "shine through"—to correct their weaker moments—when the Gospel is being obscured in favor of this or that philosophical system. It is this that helps to account for Balthasar's rather nuanced approach to the thought of the past.

In order to make this more concrete, Balthasar has provided us with three "rules of discernment."[9] First, because of the doctrine of the creation of all things in and for Christ, there is no such thing as a purely natural religion or worldview. "Every religion stands in a more or less direct . . . light of Christ's revelation . . ." The same goes for thinkers like Plato and Plotinus. Even here an act of Christian discernment is needed to determine what aspects are more or less compatible with the Gospel. Second, however, "we must not underestimate the element of original sin in these worldviews." This is especially the case when these worldviews claim the same sort of catholicity as the Christian faith. As such, it can never be a matter of simply adding Christian specifics on top of a purely natural, philosophical worldview. What, for instance, happens to the relationship between God and the world when it turns out that God is a Trinity of loving persons and not Plotinus's One or Aristotle's "unmoved mover?" Third, even though the Church has been promised infallibility in terms of her dogmatic decisions and in terms of a general orthodoxy—and here Balthasar appeals to the old maxim that "the *whole* Church cannot go astray *for long* in *important* matters"—it is not above making particular errors stemming from the influence of this same original sin, on account of the sinfulness of her members. Finally,

> [t]here is a true development and unfolding of dogma. The Church has never subsequently fallen once more into the confusion of Arianism, Donatism, Pelagianism. And what remains to her from these dearly bought experiences are not just a few dry dogmatic formulae but a living knowledge of the disadvantages and dangers of entire worldviews.[10]

In other words, the Church, in overcoming the various heresies of each time and place, has increased her ability to perform the very act of discernment which Balthasar is commending.

The Cosmocentric Method: The Fathers

The early Church worked out its theology in the context of philosophy's triumph over and subsumption of the world of ancient myth. In a perceptive comment, Joseph Ratzinger has noted that the early Church surprisingly sided with the philosophers (the "atheists") instead of the poets (the "believers") in this conflict.[11] In other words, the Church Fathers were sympathetic to the philosophical critique of the pagan gods in the light of the True and the Good as executed by a Socrates or a Plato. Indeed, the Fathers saw this critique as a move in the direction of monotheism and an understanding of the material world as a manifestation of and a participation in that which is simply One, True, Good and Beautiful. We can see this worldview quite clearly, for instance, in Plato's *Symposium*, where *eros* is finally depicted as the human desire to transcend the world of matter and change into the direction of that which is unchanging and immaterial, from beautiful things to "beauty itself." In Plato's view, the gods of the ancient myths were still too much a part of the world of finitude and change and so had to be transcended in the direction of the unchanging and unified Good. This philosophical critique should not be confused with the modern, scientific form of demythologization insofar as Plato's cosmos, as a pale reflection of the world "above," is still rife with mystery, and the human being, as "microcosm," is still "possessed" with a strong desire for that which transcends all that is finite and material.[12] In short, Plato's critique of myth does not amount to a simple rejection, but is, rather, a purification. "It is therefore impossible for Plato to do as the moderns would like and make a sharp distinction between 'scientific understanding' and 'mythical statement'."[13]

Still, Plato's—and philosophy's in general—incorporation and subsumption of the mythical into the philosophical is not without danger in Balthasar's view, for it tends to bring the divine under the control of human thought. And so he must ask whether or not the act of transcendence on the part of philosophy has not already found its transcendent object. And if it has, can such an object still be worthy of awe or worship? Can one still pray to it? Almost imperceptibly the *glory* of the gods found in the poets has passed, in philosophy, to the *beauty* of the cosmos. "Reason which inquires about being as a whole is a 'monological' act . . . [T]he dialogical act of prayer is cut off at a stroke . . . [W]hat had hitherto been depicted as 'glory' . . . in the age of philosophy will be called 'beautiful'."[14] Now, it is precisely into this thought-world—what Balthasar calls the "cosmocententric"—that early Christianity was born. And, as then Cardinal Ratzinger pointed out above, the Christians tended to take the side of the philosophers against the polytheism and moral confusion of the poets. Indeed, the entire schema of a world which had fallen from some pre-cosmic heights, but which was, explicitly in the *eros* of the human being, longing to return to those heights, was taken over almost whole cloth by the Fathers of the Church.[15] All of the classical spiritual treatises which involve some sort of an ascent—up a mountain, up stairs, up ladders, and the like—are based at least in part upon this egress/regress pattern.

Of course this is not the whole story. Balthasar's interpretation is far too nuanced to amount to the typical Harnackian charge that the Church Fathers were just crypto-Platonists, who happened to be using Christian images. Nevertheless, there exists a real danger that the pantheistically tinged worldview of the Greeks holds too much influence over the Patristic period of the Church. And Balthasar will point out that it is often only the heretics—the Gnostics, the Arians, the Pelagians, etc.—who will force the Church to delineate a more distinctively Christian vision.[16] In fact, it is precisely in the creedal pronouncements which defend the full divinity and humanity of Christ, the three-in-oneness of the Triune God, the fact that salvation comes from the One who "came down from heaven," etc., that the Church preserves the Gospel in the face of this overarching Platonism.

Still, these theological pronouncements are not always sufficiently interwoven into the whole of their works, and Balthasar finds three areas in particular in which the Platonic outlook tends to drown out the specifically Christian. First, the Platonic scheme is one of emanations *descending* from that which is highest ("god," the Good), down into the world of ideas or forms (*ideos*), and down, farther, into the world of matter, to the things which we can actually perceive through the senses. This theme of descent not only sometimes displaces a proper emphasis on the goodness of creation, it also enters into the Patristic treatment of the Trinity, so that the persons of the Trinity can be seen in terms of a gradual descent from the Father down to the Son down to the Spirit. Origen's tendency towards subordinationism is a classic example of this. Again, Balthasar will point out that it was only Arius who finally forced the Church to draw a harder line. Next, Balthasar mentions the fact that, even if the Fathers devised an orthodox view of the Trinity, this Trinitarian theology too often had an insufficient impact on their spiritual writings. It often seems that the ascent of the soul is not to the Triune God but to a simple essence of a God standing "on the summit of the Platonic pyramid."[17] This spirituality of egress-regress also often replaced a proper emphasis on mission, on the fact that just as the Father sent the Son, so he sends human beings into the world. Finally, there is a tendency, especially on the part of the Alexandrians, to see the incarnation almost as a distortion of the purely spiritual, resulting in a Christology that is tinged by docetic and Eutychian elements. It must be stated that Balthasar will wish to balance out this negative assessment by pointing out that it was precisely the Fathers who resisted the full blown implications of these Platonic tendencies in their doctrines of creation *ex nihilo*, the incarnation, the gratuity of God's gift of salvation, the full humanity and divinity of Christ, the Trinity, and so on, but in their overall approach he will still see evidence of the above-mentioned emphases. At its root, Balthasar's concern will be that a general Platonic worldview is allowed to establish the context into which the positive doctrines of Christianity take their place. In *Love Alone* he expresses this concern accordingly:

> The transition that fulfilled the philosophical universe in the Christian-theological one granted to reason, enlightened and strengthened by grace, the highest possible vision of unity. Because of this unity, the question whether revelation introduced a special principle of unity was all but left behind.[18]

It was not until the High Middle Ages, in fact, that, with the help of Aristotle, lines would be drawn a little clearer. It is here that Thomas Aquinas plays such a central role in Balthasar's account of the history of theology, for it is precisely Thomas, under the influence of Aristotle, who draws the sorts of distinctions sometimes lacking in the more Platonic approach of the Fathers. Since Thomas's role in this story is such a pronounced one in Balthasar's telling, it will do us well to take a closer look at it.

Scholasticism, Thomas Aquinas and the Real Distinction

There are times, for instance when Balthasar is dealing with history in terms of a transition from the cosmocentric to the anthropocentric, when Thomas will be included in the Patristic tendencies discussed above. In fact, in the essay under discussion Balthasar has this to say about Scholasticism in general and Thomas in particular,

> However strange it may sound, the actual dangers of Scholasticism do not come from Aristotelianism . . . but from the residue of Platonism that had still not yet been overcome. That is why, to

name the most important and controversial point, the material separation of nature and supernature . . . was never fully realized, even in Thomas. For Thomas still knew nothing of a natural final goal of man that pertains to the nature of the creature as such . . . So he had to come to the conception of a 'natural longing' of the creature for the supernatural vision of God. But this then entails, of course, the danger of interpreting the *potentia oboedientialis* as a *potentia naturalis*, which corresponds to the patristic danger of looking on the *pneuma* as an essential component of man.[19]

In other words, in spite of the Thomistic emphasis on the real otherness which pertains between God and the world, there is still the tendency to see the human being's orientation to the divine as a capacity which belongs to the human being, a capacity which reaches it goal precisely in the movement away from the material and particular and to the spiritual and universal. In short, the egress-regress schema, which comes directly from Plato and which cannot help but result in a general disparagement of difference, materiality and particularity, is not totally absent from Thomas's thought. However, in keeping with Balthasar's tendency to build on the strongest elements of a person's thought, Thomas's role in intellectual history will, in Balthasar's final analysis, be that of a kairos, mediating at once between the ancient tendency to subsume the world into God and the modern tendency either to subsume God into the world (Idealism) or to reduce the world to mere world (Empiricism). Balthasar will accordingly find in Thomas's treatment of *esse* (Being) and *essentia* (essence) the clue to negotiating the proper relationship between God and the world that will mark Christianity's unique contribution to the history of thought.[20]

In the early part of the twentieth century there was a revolution in Thomistic studies which focused on the revolution in philosophical thought initiated by Thomas. It is true, as Balthasar stated above, that this revolution was initiated in part by the recent discovery of the philosophy of Aristotle, a discovery which made it possible, on account of Aristotle's notion of causality, to grant a greater autonomy to the natural order. For Aristotle, forms (essences) inhere in the things which actually exist, bringing them from potency to act. For instance, for Aristotle, the rational soul is the form of the body; it is the actualizing principle in the rational animal that the human being is. Furthermore, Aristotle teaches that all things that exist owe their existence to something that came before them; that is, all things are caused. Unless this relationship of cause to effect is to go on forever into an "infinite regress," Aristotle maintains that there must be some first cause that is not itself caused by anything else. However, the relationship between this cause and the subsequent causes caused by this cause remains problematic for the Christian insofar as this "unmoved mover" seems still to belong to the chain of things in this world, even if it is the highest thing in that chain. Or, to put it another way, Being seems to include both Aristotle's god and the world within itself.

Enter Aquinas. As Gilson is constantly insisting, Aquinas is first and foremost a theologian. And yet, in order to make sense of what he has received in faith and in order to articulate that faith in a reasonable manner, Aquinas made generous use of philosophy. Indeed, in Aquinas there is a concerted effort to make a distinction, if not a separation, between philosophy and theology, an effort that one does not find to this degree in the Fathers of the Church. Still, this does not amount to anything like a totally autonomous or independent philosophy, for Aquinas will always philosophize in the light of his faith. This is nowhere more evident than when he is dealing with the question of Being. How, namely, do we account for the existence of anything at all? Where do things come from? If all things are contingent, that is, caused by other things, how can there be anything at all? Such questions are not strictly speaking of interest only to the religious believer; they are of interest to human beings as human beings. And yet, once one has come to believe in Christian revelation, with its doctrine of creation, it is impossible to approach these questions in the same way. In short, even if Aquinas wants to persist in a way that rightly distinguishes philosophy from theology, his philosophy does not remain untouched by the light of faith.

The aspect of Thomas's thought that Gilson and others have latched onto in order to speak to the revolution under discussion concerns the revelation of God's name to Moses in the book of Exodus. When Moses asks God his name, God replies: "I am who I am" (Exodus 3.14, RSV). Whatever else this text means, Thomas understood it to reveal something unique about the nature of God, namely, that God is uniquely the "pure act of to be itself." And Thomas would unpack the meaning of this in order to illustrate the fundamental difference between God and everything else that exists. For everything else that exists, Aquinas insists—and this goes even for angels and intelligible forms—there is a polarity between *what* they are and *that* they are. In other words, a human being *exists* and it exists as this or that human being. To its essence (human being) is added its existence (that it is this or that individual). And since there are any number of human beings, no one human being can exhaust what it is to be a human being. With God, on the other hand, *esse* (the fact that God *is*) is perfectly one with *what* God is (essence, *essentia*). We might say that God exhausts what it means to be God. Or, if we are to follow the Thomistic language, in God there is no potentiality at all inasmuch as God is pure act of to be itself.

The following two quotes from Thomas should clarify what has been said to this point about the relationship between *esse* (Being) and *essentia* (essence):

> Everything which comes after the first Being, since it is not its own *esse*, has an *esse* which is received in something by which the *esse* is limited; and thus in every creature the nature of the thing which participates in *esse* is one thing, and the participated *esse* is something else. And since every thing participates in the first act by assimilation insofar as it has *esse*, the participated *esse* in each thing must be related to the nature which participates (in) it as act to potency.[21]

And then,

> Every created substance is composed of potency and act. For it is manifest that only God is his own *esse*, as though essentially existing, insofar, that is, as his act of existing [*suum esse*] is his substance. And this can be said of no other being: subsistent *esse* can be only one. It is such that in it the substance participating in *esse* is other than the *esse* itself that is participated. But every participant is related to what it participates as potency and act, that is, of that which is and its act of *esse*.[22]

Building on what has been said so far, and from the two quotes just given, the first principle of Thomistic metaphysics can be named the real and fundamental distinction between God, who simply is his own Being, and everything else which exists, for which there is a necessary polarity between Being and essence. Yet there is another distinction in Aquinas's thought that is of fundamental importance for Balthasar, and it concerns the distinction between that Being which subsists—namely, God—and that Being which does not subsist, or, that Being which only subsists in the things which actually exist—namely, created Being. As Balthasar puts it, "It [created *esse*] only realizes natures in so far as it realizes itself in natures. In itself it has no subsistence but inheres in natures: *esse non est subsistens sed inhaerens* . . . It is only in them that it comes to 'standing' and subsistence."[23] This latter point can allow Balthasar, building on Thomas, to speak of a mutual interdependence between created *esse* and the natures (essences) of existing things. In some strange way we can see that *esse* only gains itself, so to speak, insofar as it is willing to give itself away, or, better, insofar as it allows itself to be given away. This also points to the uniqueness of Thomas's philosophy vis-à-vis that of Aristotle: for Aristotle, the highest principle of unity in a thing was its form. What struck Aristotle about a tree, for instance, was its tree-ness. The differences between actually existing trees could now be attributed to accidents. But for Aquinas, more important than the form of a thing is the fact that the thing exists at all, the fact that it has been granted a participation in the act of Being!

From the two distinctions just sketched—between God who is his own Being and beings which are a combination of Being and essence, on the one hand, and between uncreated and subsistent Being and created and non-subsistent Being on the other—Balthasar can draw four important principles from Aquinas' thought upon which he will build. First, on account of this latter distinction, between God and non-subsistent Being, it is no longer appropriate simply to equate God with the being of things, except insofar as he is considered their first and exemplary cause. This allows for a greater understanding of the transcendence of God than we get in Greek thought.[24] Second, on account of God's transcendence as the one who simply is his own Being, we can know that God exists, but not "what" he is. Our knowledge of him works backwards from effects to their cause and so is not direct knowledge. Far from making God an object of human knowledge, Thomas's proofs are necessary precisely because God's existence is neither self-evident nor immediately comprehensible to the finite mind. Third, moving from effects to their cause is a knowing through remotion or negation. And this is why Thomas actually heightens rather than decreases the need for faith and revelation. The God we come to know about on account of the *via negativa* is precisely a God who is infinitely above our natural ways of knowing. And, finally, none of this is to gainsay the fact that there is also a positive likeness between God and things which the *via negativa* presupposes: it is the likeness of a cause in its effect. This proportion between God and the world provides the basis for Thomas's notion that there is no excellence found in the created order that is not found preeminently in God. As we will see later, this last notion will become very important in Balthasar's development of Thomas's thought.[25]

By allowing the light of faith to fall upon questions which naturally arise for philosophy, Thomas is able to overcome the tendencies in ancient thought towards pantheism on the one hand and a view of the material world as a fall and diminution of Being on the other. In other words, ancient philosophy has always had a difficult time accounting for the why of the material world. Paradoxically, by establishing a greater distinction between God and the world, Thomas is simultaneously able to establish a greater intimacy between them, inasmuch as everything that exists owes its existence to a free act of God, while at the same time affirming the goodness of all that exists.

> It is precisely here that a new kind of intimacy of God in the creature becomes clear, an intimacy which is only made possible by the distinction between God and *esse*. Allowing natures to participate in reality—God's most proper prerogative—is not to be understood as the disintegration or diminution (on the part of the creature) of God's Being and unicity (which is how it is invariably seen outside the Christian tradition) and the essences of things must not appear as a simple fragmentation of reality, in a negative sense, but must be seen positively as posited and determined by God's omnipotent freedom and therefore are grounded in the unique love of God.[26]

This approach helps to alleviate many of Balthasar's concerns about the cosmocentric method, especially its tendency towards a disparagement of the material world and the escapist spirituality which this sometimes engenders. Recall, also, the Platonist tendency to swallow the glory of the gods into the beauty of the world. In Aquinas's approach, the act of creation provides the basis for affirming both the world's beauty and the glory of the God who created it.

The Anthropocentric Turn

Still, Thomas's synthesis was a delicate one, and after his death it would soon break down in two directions: on the one hand, Scotus and his disciples will reduce "Being" to an abstract concept which can be applied at once, and in the same way ("univocally"), to God and the world (rationalism), and on the other, Eckhart and his disciples will simply equate Being with God (idealism), a move that will only exacerbate the tendencies that Balthasar saw at times in the Fathers of the Church. The approach of Scotus, especially as taken up by his disciple Ockham, will eventually lead to the notion of the world as "mere world," as no longer reflective, as it still was in Aquinas, of the glory and intelligence of God. Part of blame here belongs to the disciples of Averroes and their attempt to determine just how far human reason could go in its investigation into Being when it bracketed off divine revelation. Unfortunately, the Church's (justified) response to the false philosophism of the Averroists led to an even greater demarcation between philosophy and theology than Aquinas had already achieved. In other words, the exaggeration of philosophy's reach as articulated by the Averroists, a reach that would extend quite directly to the very Being of a God who now created the world out of a rational necessity, would lead to the opposite reaction among the theologians: namely, to a philosophy that was limited to but given control over this world, and to a theology which alone could offer us reliable knowledge of the invisible (theologism). As many of the Nominalists were fond of saying, reason and this world go together, faith and the next world.[27] And the distinction, in Aquinas, between the God whom we can know exists through reason, but whom we can only know through faith, becomes in Ockham an abyss.[28]

Balthasar's reading of the history of Western thought, therefore, endeavors to get to the roots of the transition from the cosmological approach of the ancients to the anthropocentric approach of the moderns. Already in Ockham we have a notion of an external world of pure singulars which do not, of themselves, bespeak any unifying or intelligible order; if such an intelligible order exists, it must be a property of the mind. The "natures" of things, therefore, do not come from the things, but are attributed to the things from the soul of the one knowing them. Whereas according to Thomas the natures or forms of things are "nothing other than a kind of seal of the divine knowledge in things" (De Ver., 2.1, ad 9),[29] for Ockham such "natural universals" are "notional signs," mental images, for instance "dog," which can apply to any single dog, and are "cognitions in the soul."[30] Even if Ockham will agree with Thomas that the forms for things are first in the mind of God, he differs insofar as it is the spiritual subject with its capacity to know that provides the link between God and this world. Of course I am not interested here in trying to do justice to Ockham's philosophy, but mention him to show the gradual transition from a cosmos which is itself pregnant with meaning to the human being who alone is able to offer spiritual meaning to an otherwise mechanistic world. The step from Ockham to Descartes, with his notion of the universe as a machine over which reason is given absolute control, is not an altogether improbable one.

What interests Balthasar is what happens to the nature of theology after this transition occurs. Recall the assertion made above that, after Aquinas, there will be two tendencies: either Being will be reduced to a concept which can at once be applied to both God and the world (Scotus) or Being will simply be equated with God (Eckhart). The first will lead, via Ockham, to a philosophy which can only concern itself with singulars in this world (empiricism) and a theology which is increasingly Biblicist and fideistic in nature; the second will lead to an equation of God with the unfolding of Spirit in the world (idealism), and theology will simply be absorbed into philosophy. And it is Kant who provides the transitional link from the former empiricism of Hume, which, if taken to its logical conclusion cannot account for the success of modern science in finding law-like behavior in reality, to the idealism of a Hegel, for whom God is nothing more than Absolute Spirit unfolding and thereby coming into its own in the cosmos, as that which is other than itself. He also provides the step from the privatization of faith and revelation to their anthropological reduction.

> The fact that we *can* do what we quite easily and clearly understand that we *ought* to do, this superiority of the *supersensual man* in us over the *sensual man*, who is *nothing* in comparison with the former . . . even though the latter is *everything* in his eyes: this inalienable moral capacity is an object of supreme wonderment, and it becomes all the more amazing the longer one contemplates this true . . . ideal, so much so that we can forgive those who, misled by the inconceivability of this capacity, which is after all practical, this *supersensual* power in us, take it to be something supernatural. By supernatural, I mean something that does not lie within our own power and does not belong to us, but is rather the influence of another, higher spirit. Nevertheless, they are quite wrong.[31]

The particular teachings of the Christian faith are absorbed, after Kant, into a universal ethic which can, in theory, be deduced by human reason. If one were to ask Kant the question which was asked to Blondel, mentioned above, Kant would reply that Jesus is still relevant insofar as he exemplifies the "inalienable moral capacity" found in all of us. This led the theologians after Kant to try to find new ways to salvage the particular contents and teachings of Christianity, and the predominate way of doing this was to show that such teachings and doctrines both arise from and fulfill the individual, human subject. If the famous quest for the historical Jesus had proved that we either: (a) have no access to the Jesus of history on account of the fact that the real Jesus is overlaid with so much theological baggage already in the New Testament; or (b) have access to a Jesus that is in fact very different from the one found in the Gospels and, even more so, the creeds, then the theology which dominates the nineteenth and early twentieth centuries would have to be built on more subjective and immediate grounds. From Lessing to Schleiermacher to Bultmann there would be an attempt to found, upon human subjectivity, an immediate contact with a Jesus who transcends history. In a strange and paradoxical way, however, we can see that Bultmann's fideism is just the logical conclusion and flipside to D. F. Strauss's rationalism and skepticism. In short, the anthropological turn in philosophy led to a concomitant anthropological turn in theology, a turn for which the objective contents of history and dogma are only important to the degree that they fulfill corresponding needs in the human subject. Whether or not the resurrection happened is irrelevant, provided that the message about it is able to give rise to the same sort of authentic existence in the believer that it had given rise to in Jesus Christ. That this anthropological turn came to the fore also in Catholic theology should be obvious from the Tyrell quote mentioned in the previous chapter. And theologians would now have to work hard to show how a doctrine such as the Trinity fulfilled some innate need or disposition of the subject. As much as one might sympathize with these endeavors to reconnect theology to the lives of human beings as such, it is hard not to notice that something novel has occurred in this approach which can only mean the abandonment of the traditional contents of Christianity in the interest of their relevance to the individual subject. Balthasar concludes this section of *Love Alone*, after commending the intentions of the anthropological approach, by distinguishing it from the former, cosmocentric approach.

> Nevertheless, the tradition never set the criterion for the truth of revelation in the center of the pious human subject, it never measured the abyss of grace by the abyss of need or sin, it never judged the content of dogma according to its beneficial effects on human beings. The Spirit does not reveal himself; he reveals the Father in the Son, who has become man. And the Son never allows himself to become reabsorbed in the human spirit—and not even the Holy Spirit.[32]

CONCLUDING REMARKS

According to the reading of intellectual history presented in this chapter, theology has historically worked in two predominant intellectual milieus: the cosmocentric viewpoint of the ancients, for whom the Christian message was situated in the context of a world which had come from and was reflective of a higher, invisible and unchanging order, and the anthropocentric approach of the moderns, for whom the human subject alone still provided a connection between the material and now mechanistic cosmos on the one hand and the realm of Spirit on the other. The dangers of both of these approaches should now be obvious.

> [F]or neither the world as a whole nor man in particular can provide the measure for what God wishes to say to man in Christ; God's Word is unconditionally theo-logical, or, better, theo-pragmatic: what God wishes to say to man is a deed on his behalf, a deed that interprets itself before man and for his sake (and only therefore to him and in him).[33]

But this is not to say that Balthasar will now wish to subscribe to the Barthian method outlined in the beginning of this chapter. The problem is not with the attempt to make use of a philosophical foundation. Balthasar is very clear that without philosophy there can be no theology. A problem only arises when a particular philosophical approach, one that has not been sufficiently bathed in the light of faith, has been allowed to establish a measure outside of Christ either for the contents of the Christian faith or even for the relationship between God and the world. And, as we have seen, this can happen with both of the approaches outlined in this chapter.

Furthermore, like Rahner and Barth, Balthasar will have to work out his theological method in the context of modern secularism. As such, if he is to avoid the Scylla of immanentism, for which either the cosmos in general or the human subject in particular becomes the measure of the Christian message, or the Charybdis of sectarian fideism, for which the Christian message requires not only a blind leap of faith, but for which also any connection between the God of creation (and thereby "this world") and the God of redemption (and thereby the "world to come") has been severed, then he will have to lay a philosophical foundation for which neither the notion of a God who is love nor the goodness of a material world distinct from that God proves to be too scandalous. We have already seen the beginnings of such an approach in Thomas's real distinction, a distinction which maintained at one and the same time the absolute transcendence and yet most radical immanence of God vis-à-vis the creation order. It will only be left to work out this relationship, articulated by Balthasar in terms of the analogy of Being, in terms concrete enough to do justice to the subject matter at hand. In short, to come full circle, the method will have to be determined by the object: in this case, this means the method will have to be determined by the figure of Jesus Christ, fully God and fully man.

CHAPTER THREE

BALTHASAR'S THEOLOGICAL STYLE

Humanity will prefer to renounce all philosophical questions—in Marxism, or positivism of all stripes, rather than accept a philosophy that finds its final response only in the revelation of Christ. Foreseeing that, Christ sent his believers into the whole world as sheep among wolves. Before making a pact with the world, it is necessary to meditate on that comparison.[1]

Since the purpose of the present chapter is to present Balthasar's theological style, the sorts of questions which were raised in the last chapter—What role does philosophy play for theology? What is the relationship between reason and faith? What is meta-anthropology? What role, if any, does the classical question of Being play for theology today? What is Christocentrism?—will be with us in this chapter as well, the difference being that in this chapter they will be dealt with in terms of Balthasar's own solutions. In order to do this, I will examine Balthasar's retrieval and development of the cosmological and anthropological methods described in the last chapter. Therefore, I will, first, deal with the meaning and role of "meta-anthropology" in Balthasar's theology. Second, I will examine the place of reason and philosophy in Balthasar's theological method. Third, I will show how what has proceeded in the first two sections comes to bear on the famous fourfold distinction of Being found in the fifth volume (in English) of *The Glory of the Lord*. If the impression was given that Balthasar's method amounts to a simple rejection of the cosmocentric or anthropocentric approaches, this chapter should serve to correct that impression. Fourth, I will offer a brief account of what Balthasar means by Christocentrism. Finally, I will offer a brief overview of the trilogy, *Theological Aesthetics*, *Theo-Drama*, and

Theo-Logic, not so much in terms of its contents, which will come out in varying degrees in the subsequent chapters, but in terms of its overall structure, as well as in terms of what it tells us about Balthasar's theological method.

THE MEANING AND PURPOSE OF META-ANTHROPOLOGY

In the extremely helpful overview of his work, written in 1988 under the title, "Retrospective," Balthasar has the following to say about "meta-anthropology,"

> It is here that the substance of my thought inserts itself. Let us say above all that the traditional term "metaphysical" signified the act of transcending physics, which for the Greeks signified the totality of the cosmos, of which man was a part. For us, physics is something else: the science of the material world. For us, the cosmos perfects itself in man, who at the same time sums up the world and surpasses it. Thus our philosophy will be essentially a meta-anthropology, presupposing not only the cosmological sciences but also the anthropological sciences, and surpassing them toward the question of the being and essence of man.[2]

Let us recall that what Balthasar appreciates about Aquinas's philosophical approach is his ability to account for the goodness of the world in its distinction from God, which, for all of that, does not lose a genuine similarity to God. Recall, furthermore, that Balthasar sees Thomas as a transitional figure in the history of Western metaphysics between the cosmocentric approach of the ancients, which threatens to reduce all finite reality to the level of a mere reflection of that which is really real, and the anthropocentric approach of the moderns which severs the intrinsic connection between God and the world in order to salvage the autonomy of a natural order operating according to mechanical laws. Recall, finally, that Balthasar also worries that Aquinas is still sometimes too beholden to the old *exitus-reditus* framework, so that there can be a tendency to privilege the path to the infinite in terms of the *via negativa*, such that one must negate all that is finite and transitory in order to arrive at that which is infinite and intransitory. This tendency is compensated for when we insist, as Aquinas himself does, that nothing excellent is found in the finite realm which is not found preeminently in God. If this latter is the case, then, as Nicholas Healy puts it, "[t]he analogical movement toward God can leave behind precisely nothing created if we are to attain perfect knowledge of God."[3]

Before drawing the sorts of conclusions from the foregoing which Balthasar is going to want to draw, a further historical point must be made. If Balthasar is going to retrieve the Thomistic metaphysical heritage, he knows that he has to do so with an eye towards the conception of truth and knowledge that accompanies the modern, scientific worldview. The first revolution in this scientific turn is linked closely with the anthropocentric method discussed in the last chapter. Here it is the spiritual subject that is able to read off the mathematical necessity inherent in the cosmos, now mechanistically conceived. If the spiritual or immaterial is to be salvaged in such an approach—and the moderns knew that it was necessary to do so—it is relegated to the soul of the human subject, who is now, through the scientific method, given an unprecedented mastery over the world. But now the further question (arising from the second revolution in modern science) arises as to what happens to the soul—now dualistically conceived in the light of Descartes—after Darwin. It seems that things can proceed in one of two ways: either now the human person too will be understood as a mere epiphenomenon of this purely mechanistic and material world, or the human person will be seen as the culmination or *telos* of the natural order, the place, that is, where nature comes into its own. If one proceeds along the lines of the first alternative—as all science of a positivistic bent does—then one not only fails to ask the fundamental question as to why there is anything at all rather than nothing, one also fails to account for how spiritual Being, which is able to discover in the realm of nature the intelligible order which science presupposes, is produced by that which is allegedly sub-rational, sub-spiritual and sub-free.[4] In this latter case an ironic turn of events comes about in which the human subject, who was announced to be absolute master over the natural order by the pioneers of modern science, becomes the absolute slave of a now technologically and economically subservient science which knows no limits beyond what it *can* (there is no longer any basis for a *may*, for there is no longer any basis for freedom) do.[5] The point is simply this: Balthasar thinks that there are very good reasons to opt for the latter of these alternatives, namely, to see the human person as the *telos* of worldly Being.[6]

The two points made so far—the first about the goodness of the created order not being left behind in our ascent towards God, and the second about the human being as the place where the Being of the world comes into its fullness and even surpasses itself—help to account for Balthasar's use of meta-anthropology. It should be noted that meta-anthropology is not opposed to metaphysics, insofar as the questions of Being *qua* Being are taken up into this approach. The point is rather that meta-anthropology allows Balthasar to examine Being in its fullest and most concrete expression: the human person. The starting point enables Balthasar to avoid all of the ancient tendencies towards the disparagement of multiplicity, individuality, embodiment, relationality, and even, as we shall see, receptivity. It also enables him to do justice to the modern concern for individual rights, freedom, personhood and the like, without for all of that failing to attend to the deeper questions that make these things meaningful or possible in the first place. In short, unless we are to fall into the dangers of a modernity that can no longer defend the very freedom for which it is constantly clamoring, we must still attend to the old metaphysical questions. Why is there something rather than nothing? What is it about things which enables us to name them, and name them rightly or wrongly? Why do human beings hold each other responsible for their moral actions and does it make any sense to do so? Why does the universe open itself to human investigation without for all of that losing its fundamental mystery? It is just that now, these, and questions like them, will be examined from a vantage point which is both highest—insofar as worldly Being reaches it highest point in the human person[7]—and most concrete—insofar as it begins with the living, breathing human person, right before our eyes.

Meta-anthropology, therefore, can enable us to take up the classical questions of metaphysics, with which the modern world cannot dispense without contradiction, while acknowledging the truth of modernity's focus on the particular, subjective, experiential, historical, individual, and the like. One other point should be made before concluding this sub-section on meta-anthropology, a point that will provide a fitting transition to our next section on philosophy. It must be remembered that the classical philosophical project was also undertaken in a more or less consciously religio-theological context. There is, at least implicitly, a "god" in Plato's, Aristotle's and Plotinus's systems which cannot simply be equated with the God of Christianity. It may very well be that the reason that these three philosophers all tended towards pantheism (the absorption of the finite into the infinite) was that the image of god that is implicit in their respective philosophies is not the God of love that is revealed in Jesus Christ. This may also help to account for the general neglect of the importance of human relationality—especially the relationship between male and female—in their philosophical approaches. Indeed, it is hard to underestimate just how significant the classical view of women was in their philosophies, and in this sense we—with Balthasar—can give an appreciative nod in the direction of legitimate feminist concerns. At any rate, when Balthasar begins the final and important section of the fifth volume of *The Glory of the Lord*, he says: "In surveying Western metaphysics in its entirety, we must be amazed at how little the enigma of reproduction—not only of organic natural creatures but above all of man, who is Spirit—has concerned philosophers."[8] Meta-anthropology is appealing to Balthasar, then, because it provides a more fitting philosophical starting point for a style of thinking that is eventually going to culminate in a God who is three persons united in love in one being. This final consideration should help to prepare us for Balthasar's treatment of the relationship between philosophy and theology.

THE ROLE OF PHILOSOPHY

The first point to be made in regard to this question is that the relationship between philosophy (the consideration of Being in the light of natural reason) and theology (a reasoned reflection upon the contents revealed to faith) is embedded within the broader framework of the relationship between nature and grace. In the background of all of Balthasar's considerations regarding this relationship, implicit or explicit, lies the paradox found in Thomas Aquinas but retrieved by Henri de Lubac that the human person is the only creature of God who is oriented to an end that surpasses its natural abilities.[9] It should further be pointed out that this natural desire to know and love God has not been abrogated by sin, a fact that seems obvious if we consider that it was human nature that God expropriated in order to redeem human beings. The fact that when God speaks he speaks "as man" suggests that the human capacity for God, which is a gift itself within the broader gift of creation, has not simply been destroyed by sin.[10] This means that humanity's search for God—what in Plato receives the name *eros*—is not denounced but is, rather, appropriated when God seeks out humanity (*agape*). And this has two further implications for the relationship between philosophy and theology.

First, philosophy's search for answers to the so-called "big questions" is itself a result of the fact that human beings were made for God in the first place. In this sense, there is no such thing as a *purely* natural philosophy, insofar as the human capacity for philosophy stems from the first gift of God to human beings, the gift of creation. But, second, because this end—union with God—is not an end that human beings are naturally capable of achieving (the second part of the paradox), philosophy is by nature limited in what it is capable of achieving. There must, therefore, be a humility or childlikeness even at the level of philosophy which acknowledges its limits and which is ready to receive help when it arrives.[11] As we will see, this humility arises from the proper notion of truth itself. And since human sinfulness finds its center precisely in this lack of humility—recall, for instance, Eve's grasping for the fruit that will make her "like God"—Balthasar will not allow us to forget the effects of sin on human reason. A human reason which is not marked in some sense by a childlike or Marian receptivity will not only not achieve the knowledge of faith, it will cease even to be good reason. It is here that Balthasar can do justice to Martin Luther's notion of "whore reason," or Karl Barth's "idol factory."

The second point to be made about the role of philosophy goes back to notion of "meta-anthropology." Because created being finds its highpoint in the human person, reason also should be understood at its highpoint in inter-personal knowledge. The give and take, that is, that is witnessed when one person comes to know another person is present, in an analogous sense, all the way down to the level inanimate beings. This enables Balthasar to overcome a fateful decision which marks the beginning of modern philosophy, the decision to understand knowledge as "power" over the object of knowledge. With this decision came the related one to treat all reality as "artifice."[12] Since I can have a complete knowledge only of that which I have made (from the ground up), there is a great temptation on the part of the modern philosopher and scientist to conceive of the universe as a machine, literally. Notice, again, that the pure "given-ness" of the natural order is bypassed here and the question as to why there exists anything at all rather than nothing is forgotten. But the epistemological consequences of this decision are also deeply problematic. It is this that prompts Balthasar to begin with human knowing— where the freedom of the other is most fully realized—as a model for all knowing.

The crucial point for the question of the relationship between philosophy and theology is this: even natural knowledge is not something that the subject achieves on its own, but is marked by such things as receptivity, faith, mystery, love, dialogue and the like. In other words, knowledge has as much to do with worldly Being offering itself to be known (cf. Heidegger's recovery of the primary meaning of truth as "unconcealment") as is has to do with the *a priori* structures of the human mind. Notice that there is a revelatory dimension to knowledge all the way up from inanimate objects, which offer themselves to be known and must be given a space by the subject to do so, through human knowledge—and here Balthasar makes the more obvious point that one cannot get to know another person unless the other person freely opens up—to our knowledge of God, who also cannot be known apart from his self-revelation. This enables Balthasar to address the Kantian concern over heteronomy, insofar as Kant's rejection of either the possibility or necessity of divine revelation stemmed from his overly *a priori*-istic understanding of human knowing, even at the natural level. It also helps to explain why the various sections of the first volume of *Theo-Logic* have titles like, "Truth as Freedom," "Truth as Mystery," and "Truth as Participation."

The final point to be made in this regard is partially historical in nature, and stems from Romano Guardini's insistence that in addition to nature and supernatural grace "there is a third domain: the depths of nature that do not emerge into visibility until the light of grace falls on them."[13] Or, as Guardini puts it,

> There are realities that in themselves belong to the 'world', to the whole of immediate existence, and thus are in principle capable of being grasped by refined and deepened experience but de facto are grasped only within the encompassing grasp [*Übergriff*] of the corresponding realities of revelation.[14]

This third realm is what Balthasar sometimes refers to as Christian philosophy, but we must be careful not to misunderstand what this means. First, Balthasar sees it as obvious that there is a perennial human nature which, in turn, presents a series of perennial problems which give rise, in turn again, to a series of perennial questions. Why am I here? Where did I come from? How should I live? Where am I going? Questions such as these follow from the fact that human beings are *naturally* religious and philosophical beings.[15] Since Christianity enters into this fray, so to speak, and offers its own insights into these perennial questions, there can be no absolute separation between Christianity as revealed (from above) and religion and philosophy as natural (from below). It is inevitable, then, (and this is the second point) that when Christianity appears within human history, it will make an impact not only upon the faith of its adherents but also upon the intellectual climate of human civilization. Certain things will be brought to light that make it impossible to go on with business as usual. As Guardini puts it, the light of grace "refines and deepens" human experience, thus opening it to truths that are at the level of natural being but which, in fact, have only come to light in grace. This helps to account for why this "third domain" is not simply to be equated with theology. Because the natural realm, and therefore the realm of philosophy, is embedded within the supernatural realm, it can at once be said to have a proper autonomy as philosophy[16] (and this is because grace does not destroy but rather perfects nature) and at the same time be said to be oriented either towards belief or unbelief.[17]

The final point to be made with regard to this "third domain" is more historical in nature. Balthasar draws three possibilities from what has just been said. "First, one can take over unconsciously the theological data inherent in all philosophy, as Plato, Aristotle, and other pagan philosophers did."[18] In other words, theology was an intrinsic part of ancient philosophy. Second, "one can consciously reject them, secularize them, and reduce them to immanent philosophical truth . . . "[19] This is the move of various strands within modern and post-modern philosophy, so that the Christian entering into dialogue with such thought needs to be aware of its theological non-neutrality. This point is hard to overstress insofar as there has been a tendency on the part of a great deal of modern theology simply to make use of various philosophies and thought forms (Marxism, Freudianism, historical criticism, etc.) as if they did not already contain certain implicit (or explicit) theological commitments. Third, "one can acknowledge and accept the indelible presence of such theologoumena at the heart of concrete philosophical thinking. This is the Christian option."[20] This last quote helps us better to understand what Balthasar means by Christian philosophy. It is not that philosophy has simply been swallowed up into theology. It is rather that, in recognizing the necessarily (even if implicitly) theological dimension of all philosophy, Christian philosophy allows the light of grace to purify the act of reason *as reason.*

THE CONCRETIZATION OF THE PHILOSOPHICAL ACT: THE FOURFOLD DISTINCTION

Before we will be in a position to understand the full implications of what has just been said, especially in terms of what sets him apart from the other approaches to theology discussed above and in the previous chapter, it will be helpful to see Balthasar the philosopher at work. It is here that we will not only see his difference from the methods depicted in the Tracy quote from the previous chapter, but we will also see how he incorporates the Thomistic approach outlined there as well. It is here that we will see exactly how Balthasar retrieves the cosmocentric and anthropocentric approaches, integrating them into a third way, the way of "love alone." This "third way" is not an attempt to replace classical metaphysical concerns with a new, personalist approach. Rather, in the light of the insight mentioned above, that worldly Being both finds and surpasses itself at the level of the human person, Balthasar begins his investigations into the nature of Being with the inter-personal. By beginning accordingly, Balthasar is able to deepen Aquinas's "real distinction" into a "fourfold" distinction. It must be kept in mind, however, that these four distinctions are really aspects of the original and real distinction between God and the world.

Balthasar begins this discussion, famously, with the experience of the child and his mother. The child's first experience of the all-encompassing reality in which he finds himself is precisely in the smile of his mother. The first distinction, then, is the distinction that the child immediately recognizes between himself and his mother. But a number of important truths come to light when we think of the first encounter with Being in this way. First, the child intuitively knows (even before he is consciously aware of this) that he has been granted entry, that he owes his very existence to another. Second, for the child—and this becomes clear as soon as he returns the smile—this is always an experience of the purest joy. Pure joy is always a response to some sort of grace or gift, and this, Balthasar reminds us, is why children find it so easy to play. Third, the child can in no way conceive of his own existence as having the sort of necessity that the Being of all that surrounds him must possess. In other words, the child will eventually come to realize that the reality in which he lives could go on rather easily without his being there at all, and that there is no necessity which can account for his *individual* existence. This, too, ratifies the fact that the child's existence is pure gift and grace. Finally, the child's distinction from his mother is enveloped always, already in a prior unity of love. The eventual distinction and difference, which will become more obvious over time, can never gainsay the fact that the relationship between the two exists in the first place in the realm of a unifying love. This insight enables Balthasar to correct the modern tendency to see the other as a threat to the autonomy of the subject and has enormous implications, in my view, for political philosophy.

Once the child realizes that his existence is not a necessity of logic, but a gift of grace, once the child realizes, namely, that he has been permitted entry, he will soon come to realize that this is also true of all other existents that he will encounter: they, too, have been granted entry. And this gives rise to the second distinction: specifically, that all beings are indebted to the gift of Being in general. Balthasar makes the important further point with regard to this distinction that one cannot simply understand Being as the totality of existing beings. The contingency and particularity of existing beings cannot account for universality of Being, and thus, within the distinction between beings and Being we arrive at the dependence of beings upon Being.

The third distinction is tied up with this second insofar as it, too, arises within the distinction between Being and beings. Phenomeno-logically speaking, we never encounter "Being." We only ever encounter actual things. This goes back to the Thomistic notion, discussed above, that running does not run, only runners. Nevertheless, it still makes sense to refer to the thing *which* exists and to the fact *that* it exists. If, then, we never encounter running, but only runners, we must conclude that Being only comes to subsist in the things which actually exist. But this leads to a further question. How does the impersonal Being of all things issue forth in these things? In other words, if the Being of all things which exist only comes to subsist in those things which actually exist, if, that is, it is not subsistent, does it make any sense at all to attribute any creative capacities to this common Being? Balthasar's negative answer to this seems to be rooted in two things. First, that which does not subsist cannot be said to be responsible for the existence of actual existents. Second, that which is not itself personal or free cannot be responsible for beings which reflect both intelligence and freedom.

This third distinction, then, opens up, on its own steam, so to speak, to a fourth distinction. Indeed, Balthasar will fault a great deal of modern philosophy for not pressing past this third distinction. This can happen in Hegelian fashion when "Absolute Spirit" is simply equated with the process of worldly Being. Here the mutual interdependence of beings upon Being and of Being upon beings is simply all that there is: God is swallowed up into the world and theology is swallowed up into philosophy. But, as Balthasar points out, "[Hegel's approach] does not explain how the Spirit which is still only in search of Itself achieves such perfection which presupposes, not only a luminous intelligence . . . but a superior and playful freedom beyond all the constraints of Nature . . . "[21] Heidegger's philosophy runs into similar problems, for he also "offers us no information regarding the underivability of the interrelation between essential form and Being . . . "[22] Before Balthasar proceeds to the fourth distinction, he offers a succinct summary of the first three that deserves to be quoted in full.

> I find myself in a world in whose necessity my accidental existence cannot find a place as *pars integralis*. But all existents are in an analogous situation, since they too—either as fragments or as world-wholes—do not fit into Being as *partes integrales*. Here a third point comes into view: namely, that Being as a whole or the actuality of all that is actual does not generate from itself the actual entities, for the responsible generation of forms would presuppose a conscious and free spirit . . . It is precisely this which points inexorably beyond itself to the fourth and final distinction, which alone provides an answer to the opening question.[23]

Notice that philosophy itself, and not theology, demands that we push on beyond the first three distinctions. Only a free and self-subsistent being—for whom Being and existence are absolutely one, in whom there is no potentiality—can account for the existence of finite essences in their actual forms. In short, if the third distinction—which highlights the dependence of Being upon beings—does not open up to the fourth, Being is just as much left "hanging in the air" as the actual existent finds itself hanging in the air. "The consequence is that the grounding in God of this Being which does not depend upon any necessity, points to an *ultimate freedom* which neither Being (as non-subsistent) could have, nor the existent entity . . ."[24]

It is important to note that Balthasar is not under the impression that this fourfold distinction leads inexorably to the Christian notion of God. It could, he notes, lead just as easily to a more Platonist notion. Still, there are signposts in the philosophical investigation of Being which point to the fittingness of the Christian solution once it comes into view. In other words, even if it could not have been guessed in advance, it certainly seems uniquely suited to safeguard the sorts of truths that one has discovered, even from the side of philosophy. One can compare philosophy's role to that of John the Baptist's in the gospels: John's genuine adherence to the Old Covenant (it is not uninteresting that it is John's *Jewishness* and not his Christianity that brings him into conflict with the Pharisees and Sadducees) enables him to recognize the genuineness of Jesus' mission, even if it ultimately means that he must decrease so that Jesus can increase. In other words, John's Old Covenant faith leads him to the place where he is prepared to hear a new word, a new word that he could not have foreseen, but which helps him better to preserve all that he wanted to preserve, even from his former position. Just, then, as the New Covenant is able to fulfill without destroying the Old, so the new word of Christianity is able to fulfill without destroying all that is true from the side of humanity's natural reason and religiosity.

With regard in particular to the fourfold distinction, this can be seen especially in two ways. First, if the first three distinctions do not open up, in the fourth, to a God who, out of a free act of love, creates the world as a gift, it is very difficult to defend the goodness and freedom of the created order in its distinction from God. Again, to go back to what has been said before, either the world will be swallowed up into God—and not really have a genuine integrity of its own—or God will be swallowed up into the world, and thereby lose the very thing which makes God God. The Christian solution at once guarantees the proper autonomy of the created order vis-à-vis God, without for all of that undermining the relationship of intimacy and dependence between the world and God. If we think about these things in terms of Giver and gift—as Balthasar's metaphysical approach encourages us to do—this becomes clearer. First, God as Giver is delineated in his proper transcendence vis-à-vis the world, just as a

Giver cannot be equated with his gift. Second, as gift, the world is precisely distinct from its Giver, God. This gives the gift a worth that is proper to itself and which is not simply that of the Giver. Third, however, the gift has no worth that is absolutely autonomous from that of its Giver. In other words, the worth of the gift is derived precisely from the Giver. An expensive ring from an unloved suitor is worth less than a cheap ring from one who is loved. The "worth" of the ring, in short, stems exactly from the "worth" of the Giver, or, better, from the presence of the Giver in the gift. This means that the goodness of the world *as world* is rooted in its prior given-ness by God. As Alexander Schmemann puts it in *For the Life of the World*, the sin of Adam and Eve consists precisely in their desire to make the world an end in itself. What is interesting is that they not only lost God in the process, they also lost the world. A piece of fruit that is not seen as a gift of God, blessed by God, ceases to give joy even as a piece of fruit.

Second, when we read the fourfold distinction in the light of the fact that no excellence can be found in the created order that does not originate in God, a new possibility opens up with regard to the question of relationality and God. It should be remembered at this point that when asked about the relationship between God and the world, Aquinas responded that the relationship was rational rather than real.[25] Of course the reason for this assertion is to emphasize the absolute non-dependence of God upon the world. If the relationship between God and world were simply essential to God's nature—as it is in the case of the relationship between the world and God—then God would stand in need of the world in the same way that the world stands in need of God. As Aquinas puts this,

> Since, therefore, God is outside the whole order of creation, and all creatures are ordered to Him, and not conversely, it is manifest that creatures are really related to God Himself; whereas in God there is no real relation to creatures, but a relation only in idea, inasmuch as creatures are related to Him.[26]

Again, the fear here, as is standard in classical, Christian metaphysics, is that a real relation between God and the world would imply that God receives something from the world that God does not already have, and this would imply the very sort of potentiality in God that we have been trying to guard against in terms of the real distinction.

Certain twentieth-century Thomists, however, have noticed that the ability to "receive" seems to be of the essence of all authentic love: the higher the ability to receive, the higher the love.[27] Such discussions always seemed to get bogged down, however, in the inability to conceive receptivity apart from potentiality. Kenneth Schmitz, for instance, makes a distinction between God's Being, *per se*, and his Being "as a lover."[28] With regard to the latter, says Schmitz, God can receive something from the world—for instance, a "wound" when the world, in its freedom, decides to reject God's love. But, as Nicholas Healy points out, this is a "curious distinction," and may not do full justice to the New Testament notion that God simply *is* love.[29]

This seemingly rather esoteric discussion helps to shed important light on the full implications of Balthasar's meta-anthropological starting point. By highlighting the Thomistic notion that the Being of the world is not self-subsistent, but, in some sense, receives something from the essences to which it gives itself, and coupling this with the further Thomistic notion that no excellence is found at the created level that is not found pre-eminently in God (the "positive" aspect of the analogy of Being), and placing all of this within a personological/dialogical setting, Balthasar is in a position to assert that this give and take at the level of created Being must have its source in God. Balthasar expresses this accordingly,

> God-given Being is both fullness and poverty at the same time: fullness as Being without limit, poverty modeled ultimately on God Himself, because He knows no holding on to Himself, poverty in the act of Being which is given out, which *as* gift delivers itself without defense (b/c here too it does not hold on to itself) to the finite entities . . . Here through the greater dissimilarity of the finite and the infinite existent, the positive aspect of the *analogia entis* appears, which makes of the finite the shadow, trace, likeness and image of the Infinite.[30]

In other words, this "laying down one's life," found even at the level of finite Being, has for its prototype a God who does not just love, but a God who *is* love. It only stands to reason that the image of this love, found at the level of creation, should also be marked by such love, a love which finds its fulfillment and surpasses itself at the level of inter-personal relationships. And such give and take—the ability, namely, to give and also to receive from the beloved—should surely not be seen as a weakness or flaw, but rather as the very essence of love. As Nicholas Healy concludes,

> Nevertheless, to the extent that the perfections of being are concretely revealed in the love between persons, Balthasar . . . [has] provided good grounds for seeing receptivity as a metaphysical perfection. The implication is that act in its purity and fullness must include in some genuinely analogous sense all the perfections of love such as life, movement, even mystery and surprise. To say otherwise would be to ascribe more perfection to human love than to God's love.[31]

All of this will have to be kept in mind when we proceed to questions of an explicitly Trinitarian nature in Chapter Six below.

FOUR NOTES ON BALTHASAR'S CHRISTOCENTRISM

Since I will be addressing specifically theological questions in the remaining chapters, this section will only touch on the methodological implications of Balthasar's Christology. The late John Paul II never allowed an encyclical to pass him by without quoting the important passage from *Gaudium et Spes* 22 which states that "only in the mystery of the incarnate Word does the mystery of man take on light." I would like to think that this passage, along with John Paul II's repeated quoting of it, owes a great deal to Balthasar's call for a "Christocentric" approach to Catholic theology. Such an approach would allow the Church to preserve what was best in the Patristic and Medieval periods without for all of that neglecting truths that were now being emphasized in the Modern age. In fact, as early as 1948, in the programmatic essay entitled, "Theology and Sanctity," Balthasar made a statement that sounds strikingly similar to the famous passage so often cited by the late pope.

> Human nature and its mental faculties are given their true center when in Christ; in him they attain their final truth, for such was the will of God the Creator from eternity. Man, therefore, in investigating the relationship *between* nature and supernature has no need to abandon the standpoint of faith, to set himself up as the mediator between God and the world, between revelation and reason, or to cast himself in the role of judge *over* that relationship.

All that is necessary is for him to understand "the one mediator between God and man, the man Jesus Christ" (1 Tim. 2.5), and to believe him in whom "were all things created in heaven and on earth . . . all by him and in him" (Col. 1.16). Christ did not leave the Father when he became man to bring all creation to fulfillment; and neither does the Christian need to leave his center in Christ in order to mediate him to the world, to understand his relation to the world, to build a bridge between revelation and nature, philosophy and theology.[32]

In what follows I would like to sound four "notes" with regard to Balthasar's Christocentrism which should help to illuminate this central passage.

First, when people speak of Balthasar as a Christocentric theologian, it must be clear that this does not mean that somehow Balthasar neglects the proper autonomy of the natural or philosophical order of things. Rather, as Balthasar insists repeatedly, it is actually on account of Christology that the Christian must be the first to preserve the legitimate autonomy of the created or natural order, for it is precisely in the person of Christ that the divine and the human come together "without confusion, without separation, without admixture." In short, Jesus Christ is at once fully human and fully divine, and he is so in such a way that the divinity is not diminished by its contact with the humanity and the humanity is not diminished by its contact with the divine. Indeed, we could say that just as created Being reaches its *telos* at the level of human being, so human being reaches its *telos* when it is united to God in the one person of Jesus Christ. It therefore follows that all that has been said to this point about the analogy of Being— the relationship between God and the world—finds in highest and most concrete expression in the person of Jesus Christ. This is why Balthasar can refer to Jesus Christ as the analogy of Being in person.

Since the person of the Logos is the ultimate union of divine and created being, it must constitute the final proportion [*Mass*] between the two and hence must be the "concrete *analogia entis*" itself. However, it must not in any way overstep this analogy in the direction of an identity.[33]

It should not surprise us then, that everything that we have discussed to this point, in terms of the simultaneity of the wealth and poverty of created Being, should be recapitulated at the highest level in the person of Jesus Christ. When Jesus says, "He who wishes to save his life must lose it," he is speaking of a general rule of creaturely being for which he is the source and measure.

Second, to be a Christocentric theologian means that Christ defines the standard by which we speak about God. This does not mean that Balthasar rejects so-called natural theology, because, as we have just seen, the natural is not destroyed but preserved and elevated precisely in Christ. It does mean, however, that our natural knowledge of God will always have to be measured against what has been revealed about God in Christ, for it is in Christ that God speaks for himself. It means, furthermore, that we really do see God for who he is when we see Jesus Christ. Balthasar, therefore, prefers Irenaeus's approach to that of Gregory Palamas, insofar as the latter seems to want to separate the revelation of God in Christ ("energies") from God himself ("essence"). Rather, for Balthasar, as for Irenaeus, the mystery of God's essence is preserved precisely *as* revealed in Christ. And that is because Balthasar's model for knowledge is always the knowledge of love. When one knows the beloved, knowledge and mystery grow, paradoxically, in direct proportion to each other: as the knowledge increases, so the mystery increases. Balthasar can, therefore, quote Irenaeus accordingly,

> According to his majesty he is unknown to all those whom he has created, for no one can climb up after him into the lofty heights where he is removed . . . but according to his love he is forevermore known through the one by whom he created all; and this is his Word, our Lord Jesus Christ, who in the last days became man among men.[34]

Or, he will often quote Paul's famous paradoxical hymn, "To know the love of Christ which surpasses knowledge" (Eph. 3.19). And this explains why Balthasar's Christocentric approach does not do away with a proper attention to silence and mystery: the God who is revealed in Jesus Christ is even more incomprehensible to human reason than the God of negative theology and philosophy.[35]

Third, Christocentrism cannot be opposed, for Balthasar at least, to a Trinitarian approach, for it is precisely the Trinity and the Trinitarian relations that are revealed to us for the first time in Christ. "It is thus that the trilogy, in spite of, or precisely because of, its Christocentrism, proves, at a deeper level, to have a Trinitarian structure in each of its three parts."[36] This is because the immanent Trinity can only be known to us through the economic Trinity, and it is in Christ that God's economy of love is uniquely and quintessentially revealed. Balthasar would therefore concur with Aquinas when the latter says, "The Son of God came and he caused the hidden rivers to gush forth, making known the name of the Trinity."[37]

Finally, Christocentrism implies revelocentricism. Again, we must be careful here not to assume that a revelocentric approach, one that begins and ends with God's self-revelation in Jesus Christ, is simply opposed to all philosophy and natural knowledge of God, or to all "movement towards God." As we have seen, even at the natural level, the subject is never the measure of the knowledge of the object. First, the object must offer itself to be known, must, in some analogous sense, reveal itself. And it is precisely receptivity, indifference and even a certain type of childlike wonder which mark the proper attitude of the knower before the object of knowledge. Nevertheless, just as the subject would know nothing if it were not for an object offering itself to be known, so, too, the object in some sense needs the subject in order to unfold as it really is. Of course, this can be seen most fully at the level of inter-personal relationships when the child comes to know himself only in the smile of his mother. Similarly, a revelocentric approach is not a merely "from above" approach. Just because Jesus Christ is the measure of our knowledge of God, does not mean that Christ himself does not appropriate humanity's search for God. Again, it is on account of, and not in spite of, his Christocentrism and revelocentrism that Balthasar will insist upon defending the proper autonomy and integrity of humanity's natural search for God.[38]

PRELIMINARY SUMMARY

Before proceeding to the final section of this chapter concerning the structure of Balthasar's trilogy around the transcendental properties of Being, it should be helpful to draw some preliminary conclusions concerning what has been said to this point. At the bottom of the contemporary debate over theological method lies the question of the relationship between philosophy and theology, which is a part of the more basic question of the relationship between nature and grace. At the risk of oversimplification, modern theology seems to be at an impasse between a position which, on the one hand, tends to reduce the distinctively Christian to the highpoint of natural capacities. By emphasizing the fact that the world is a "world of grace," this approach has always had trouble accounting for the newness of Christianity and the so-called scandal of the cross. On the other hand stands the temptation, therefore, simply to reduce everything to theology. If human reason seems inevitably to be marked by this tendency towards overreaching, would it not be better simply to insist that anything that does not come explicitly from the side of God's self-revelation is not only not helpful, but even idolatrous and harmful? I will not repeat the respective weaknesses of these approaches at this time, but mention them only to help us better grasp the uniqueness of Balthasar's approach.

With the Fathers, Balthasar understands that Christianity necessarily enters into humanity's philosophical and religious fray. As distinct and new as it may be, it comes to us at the level of the human and through the human. "God," Balthasar reminds us, "speaks as man." This means that it must take up, in order to heal and renew, the human search for God. God's "*agape*" is not simply opposed to human "*eros*," if for no other reason than that God is the source of human *eros* in the first place. Nevertheless, even if human *eros* is oriented to the infinite and transcendent, it is not equipped by nature to get there. Balthasar's theological method is found precisely in this delicate paradox. As such, in Balthasar's view, the Christian must be the first to preserve the proper place for the human search for God. The Being of the world will always be marked by its orientation towards that from which it came and to which it is destined, *by nature*. However, lest our conception of Being is too abstract, Balthasar's investigations begin at the level at which Being reaches its fulfillment, at the level of the human person. This starting point enables Balthasar to do justice to both sides of the impasse mentioned above. First, it enables him to emphasize Being's self-transcendence towards its Source. But, second, it enables him to emphasize the need for revelation, for even at the level of worldly Being, truth is marked by the give and take of inter-personal relations. This cursory summary will both prepare us for Balthasar's use of the transcendental properties of Being, even as it will be made clearer by our examination of them.

THE TRILOGY AND THE TRANSCENDENTALS

Not many theologians in our current setting are willing even to talk about the "transcendental properties of Being," much less structure their entire theology around them. Such talk may even seem anachronistic. Is Balthasar's theological project, then, simply anachronistic? Let us recall for a moment that Balthasar is at once trying to retrieve what is of lasting value from the great intellectual and theological tradition of the past, while at the same time addressing modern concerns over individuality, difference, personhood, historicity, event, freedom, etc. It is not so much that Balthasar's theology strives for a synthesis of these two approaches as it is that, by looking at the question of Being in terms of the concrete encounter between the child and his mother, he can affirm what is true in both of them while avoiding their respective dangers. If, again, we begin with the encounter between the child and his mother and understand Being in this light, we will see that Being appears (the Beautiful), Being gives itself (the Good), and Being speaks (the True).[39] Why Balthasar begins with the Beautiful can likely be attributed to three things. First, phenomenologically, Being first *appears*. Second, modernity—in both its progressive and conservative guise—is more forgetful of beauty than it is the other two transcendentals (cf. rationalism and moralism). Finally, if Being reaches its highpoint in the realm of the personal, then the concrete encounter between loving persons should be more central to our understanding of Being than it has been in the past.

Furthermore, the division of the trilogy into an aesthetic, dramatic and logic, should in no way give the impression that the transcendentals are in fact separable. They always run together. Balthasar distinguishes; he does not separate. It will also become clear that no one part of the trilogy serves as Balthasar's "natural" theology so that the others could take up his theology proper. Rather, in each part of the trilogy Balthasar begins with the Being of the world before he makes his way to the Source of this Being. For instance, in the volumes on aesthetics, Balthasar begins with inner-worldly beauty before addressing the direct question of the "Glory of the Lord." In each case, he respects the notion of analogy that we have outlined in these past two chapters. There is, thus, an analogy between inner-worldly beauty and God's glory which presupposes a greater dissimilarity on account of the real distinction between God and the world. It is this real distinction that accounts for the "polarity" at the level of inner-worldly Being, and this polarity will have its effect on each of the transcendentals. At the level of Being in general, as we have already seen, this polarity can be seen from the fact that Being does not subsist apart from the individual beings in which it actually appears, and yet these beings cannot attribute their existence to themselves. Balthasar applies this polarity to the beautiful in the following quote.

Every worldly being is epiphanic, in the difference just described. The life principle of the tree invisible in itself, is essentially shown in the form, growth, and gradual decline in the appearance of the tree.[40]

And, finally, in this very polarity, each of the transcendentals points beyond itself to its Source in God. Again, in the case of beauty, Balthasar illustrates this accordingly, "It is the way in which things express not only themselves but the whole of reality existing in them as well, a reality that, as *non subsitens*, points to the subsisting real . . ."[41] This cursory introduction will help us better to give a brief overview of each part of the trilogy. This very brief overview will be filled out in the next three chapters.

Aesthetics: The Glory of the Lord

In the English language edition, *The Glory of the Lord: A Theological Aesthetics* is broken into seven (thick!) volumes. The first volume addresses the basic question of how a form appears (objective) and how it can be perceived (subjective): it constitutes, then, a general theory of the appearance and perception of Being. In volumes two and three Balthasar introduces the readers to a host of thinkers, clerical and lay, from the tradition, who exemplify theological aesthetics. Volumes four and five offer an overview of the history of the Western metaphysical tradition (and for Balthasar this includes poets and saints) in the light of the question of beauty/glory. And, finally, volumes six and seven offer an account of beauty/glory in the Old and New Testaments. They offer nothing less than a biblical theology of glory: the appearing of the beauty of God.

But why, again, begin with beauty? What does theology have to do with beauty? In focusing, first, on the appearance of Being, Balthasar can address perhaps the single greatest obstacle to the Christian faith for the modern person. Balthasar repeatedly warns that the person who is incapable of seeing worldly beauty will be the last one who is capable of seeing the glory of God when it appears. Moderns, in short, tend to get stuck on the surface of things, equating knowledge of a thing with knowledge of its appearance, reducing things (whole forms) to the sum of their measurable parts. But is it not a miracle, giving rise to awe, that this thing is here before me in the first place, and that it is appearing to me precisely as this or that *thing*? And what is it about this thing that enables me to name it, and name it correctly or incorrectly? Indeed, is not the fact that I can mistake a thing for something else, the fact that I can be mistaken about its appearance, evidence enough that a thing is more than just its appearance, or the sum of its parts? In other words, at the heart of Balthasar's aesthetic lies the notion that when an object gives itself to be seen, it gives more than itself. It gives something which ultimately transcends it and thereby points to the very polarity mentioned above. The invisible thereby comes to presence in the visible.

Of course the source and end of all of this is Jesus Christ, who is the appearance of God in the flesh. However, if the modern person is incapable of seeing the whole manifested in the part, how will he be able to see either God, manifested in the person of Jesus, or the figure of Jesus, manifested in the plurality of the biblical witness? Beginning with beauty, in short, is Balthasar's way of helping modern persons regain their vision for wholeness.[42] It also enables him to overcome the Kantian notion of revelation as "heteronomous," for even at the level of worldly truth, knowledge comes to us through an act of revelation, an act of unconcealment. Finally, it helps Balthasar to answer the question posed to Blondel in Chapter One above as to why one should be concerned about a single, individual person at a single point in history 2,000 years ago. Even at the level of worldly Being, that which is universal comes to us through what is concrete.

Dramatics: *Theo-Drama*

Being not only appears, it also gives itself. Notice the almost extreme degree to which the mother avails herself to the needs of her child (morning and night!). But if Being has been so generous to me, am I not under an obligation to be generous to those around me? Here we come to another dimension of the polarity of Being: there is the objective demand for me to be a certain sort of person, and then there is my subjective freedom which chooses whether or not to comply with the demand. Here, again, the freedom which can be witnessed in some way at all the levels of Being, finds its highest creaturely expression in human persons and their moral freedom. And does it not make sense to suppose that such freedom, found in this imperfect and differentiated manner at the level of the human person, must find its source in One for whom the objective good and subjective freedom are of a piece? In other words, must not the freedom found at the level of the creature in a partial way have its source in a perfect freedom?

Already at the level of nature, then, a problem arises which cannot be solved strictly from the side of that nature. Finite freedom points towards an infinite freedom which it cannot, of its own power, attain. We are back to the famous Thomistic paradox. For Balthasar, the tension that is already present at the level of worldly freedom, points beyond itself, so that the reconciliation of finite and infinite freedom that is given to us in the person of Jesus Christ is in no way extrinsic to human concerns. Furthermore, by emphasizing the situatedness of all finite freedom in infinite freedom, Balthasar can achieve two important things in his *Theo-Drama*. First, he can present an account of the relationship between divine and human freedom, which does not amount to a competition between two separate freedoms. Next, if finite freedom is already located within infinite freedom, it is nonsense to see Jesus' vicarious representation of human freedom on the cross as a false imposition or interference from the outside. Both of these things will receive fuller development in Chapter Five.

Logic: *Theo-Logic*

In the short work, *The God Question and Modern Man*, Balthasar says the following about the nature of truth and knowledge,

> That is why knowledge that occurs in this space [the space between the subject and the object] cannot be interpreted by any defective case but solely by the highest, adequate and fully valid one, that is by the meeting of another person. For this is not a special case of knowledge beside others, but that which gives direction to all other cases of intellectual or sense knowledge which are below it, because they are inferior in depth of meaning; they all are, at least inchoatively, forms of meeting and letting meet, and thus of the being-for-another of the world's creatures. A theory of knowledge that resolutely starts from the case that sets the norm of all knowledge, i.e. the meeting between persons, saves itself a good many false problems.[43]

This quote only affirms what was said earlier regarding the teleological nature of Balthasar's thought: namely, that creaturely being finds its goal and surpasses itself in human being, and that knowing finds its highpoint, therefore, in the knowledge that occurs between persons. This basic opinion does not change when Balthasar caps off his trilogy with the three volumes on "logic": the truth of the world, the truth of God, and the truth of the Spirit. Indeed, Balthasar is able to use the extended essay on truth that was originally written in 1947 (*Warheit der Welt*) as the first of these three volumes, an essay which was written before the above mentioned quote.

By taking inter-personal knowledge as the standard for all knowledge, Balthasar is able, in the first volume, to avoid both the false objectivism and naïve realism which mark so much modern rationalism/empiricism, while at the same time avoiding the false subjectivism and skepticism which marks the various forms of modern idealism/postmodernism. True knowledge can only occur, in short, if the object of knowledge gives more than just its appearance to the subject, if it gives, that is, something akin to its "word." And its ability to give its word, or its essence, to the subject presupposes, of course, that it has such a word to give. In the entirety of *Theo-Logic* I, which reads like an extended commentary on Aquinas's *De veritate*, the only contemporary thinker who is explicitly cited is Josef Pieper, whom Balthasar draws in to remind us of the important medieval notion that a thing cannot be known unless it is first known in a pre-eminent way.[44] In other words, the intelligible order of the cosmos, which science simply takes for granted,[45] points to an intelligent creator who holds the measure for things in himself. Balthasar therefore agrees with Aquinas that when we know things we implicitly know God. It is important, then, to note that knowledge presupposes the intelligibility of Being as a whole, a Being which envelops both the subject and the object. Knowledge, in fact, can be spoken of as the fruit of the encounter between the subject and the object in the common space of Being. This allows Balthasar, finally, to give proper due to the subject's role in the process of knowing. It is not only that there would be no knowledge if the object were not capable of giving its essence to the subject, it is further the case that the object finds a place to unfold in its reality in the subject, a subject who can see its colors, smell its odors and hear its sounds. The subject is not to be reduced, then, to a mere recorder of impressions, for, as Aquinas and Aristotle remind us, in order to know things the soul must in some sense be all things.[46] Balthasar simply develops this notion further to suggest that a thing only really becomes what it is, in some sense, when it is known by another. Of course this must be rooted in the fact mentioned above that things are first known and measured by God, and not by the finite subject. But we could very well say that they were made by God with a view to being known, also, by a finite, spiritual subject.

But, furthermore, since the measure of all things is finally in God, and since God is a Trinity of persons in one Being—and this is something that comes out in the explicitly theological second volume—it should not surprise us that reality itself is structured trinitarian-ly. So, in volume two Balthasar shows us that "ana-logically" the truth of the world points, from its triadic structure, to the truth of God, and that "cata-logically" (from above) Christ reveals to us a God who is, in his inmost essence, constituted by Trinitarian love. With regard to the former, for instance, in the act of knowing, there is the knower, the known, and the knowledge event that occurs on account of their encounter, which, incidentally, leaves neither of them unchanged. With regard to the latter, Balthasar steers a middle course between those who would want to find some essence lying behind the loving, Trinitarian persons on the one hand, or those who would want to dispense with the language of Being altogether in order to focus simply on a language of love. Rather, Balthasar will insist that the essence or Being of God is constituted always, already by love. It will be the final purpose of the volumes on truth to show that the loving unity in difference of the Trinitarian persons provides the possibility not only for the otherness of creation, but also for the eventual reconciliation in love of that otherness to God through Christ. Or, as Balthasar puts it,

> And thus this-worldly being will then necessarily contain within itself traces and images of the intradivine difference, which means that it can then appropriately enter upon a union with the divine unity. These traces will then explain the ground and goal of this divine world enterprise: to show that, just as God can be one with the other Divine Persons *in* himself, he is just as capable, in his freedom, of becoming one with the others outside of himself.[47]

This brief overview of the trilogy will receive the necessary detail in the chapters that follow.

CHAPTER FOUR

JESUS CHRIST AND THE MEANING
OF SCRIPTURE

The Word that is God became man, without ceasing to be God. The Word that is infinite became finite, without ceasing to be infinite. The Word that is God took a body of flesh, in order to be man. And because he is Word, and, as Word, took flesh, he took on, at the same time, a body consisting of syllables, Scripture, ideas, images, verbal utterance and preaching, since otherwise men would not have understood either that the Word really was made flesh, or that the divine Person who was made flesh was really the Word. All scriptural problems must be approached through Christology: the letter is related to the Spirit as the flesh of Christ [is related] to his divine nature and Person.[1]

At the center of all Christian theology stands Christology, and this is true even of those modern theologies which, for a variety of reasons, try to downplay the centrality of Christ in favor of some other center (anthropocentrism, theocentrism, etc.). For even a theology which considers it necessary to marginalize Christ in lieu of some other center has decided to do so on the basis of some previous Christological consideration: e.g. the notion that Paul's Christ-centered approach is a betrayal of the historical Jesus' God (Father)-centered approach; the notion that the Gospels, especially John, with their "high" Christologies are a betrayal of the simple, humanistic message of Jesus; the notion that in a pluralistic world it amounts to theological hubris to ascribe unique mediatorial and divine status to Jesus Christ; etc. In the next two chapters, then, I will show how Balthasar's Christocentrism is applied, first, to the problem of Scripture—this chapter—and then to the problem of finite and infinite freedom—the next chapter. This will also afford us a glimpse into the first two parts of Balthasar's trilogy: the aesthetics and dramatics.

It would be a mistake to try to locate Balthasar's Christology in one part of the trilogy—in *Theo-Drama* III, for instance—for, as we shall see, Christ plays the central role in each part of the trilogy. In the first part—the aesthetics—it is in Christ that we see the source and measure for the idea that the universal appears in that which is concrete, resulting in a simultaneous veiling and unveiling of the universal and infinite (God) in the particular and finite (Jesus of Nazareth); in the second part it is Christ, in whom person and mission are one, who reveals the proper relationship between divine and human freedom, and therefore the meaning of the divine-human drama; and in the third part it is Christ who reveals the meaning of truth, who, rather, simply *is* the truth, both the truth (logic) of the Trinitarian God and the truth (logic) of this world. In each of these cases Christ presents a new scandal for human reason, for in each case a single person is put forth as the unique entryway into the universal. This is a scandal to religious as well as philosophical reason, insofar as both tend to grant access to the universal (the One) only through the transcendence and eventual dissolution of the particular. At best, as in Plato's *Symposium*, the particular can be seen as the stimulant towards the universal, as when a beautiful object evokes the beautiful in general, or a good person evokes the good itself. But even here that which is particular must eventually be left behind. Furthermore, it would be a mistake to think that the singularity and uniqueness of Christ presents a scandal only for the modern thinker, so that the question raised by Blondel's fellow student mentioned earlier would be seen as a uniquely modern problem. If one looks at the criticisms raised against Christianity by the intellectuals of ancient Rome, one finds the same sort of attitude: Why should a single man in history be considered the locus of universal meaning, and in a unique and unsurpassable way at that?[2]

So, it is not so much that the modern criticisms of traditional Christology are new as it is that, when coupled with the historical critical study of Scripture, they take on a new force.[3] It must be remembered that this modern study of Scripture is deeply entangled with questions of a Christological nature, even when such an approach pleads theological neutrality. Such neutrality cannot be maintained on either theological or historical grounds. Before proceeding to actual Christological considerations, then, we should follow Balthasar in addressing the question of the meaning of Christian Scripture in the modern world. We will also have to follow Balthasar in his refusal to isolate this question from the broader philosophical, theological and historical context in which it necessarily stands. It would do the reader well to recall at this point the discussion of de Lubac in Chapter One. First, Balthasar will agree with de Lubac that a dualism between nature and grace which seems to be a distant memory, associated only with a now nearly extinct neo-Scholasticism, has resurfaced after the Council in an attempt to find a theologically neutral method for the academic study of theology. Here, nature (the "natural" approach to the study of theology) is separated from questions of grace, faith and the supernatural. Second, Balthasar will also agree with de Lubac that the one aspect of Patristic exegesis that cannot be supplanted is its commitment to a Christocentric reading of the entire Christian Bible, Old and New Testaments.

THEOLOGICAL AESTHETICS AND THE STUDY OF THE BIBLE

In the light of the foregoing, the first step toward understanding Balthasar's Christology must begin with *The Glory of the Lord*, for what Balthasar provides there is the philosophical and theological foundation for his Christocentric approach. This will involve, first, indicating some of Balthasar's methodological principals, especially as these come to bear on his reading of the Old and New Testaments. As we will see, these principles are merely the application of his overall theological methodology to questions of biblical exegesis, and cannot be examined in isolation. The first concerns, as just stated, the non-neutrality of human reason in its search for truth. The second concerns the manner in which a renewed attention to beauty, the "forgotten transcendental," can shed light on the current impasse between scientific exegesis on the one hand and dogmatic theology on the other.

In order to address the first, we should recall the observations made by David L. Schindler with regard to de Lubac in Chapter One. In those statements, Schindler points out that, while the older version of the nature-grace dualism are now largely behind us, a newer version has inserted itself into the study of theology in the name of ecumenical sensitivity and the search for "common ground" among people with different faith commitments. It is important to note at this point that the rise of modern biblical science occurred during the simultaneous birth of modern science on the one hand and the attempt to establish earthly peace outside of a particular confessional stance on the other. As such, the proper biblical method must be "scientific" in the way that, say, Newtonian physics is scientific (empirical, based on observation, etc.), and must, at the same time, bracket "sectarian" faith commitments in order to arrive at the universally recognized facts of the matter. Of course, contemporary biblical exegetes are not as naïve regarding the possibilities of either of these ends as were their Enlightenment forebears, but this is what might be called the "hard center" of the method. As Schindler puts it,

Something analogous happens in the academy: each of its disciplines involves a certain methodological abstraction: "x" must be temporarily bracketed in order to get clear first about "y" . . . More generally, we have all frequently heard the suggestion that we should first seek to ascertain what reason alone or the empirical evidence alone has to tell us, before going on to introduce the Christian "perspective."[4]

After pointing out that there is, of course, an "ineliminable" element of truth in this approach, Schindler goes on to point out that,

[n]onetheless, the subtle but absolutely crucial point required by de Lubac's theology is that none of these tendencies can any longer be rightly understood as implying *neutrality* with respect to the truth revealed by God in Jesus Christ. Neither any "common ground," nor any "methodological abstraction," nor, finally, any appeal to reason or nature alone is ever, from its first actualization, innocent of implications (positive or negative) relative to this truth . . . The point, and it is fundamental for de Lubac, is that this abstraction must not be taken to imply that the order of grace is to be subsequently (simply) *added* to what has been first abstracted . . . The fact that the "superaddition" occurs now for methodological reasons does not render it any less problematic as a false abstraction hence as wrongly autonomous, relative to the order of grace.[5]

And, lest the reader think that these comments are only relevant to Schindler or de Lubac's view of the matter, here is Balthasar in the same vein.

First, the world as it concretely exists is one that is always already related either positively or negatively to the God of grace and supernatural revelation. There are no neutral points or surfaces in this relationship. The world, considered as an object of knowledge, is always already embedded in this supernatural sphere, and, in the same way, man's cognitive powers operate either under the positive sign of faith or under the negative sign of unbelief. Of course, insofar as it works in a relative abstractness that prescinds from creaturely nature's embedding in the supernatural, philosophy can indeed highlight certain fundamental natural structures of the world and knowledge, because this embedding does not do away with, or even alter the essential core of, such structures. Nevertheless, the closer philosophy comes to the concrete object and the more fully it makes use of the concrete knowing powers, the more theological data it also incorporates, either implicitly or explicitly . . . [T]he supernatural has impregnated nature so deeply that there is simply no way to reconstruct it in its pure state (*natura pura*).[6]

It is important to understand the implications of these quotes for the question of biblical studies so that we can see just how radical (to the root) Balthasar's critique is. It is not, that is, just a matter of Balthasar liking this and not liking that aspect of modern biblical exegesis. It is rather a root and branch rejection of any appropriation of the method which would naïvely imply that one can *de facto* prescind from questions of ultimate "value" in order to address questions of "fact." But, as Schindler pointed out, the point is a subtle one. As Balthasar acknowledges, one can bracket explicit theological commitments in order to focus on this or that aspect of the natural order—the natural order does have its proper autonomy and its own integrity—but only so long as one realizes that one has only rendered one's faith (or non-faith) stance unthematic, not *non-existent*.[7] When we couple this with the further fact that, for Balthasar, faith is already present in *all* forms of knowing[8] and the further fact that, because grace perfects rather than distorts nature, faith clarifies rather than obscures reason, then we are better prepared to understand his criticism of certain Enlightenment style approaches to the biblical text which demand pure theological neutrality. This helps us to see that Balthasar's preference for certain biblical scholars— Martin Hengel, Nils Dahl, Heinrich Schlier, Heinz Schürmann,

Gerhard von Rad, et al.—is not arbitrary, but is rather based upon whether or not their work is sufficiently reflective of the sorts of complex issues just outlined.[9]

What has been said to this point also helps to shed light on the relationship between theological aesthetics and biblical exegesis. One need only read the first volume of the theological aesthetics, or even the short essay "Revelation and the Beautiful," to see that Balthasar can never talk about theological aesthetics for long without talking about how to read the Bible. It will prove helpful, therefore, to delineate several principles of Balthasar's theological aesthetics in order to highlight their implications for biblical exegesis. First, Balthasar uses the aesthetic and the inter-personal to shed light on the rather convoluted issues surrounding epistemology. One can get the impression from modern epistemology that knowledge is an act of the subject *upon* a passive object. This goes back to our previous discussion of the fact that it no longer made sense after the breakdown of Thomas's epistemological realism to say that all that exists is true. Kant, for instance, thought that this proposition was "sterile" and "tautological." For Kant, truth does not inhere in things, but refers only to "certain logical requirements and conditions inherent in any *perception* of things."[10] A thing only gives its appearance; one receives nothing more than the surface of the thing. The unifying, categorizing and conceptualizing all come from the spiritual subject. But an aesthetic approach, for instance that of Goethe, assumes that an object always gives more than itself, that it gives that which enables the subject both to know it and to name it. Now, for Balthasar, the subject is not simply passive in this process. The subject is clearly spiritually equipped to receive, judge and name the things which appear. Knowing occurs as a result of an encounter between a subject and an object—and their common belonging in Being must always be kept in mind—but what is known is determined by what the object gives of itself. The proper attitude of the subject, then, is not that of grasping or attempting to control the object (which is why Balthasar rejects the modern notion that knowledge is power), but is that of an active receptivity which makes a space for the object to unfold for the subject. When, in the first volume of *The Glory of the Lord*, Balthasar notes that autopsies are only performed on dead bodies, he is speaking in the context of biblical exegesis. The Bible, in short, should not be treated as a corpse, but as a living document which actually gives something, something to be known, to be sure, but also something to be adored. The reader must be as willing to be measured by the text as he is willing to measure it, and this is because the text is placing more than mere text before the reader; it is presenting an event, and, ultimately, a person.

Second, aesthetics helps us to address the question of the relationship between the whole and the parts. Modern science sometimes has the tendency to treat the whole as nothing more than the sum of its parts, but, as a work of art illustrates, the whole is always greater than the sum of its parts. This or that note, or even phrase, in a Mozart symphony finds its place and meaning only within a larger whole, a whole which one must keep in mind if one is even to understand the part. The same could be said of a word, sentence or chapter in a Dickens novel, or a color, stroke or figure in a Michelangelo painting. To break down a great painting into discrete bits of pigment or brushstrokes, while possibly interesting, would be to risk losing the meaning of the work as a whole. This aspect of art, furthermore, points to something that is true of reality in general. A corpse may have indiscriminate body parts, and even this could be debated, but a person has legs, arms, a nose and a mouth which find their final meaning only in the light of the person to which they belong. This is why human sexuality cannot be sufficiently treated from a purely biological standpoint.[11] Similarly, the text of the Bible is a whole that must always be kept in mind when dealing with its parts. This gives Balthasar's approach to Scripture a certain affinity with the canonical school, provided that one keeps in mind the fact that, for Balthasar, the final referent is not the text, even if that text is the entire canon, but a person (and the events surrounding that person), who alone grants the requisite unity and meaning to that text (canon).[12] It is not an accident that the Christian canon was established only in the light of an increasingly standardized theology of the person of Jesus Christ. To go back to the first point: the text gives more than merely text.

Third, Balthasar uses the aesthetic as a way of highlighting the fact that the natural, visible order cannot be grasped through the scientific method alone, in such a way, for instance, that the Christian could now turn his attention simply to the "spiritual" or "invisible" order. It is often said, in the interest of making peace between science and religion, that science deals with the material order (the order of reason) while religion deals with the spiritual order (the order of faith).[13] Applied to biblical studies, this would result in a purely scientific approach to the text in the academy coupled with a more spiritual approach for preaching or devotion. Balthasar refuses this sort of dualism, insisting, under the notion that all methodology must be determined by the object of that method, that the material order itself cannot be adequately addressed in terms of mere matter. Indeed, even the definition of matter is not something that can be solved on the basis of empirical observation alone, a point that is only exacerbated by the fact that one never encounters "mere matter" or "brute facts."[14] Similarly, history cannot be reduced to a series of discrete facts, for even the selection of the facts to be considered betrays some posture towards the whole in which they find their meaning and place.[15] In other words, a purely scientific approach to history is not even adequate at the level of history.[16] Balthasar will often draw an analogy here with the relationship between Eros and Agape. Eros, even prior to being taken up into Agape, desires to go where Agape alone can take it. There is a *natural* orientation on the part of Eros towards Agape. Similarly, the "material" biblical text already refers to and makes present something more than itself in such a way that a purely scientific approach, while sometimes appropriate, is never sufficient. The so-called spiritual sense of the text is already latent, then, within the literal sense and is not the addition of something extrinsic to it.[17]

Fourth, the aesthetic provides a fitting analogy for the proper role of faith in the quest for truth. In the context of Enlightenment prejudice—what Gadamer has called "the prejudice against prejudice"— faith is almost always understood as that which distorts the simple and plain facts. In other words, if the faith of a writer enters into his description of a person or event, that person or event is thereby obscured. The job of the scientist would be, in this case, to try to uncover the "real" event or person beneath the faith of the one giving the account. Never mind the fact that the scientist can never rid himself of his own faith (or non-faith), Balthasar will also point to the fact that truth requires eyes capable of seeing. A mere tape recording of facts is never adequate to what has happened, for even such facts have to be interpreted. As things get more complex, for instance, when we are dealing with a person and not merely snippets of information, this becomes even more the case. And this explains why a painter is often capable of capturing the "form" of a person more faithfully than a photograph,[18] or why a great novelist can often tell us more about an event than a news reporter. The "inspiration" that goes into creating an artistic image does not merely NOT obscure the truth in such cases, but actually sheds greater light. In a similar vein, the Spirit-inspired faith of the biblical writers can just as easily be seen as a deepening of insight.[19]

Fifth, the aesthetic helps us to see the limitations of a purely genetic-historical approach to Scripture.

> Great works of art appear like inexplicable miracles and sponta-neous eruptions on the stage of history. Sociologists are as unable to calculate the precise day of their origin as they are to explain in retrospect why they appeared when they did. Of course, works of art are subject to certain preconditions without which they cannot come into being: such conditions may be effective stimuli but do not provide a full explanation of the work itself. Shakespeare had his predecessors, contemporaries and models; he was surrounded by the atmosphere of the theatre of his time. He could only have emerged within that context. Yet who would dare offer to prove that his emergence was inevitable?[20]

As helpful as it may be to get behind a given text in order to deter-mine its original form—how an original statement of Jesus has, say, been redacted by this or that evangelist—such investigation is never adequate to explain the final meaning of the text. "This narrative moment of going from beginning to end can make it seem as if the beginning accounts for the end, rather than the end representing an astonishing fulfillment and supersession of what went before." One of the greatest weaknesses, then, of a strictly historicist account of the biblical text is that it rules out in advance—with the notion that all events in history must be analogous—what is perhaps the most interesting claim of the text: namely, that Jesus Christ is unique.[21]

This fifth principle requires some elaboration, for it is the key to Balthasar's manner of relating the Old and New Testaments, just as it is the key to his biblical Christology. Again, Shakespeare is more than the sum of those things which led up to Shakespeare: e.g. his place of birth, his education, his upbringing, his involvement with the theatre of his day, etc. The final form, in other words, is both continuous with what went before it—and this is the partial truth of the genetic approach—and it is also new and unpredictable in refer-ence to it. Indeed, it is only in hindsight that we can later come to say, "It had to be this way," this latter being a judgment aesthetic in nature. As we will see, such an approach rules out a fundamentalistic approach to scripture as much as it does a pseudo-scientific one, a point that can be seen in Balthasar's criticism of the older use of the "argument from the prophets," which sees the events in Christ's life as obvious fulfillments of things predicted in the Old Testament and, therefore, as proofs of the divine nature of Scripture. Of course the modern approach to the Bible has shown that this older approach can no longer be maintained. Scholars have shown rather convincingly that the Old Testament texts were only applied to such events in hindsight, and were often forced to take on a meaning that they could never have had in their original context. However, far from seeing this as evidence that we are, at last, only dealing with a human apologetic strategy, if not an outright prevarication, Balthasar sees this modern insight as an opportunity to move beyond an overly mechanistic and rationalistic approach to the Old Testament.

> If it is true that the historical-critical method has destroyed the old form of the *argumentum ex prophetia*, which understood sayings of the old covenant as having been spoken with direct reference to Christ . . . the elimination of this all too naïve concept left space for something much more important and splendid, viz. for the prophetical character of the whole history of Israel.[22]

This "prophetic character" refers to the forward looking nature of Israel's religion and to the fact that Israel's faith issues forth in a series of forms that are tentative and non-unified by their very natures. For instance, how does one reconcile the form of the warrior king with that of the Suffering Servant Or, even more problematically, what becomes of the covenant between God and Israel in the face of death?

There are, then, two things which must be kept in mind with regard to Balthasar's approach to the Old Testament. First, in the light of the historical-critical method, it is no longer permissible simply to read promise and fulfillment in a mechanistic and pre-critical way. But, second—and this is the point addressed to the historical-critical approach—Christianity is not at leisure simply to abandon its relationship with Israel for either rationalist or political reasons. As difficult as it may be, that is, Balthasar insists that the Christian story consists of both an old and new covenant,[23] so that that which brings fulfillment cannot be understood except in terms of what it fulfills.

But in order for this approach to work in a post-critical context, three conditions must be met. First, "[t]he individual forms which Israel established in the course of its history converge together upon a point that remains open and that cannot be calculated on the basis of the converging forms and of their mutual relationship." Second, "[t]he midpoint is occupied in the fullness of time by one who lives this midpoint . . . " And, third, "[w]hen this midpoint is interpreted subsequently, it is seen at a secondary stage that the midpoint retains its place as midpoint through the crystallization of the periphery around it, and that it is only through this crystallization that the periphery acquires its point of reference which gives it form."[24]

In these three "steps," Balthasar is trying to move beyond a false alternative between a pre-critical and naïve use of the Old Testament which simply sees mechanical predictions being fulfilled by mechanical events—e.g. Isaiah predicts the birth of a messiah to a virgin; Jesus is born of a virgin—on the one hand, and a modern, critical view which discredits the New Testament's use of the Old as little more than propagandistic distortion. Indeed, it is important for theological reasons to admit, with the modern, historical critic, that Jesus' fulfillment of the old covenant was neither straightforward, nor simply obvious. Notice that it was not only the Pharisees and Saducees who failed to recognize in Jesus a fulfillment of their messianic hopes; Jesus' own disciples *as reported in the Gospels* betray almost no sense of who Jesus is or what he is about prior to the resurrection and the bestowal of the gift of the Spirit. If Jesus' fulfillment of Old Testament prophecies were simply obvious, then anybody should have been able to see them. But the fact of the matter is that they required a certain type of vision. On the other hand, after the event of the resurrection and with the eyes of faith, the followers of Jesus were enabled to see just how, in fact, Jesus did fulfill the expectations of Israel. In other words, their newfound faith was not a mere fabrication; rather, faith enabled them to see what was in fact the case. And this is why, for Balthasar, it is not so much this or that proof text that matters—the Old Testament texts which are quoted in the New Testament very often verge on fabrications, or are at least combinations and paraphrases of actual texts—;[25] it is rather the case that the general notion that Jesus brings together into a final form the disparate images and forms of the Old Testament that drives the use of particular texts. "The choice of Old Testament texts . . . is unimportant."[26] This is hardly the statement of a biblical fundamentalist.

We are now in a position better to understand what Balthasar means by the three steps listed above. First, the faith of Israel is by its very nature open in such a way that the various trajectories arising from that faith do not of themselves provide the final form to which they point. Simply put, the faith of Israel is oriented to the sort of fulfillment that is left open by that faith itself, insofar as its fulfillment is eschatological: i.e. in God's hands. Next, it is fitting that the midpoint, at which these various trajectories aim, should be occupied by a person who is in himself that very midpoint, and this is true even if it is not Jesus' explicit intention to be such. It is also fitting that this role of midpoint be filled by a person who can play out, equally, the role of God and humanity, insofar as the covenant was based on the confrontation of divine (God's initiative) and human freedom (Israel's response). And, finally, the point that was previously made, it is only subsequently that the final form, the "midpoint," will be seen as that which incorporates all of the preliminary forms into itself. This incorporation will be double faceted by being both continuous and new at the same time. In other words, it will be an incorporation which takes up all that was authentic and preserves it, while leaving behind all that was temporal and merely preliminary. This last point prevents Balthasar's theology from being simply supersessionist, insofar as the preliminary forms of the old covenant really do live on and become what they were meant to be. Only that which was "all too earthly" is left behind,[27] a point which is already present, in incipient form, in the Old Testament's prophetic critique of purely external religion.

There is one further point which Balthasar makes with regard to this fifth principle and it concerns the insurmountable obstacle which death places before the Old Covenant. "For our theme, this means that a clear boundary which cannot be crossed is drawn in the old covenant for the appearing of the glory of God: the fact that death has not been overcome."[28] This means that it is not enough for Jesus to enter into the covenantal fray as one who takes up the various images of the Old Testament into himself. For instance, it is not enough for him to take up the role of Old Testament prophet and simply heighten this role. It cannot, in short, be a matter of degree in which Jesus surpasses the various forms of the Old Testament; it has to be a matter of kind. To be sure, there will be themes in the Old Testament and especially figures who will pre-figure the role that Jesus will play: for instance, the vicarious suffering for the whole of

Israel on the part of figures such as Moses and Jeremiah. However, Jesus must fulfill the meaning of these types not only in a world-historical way, but in a way that transcends the world historical. After all, the covenant is not only a human reality; it concerns humanity in its relationship with the eternal God. "If [Jesus'] life is to be the breaching of the Old Testament boundary, then the event that is his life can only be obscure for the world, since it is an eschatological event."[29] The difference here will not so much be seen, then, in the preaching of Jesus, which can fairly easily be compared to that of the Old Testament prophets, but in his deeds, culminating, of course, in his crucifixion and resurrection. Here again we come to the theme of continuity and newness. While it is certainly the case that the faith of Israel is already "dynamic" and developmental in nature, so that the figure of Jesus really can be seen in many ways as part of a continuous development of the prophetic movement within Israel, the fact of death creates a barrier that development from the human side of the covenant alone is incapable of crossing. What Jesus brings, then, is not simply "one new stage added in this process of transcendence," but "belongs to a wholly different order."[30] The analogy with nature and grace should be obvious by now: even if grace fulfills the natural orientation of nature, the fulfillment is not something that nature could have ever achieved on its own, nor could the precise nature of this fulfillment have been construed from within the natural order. Finally, just as the natural order was made for the supernatural—and therefore is not simply destroyed when it is taken up into it—the old covenant was designed to be fulfilled in the new, and, again, is not destroyed when taken up into it.

THEOLOGICAL AESTHETICS AND NEW TESTAMENT CHRISTOLOGY

These five principles, based largely on the first and sixth volumes of *The Glory of the Lord*, put us in a better position to understand the biblical basis of Balthasar's Christology. Since the next chapter will focus on the more systematic elements of this Christology, I will use the rest of this chapter to show how Balthasar's study of the New Testament provides the groundwork for what comes later in *Theo-Drama* and *Theologic*. I make no attempt here to summarize the theology of the New Covenant that is contained in the last volume of *The Glory of the Lord*, but will touch only on those elements significant for the development of the Christology discussed in the next chapter.

In her essay, "Jesus and his God," Marianne Meye Thompson encapsulates the problem of modern Christology accordingly,

> Although Jesus of Nazareth is arguably the world's most influential historical figure, there is no agreed understanding of his aims, message and legacy. If we paint with rather broad strokes, we may divide interpretations of him into two camps. On the one hand, while traditional Christianity has described Jesus with a variety of images, it has regularly and persistently confessed him in terms of his divine identity as Lord, Saviour of the World, Son of God and, in the words of the Nicene Creed, 'very God of very God'. On the other hand, Jesus has also been characterized not so much as one to be revered and worshipped, but rather as one who taught a way of worshipping and following God. Under this rubric he has been thought of as mystic, moral teacher, religious visionary, political and social reformer, cultural critic and renewal movement leader.[31]

As evidence for the superiority of this latter approach, some modern biblical scholars have pointed to the fact that, while Jesus is busy deferring attention from himself and to God, the early Church—and even the later biblical accounts—began placing increased attention on Jesus. Although this has been articulated in a variety of ways—for instance, Jesus preached the Kingdom of God, but what came was the Church; or, Jesus preached an anti-institutional message of brotherly love and Paul invented Christianity—at bottom the charge is the same. This thesis is further supported, according to its champions, by the fact that we can still see, in the earliest Gospel strata, evidence of a lowly, humble Jesus who is quick to denounce any high or messianic titles.[32] We can see this, we are told, in Mark's "messianic secret" and his general "low Christology," in contrast to the much later and higher Christology of, say, John. Finally, the enemy in this view is the early Church with its false hellenization of Christianity, resulting in the invention of a "God-man" who is *homoousios* with the Father. In short, the early Church's standard theology of Christ is seen to have little basis in the actual Jesus of history, a Jesus who can be glimpsed in the earliest layers of the gospel traditions.

In the face of all of this, Balthasar's Johannine starting point can be seen as at best naïve and at worst evidence of a stubborn, pre-critical, arch-conservatism. This can get especially confusing when we see Balthasar in the very next breath quoting some finding or other of modern biblical exegesis, often admitting that this or that quote attributed to Jesus is actually the work of the early Christians. How are we to explain this seeming contradiction? Of course, we have already provided part of the answer to this question in the principles delineated in this chapter, but we must now turn attention to the more specific question of the Christology of the New Testament. If we are willing to get beyond the sorts of impasses noted in the Thompson quote above, we can actually see that the two images of Christ—the uniquely divine savior of humanity on the one hand and the lowly servant of God on the other—seem to rest side by side, even in the Gospel of Mark. Indeed, Mark does not shy away from the fact that Jesus teaches with a unique sort of authority, and this does not seem to be inconsistent with the humility Jesus exhibits in his deference to the will of the Father. What is strange, in Balthasar's view, is the fact that John—with his seemingly much higher Christology—very often presents the entire ensemble cast of his Gospel as quite clearly missing the point of who Jesus is. In other words, John seems to be in no hurry to present a Jesus who is so obviously divine that everybody simply immediately recognizes it. If Jesus is, in fact, God in the world according to John's Gospel, the world certainly seems slow to pick up on this. The point that Balthasar seems to be making is that a great deal of the either/or sort of thinking that is presented so accurately in the Thompson quote results from a simple failure to pay attention to what the Bible actually says about Jesus. It stems from a further failure to recognize that it was just this biblical tension that the Chalcedonian formula is intent to preserve.

At the beginning of Balthasar's depiction of the Christology of the New Testament lies a carryover from his treatment of the Old Covenant: namely, the prohibition against Israel's making any image of God. Strikingly, this carryover provides the basis for both the continuity between Israel's and the Church's faith—their common emphasis on the absolute transcendence of God—and the newness of the latter—the fact that God is revealed in a final and definitive way only when he can provide his own image of himself for the world. When we couple this prohibition against images with the facts mentioned above—that the various Old Testament figures do not come together of themselves to make a final form and the fact that the Old Testament provides no solution to the problem of death—we are in a good position to survey Balthasar's portrait of the New Testament Jesus.

First, then—to repeat the important point made with regard to the fifth principle delineated above—Jesus Christ's role in the drama of salvation consists in bringing together the various promissory figures into a final form, which at once takes up what is valid in those figures and at the same time transcends them in an entirely unforeseeable way. Next, with regard to the issue of death, we are in a position to see what it is that distinguishes a theological aesthetic from an aesthetic theology. The former, specifically, must include within its purview a robust theology of the cross, and it is here that Balthasar's theology is able to take up the concerns of a Martin Luther and his famous *theologia crucis*. Luther's emphasis here is twofold: first, the cross presents an ineliminable affront to all human philosophical and religious wisdom. "He who wishes to philosophize by using Aristotle without danger to his soul," Luther tells us in his *Heidelberg Disputation* of 1518, "must first become thoroughly foolish in Christ."[33] Second, the cross discourages us from seeking to find out who God is in his works outside of the cross—e.g. in the mighty acts in the Old Testament or in his general manifestation in creation. "That person does not deserve to be called a theologian who looks upon the invisible things of God as though they were clearly perceptible in those things which have actually happened (Rom. 1.20)." And then, "He deserves to be called a theologian, however, who comprehends the visible and manifest things of God seen through suffering and the cross."[34]

This distinction, between a "theology of glory" on the one hand and a "theology of the cross" on the other leads, in Luther, to a distinction between the hidden God (*deus absconditus*) and the God who reveals himself to us in lowliness (e.g. in the manger in Bethlehem; on the cross; etc.). There is a danger in such an approach that the God who is revealed in the cross is not exactly God as he is in himself, but, rather, the only God whom human beings are capable of confronting. What differentiates Balthasar's theology of the cross from this one is the fact that what happens on the cross—and not only on the cross, but in the Son's condescension to take on the human situation in the first place—reveals to us something about the very essence of God. As such, Balthasar does not need to juxtapose a theology of glory with a theology of the cross: in the cross we see, first, in a definitive way a God who is in his very essence self-giving love, and we see, second, the measure of all earthly beauty and love. In other words, what Jesus does on the cross may be a scandal to human reason, religiosity and pride, but Balthasar will want to insist that what we witness there really is God as he is and what his creation is called to be. This really is an act of beauty, even as it confronts everything which is ugly and formless, for it is here that God's Yes triumphs over humanity's No, and here where the last barrier of the old covenant, death, is traversed and taken up into God's infinite and eternal love.

Balthasar is trying to walk a tightrope here between, on the one hand, a theology of the cross which would see in the cross the simple contradiction to all human reason and which must then drive a wedge between God as he is in himself (the God of glory, the God of creation) and the God revealed on the cross (the God of the economy, the God of redemption), and, on the other hand, a theology which would see the cross as the necessary playing out of a philosophical principle written into the very structure of reality. The latter would be an "aesthetic theology"; the former, a denial of the category of beauty to theology altogether. And here we must allow Balthasar to speak at length for himself.

> For such obedience [the obedience of Christ all the way to the cross], a divine decision may truly be required, a decision that as such implies the 'surrender' of the *forma Dei*, and therefore we must at least attempt to consider how such a surrender can be possible for the God of whom we cannot postulate any alteration as this is found in creatures, nor any suffering and obeying in the manner proper to creatures. In order to undertake the attempt of such a consideration, it will be necessary to posit an incomprehensible freedom in God that allows him to do more, to be other, than the creature would suppose of him on the ground of its concepts of 'God.'[35]

In order to do this, Balthasar recommends, without "his sophiological excesses," the thought of Bulgakov, and his decision,

> to take the 'selflessness' of the divine persons, as of pure relations of love within the Godhead, as the basis of everything: this selflessness is the basis of a first form of kenosis, that lies in creation

. . . for the creator here gives up a part of his freedom to the creature, in the act of creating; but this he can dare to do only in virtue
of his foreseeing and taking into account the second and truest
kenosis, that of the Cross, in which he makes good the uttermost
consequences of creation's freedom, and goes beyond them.[36]

Notice the delicate balance between the human inability to figure
out God on the basis of preconceived "concepts," on the one hand,
and the fact that, in the cross, God really does reveal the truth about
himself and the world, on the other. Here a "theology of the cross"
and a "theology of glory," far from being in opposition actually come
to coalesce, and if one Protestant theologian—Martin Luther—is
opposed in this regard, another—Karl Barth—is given the last word.

God confirms that he is God 'by entering into the circumscription
and the misery of the human creature; he who is lord becomes a
servant, and in this he abases himself, unlike the false gods; and
the man in Christ Jesus, himself, without loss or limitation of his
humanity, is . . . not deified . . . but, in the power of his deity and
therefore in the power of God and thanks to the self-abasement of
God . . . is the man exalted by God'. In all this, there is 'no paradox, no antinomy, no division' in God; by 'doing such a thing, he
proves to us that he *can* do it, that it is absolutely in his *nature* to
do such a thing. He demonstrates himself then precisely to be
more sovereign, greater, and richer than we had thought before'.
Everything depends on God's triune love, which alone can explain
'that an act of obedience' need 'not be foreign to God himself'.
'The relationship within the Godhead between the one who rules
and commands on high, and the one who obeys in humility,
becomes, in the work of the reconciliation of the world with God,
identical with the wholly different kind of relationship between
God and one of his creatures, a man' (Karl Barth).[37]

It is here that the prohibition against images in the Old Testament
is both taken up and fulfilled with the definitive image of Christ in
the New. Already there is an admission from the side of the old covenant that no definitive image of God is to be found there, but only
fleeting glimpses. These glimpses are in no way intended to obscure
the fact that God is greater than anything which human beings—even
those to whom he has been revealed—can understand or fathom.

With the appearance of Jesus Christ—and here we must keep in mind Paul's words in the third chapter of 2 Corinthians regarding the glory of God revealed in Jesus Christ—we are given a definitive or normative glimpse of the glory of God with, as Paul puts it, "unveiled faces" (2 Cor. 3.18). It is here that Balthasar's analogy of beauty proves to be especially helpful. The fact that God has now appeared to us in Jesus Christ—and this is heightened by the fact that this appearance includes the cross—does in no way undo the absolute transcendence or mystery of God. In other words, even here, where the Christian faith seems to be the absolute opposite, or the simple supersession of, the faith of its older siblings in Abraham, we see the notion of God's absolute transcendence taken up and fulfilled. For who could claim that God's self-revelation in Jesus Christ does not contain within it a simultaneous hiding of God?[38]

If it is true, then, that Balthasar's Christology of the new covenant mediates between the overly dialectical version of Luther's *theologia crucis* on the one hand and an overly confident natural theology on the other, it is equally true that this Christology helps Balthasar to navigate between an overly loquacious propositionalism and a, now more fashionable, overly taciturn mysticism. Against the former, Balthasar is quick to point out that when God wanted to reveal himself to the world in a final way—and here we should keep in the mind the key opening lines of the New Testament letter to the Hebrews—he did so not in the form of a book, but in the form of a person. It should be emphasized, furthermore, that this person stood out more in terms of his actions than his words; or, as Balthasar puts it, his actions were living words. It should finally be remembered that these actions culminated in a quite literally wordless action, a wordless word, to use Balthasar's preferred expression: namely, the cross. All human words, even of the inspired sort, must, therefore, take a back seat to the events to which they give witness. The individual Gospels, each in their own way, and the subsequent Christian canon, in its own way, seem aware of this, the former by presenting Jesus as a walking paradox—at once teaching with an unheard of authority and forgiving people of their sins, while at the same time deferring all attention from himself to the Father and silencing grandiose messianic titles—and the latter by containing not one uniform but four complementary accounts of Jesus' life and deeds. It is clear, in other words, that the man and his actions transcend the words by which he is witnessed. As Balthasar never tires of repeating, only Christ can properly be called the Word of God; Scripture is the "Spirit inspired witness to the Word."[39]

However, and this time against the overemphasis on apophaticism in so much contemporary theology,[40] Balthasar does not want to downplay the proper role of words and writing for human beings in general and in Christian revelation and theology in particular. In Christ, God appears on a human stage, and part of that appearing means making use of human language and inviting human reflection. The fact that God ultimately transcends human understanding does in no way imply that true or false statements cannot be made about God or about God's appearance in history in the person of Jesus Christ. It simply means that human language can never exhaust what it means to be God. Balthasar's understanding of analogy as discussed in the earlier chapters is important here: between the image of God that is contained in the words of human beings and God there obtains a real analogy, a real likeness, and yet the very likeness points to a greater unlikeness. Just as Christ simultaneously reveals and conceals the Father, so the words of Scripture simultaneously reveal and veil Christ. Just as a sacrament contains what it signifies without for all of that gainsaying the transcendence of the thing signified, so the words of Scripture contain the truth of Christ without exhausting that truth. Just as the consecrated host is never intent upon drawing attention to itself, but to the Christ who dwells therein, so the words of Scripture are always intent upon drawing attention to the person and events to which they give expression.

Finally, the fact that these words are inspired words also militates against either a false fundamentalism or a false apophaticism. Against the former, if the words were simply equal to what they were expressing, then there would be no need for inspiration. In other words, the fact that only the Spirit of God knows God is another way of saying that human language is simply not equal to the task. And yet, that the language is not merely human language testifies to the fact that it really does give an authentic witness to the person and work of Jesus Christ. It is God, after all, who has chosen to enter the human realm and make use of human language. And this willingness to use human language presupposes the fact that human language is capable of expressing transcendent truth. Since this is a topic that will receive fuller explanation later, it will simply have to stand as stated at this point. At present it will suffice to recall the following parallelism: just as Christ, by deferring attention from himself, reveals the Father to the world, so Scripture, by deferring attention from itself, reveals Christ. And, lastly, just as Scripture defers attention from itself and onto Christ, so the words of the Councils and the theology proclamations of the Church defer from themselves to the mystery that they can never exhaust.

CONCLUDING COMMENTS

At the beginning of this chapter we referred to a scriptural approach that would relegate any doctrinal affirmations about Jesus Christ to the realm of faith, while turning the study of history and Scripture over to the realm of fact and science. The relationship between the Bible and Christology becomes very tentative in such an approach, making Balthasar's high Christological reading of Scripture seem naïve at best. In the final part of this chapter, making use of a quote from Marianne Thompson, we were given a glimpse at the impasse that has arisen between the modern portrait of Jesus as lowly, prophetic servant *of* God on the one hand and the traditional portrait of Jesus as "very God of very God" on the other. That these two issues are deeply related should now be obvious. I have tried to show in this chapter that Balthasar does not fit into the debate as it is usually drawn up. In other words, Balthasar challenges the dualism of the first approach just as he refuses the either/or of the latter. The dualism of the former is rejected on the basis of the fact that the study of the facts of the matter (the so-called parts) is never merely the study of facts. Which facts? And what is their significance? In short, the study of the part always implies some view of the whole—the two are intrinsically and not extrinsically related—just as the study of the surface (the text, the facts) always implies some view of the depths (the meaning, the theology). This required a brief look at what Balthasar means by theological aesthetics. The false either/or of the latter is addressed by Balthasar in his willingness—and here he is very close to Karl Barth—to allow the very lowliness and apparent failure of Christ to shed light on the nature of God as a Trinity of self-giving (sacrificing) persons, to allow, namely, the kenosis of Son in the person of Jesus of Nazareth to shed light on the eternal kenosis in God. Paradoxically, the very bracketing of the Chalcedonian formula—fully God and fully man—in order to facilitate a getting to the bottom of who Jesus really was, has, in Balthasar's view, blinded some forms of modern exegesis to the very thing that makes the Jesus of the Gospels comprehensible in the first place. This biblical foundation will have hopefully paved the way for the next chapter dealing with Balthasar's Christology.

CHAPTER FIVE

JESUS CHRIST AND THE DRAMA OF FINITE AND INFINITE FREEDOM

Since God does not alienate himself from himself by becoming incarnate (for the obedient Son of Man is only the illustration of the eternal relatedness and selflessness of the divine Persons), Christ does not alienate man from himself when he raises him from the apparently closed substantiality of his personal being (in which he thinks he definitively stands over against God) into the open relatedness of the life within the Godhead. Rather, Christ brings him into the genuine truth of his origin; he is a distant image of this (imago trinitatis) in the love between human persons.[1]

The fact that the drama is grounded in Christ is no hindrance to it: on the contrary, from every angle, it is what makes it possible.[2]

Christian theology has always had to work out its doctrine of Jesus Christ in the face of general skepticism and incredulity. If Jesus is the cornerstone of the Christian faith for the insider, he is no less its stumbling stone for the outsider. It was the famous Roman statesman Celsus who, perhaps, better than any other in the ancient world expressed the attitude of the typical Roman to the place of Jesus Christ in Christian thought. "If [the Christians] worshipped no other God but one, perhaps they would have had a valid argument against the others. But in fact they worship to an extravagant degree this man who appeared recently, and yet think it does not offend God if they also worship his servant."[3] It is easy to see why early Christians, such as Origen, who had to defend the Church against such attacks tended to focus on questions of Jesus' nature or essence. Just how could Christians claim to worship one God and yet give such honor to a man who "appeared recently" in history? As was stated in the last chapter, this question is not that far removed from the typical modern objection which goes something like the following: "Why should a man who appeared 2000 years ago, at a moment in history and at a distinct place in geography, hold the meaning of universal human existence?" Furthermore, with the rise of the historical consciousness in the nineteenth century, Celsus's problem not only does not go away, it takes on new force. To the question of Jesus' relationship to God is added the question of the real Jesus' relationship to the preached Jesus. Has not the latter been so thoroughly mythologized that we can no longer imagine any real connection between it and the former?

The questions raised in the last chapter are not, then, behind us. The overview of Balthasar's aesthetic approach to Scripture as well as the glimpse into his theology of the two covenants were intended to provide the presuppositions for his dramatic approach to Christology. It is not, however, that now we have moved past the biblical problems and can focus on more "systematic" ones. In Balthasar these things are never separable, not least because who Jesus is/was cannot be separated from what he does/did. Furthermore, if the impression was given in the last chapter that Balthasar is not attentive to the problems of modern exegesis, this chapter should go a long way in correcting that. But before we can proceed to a direct discussion of Christology, we must follow Balthasar in addressing Christological questions in the context of broader anthropological ones. What is a human being? What is the relationship between divine and human freedom? What is the nature of the Christian God? What is the relationship between time and eternity? If there is infinite freedom, can there still be finite freedom? If God were to enter the human drama, what would happen the rest of the actors? In this chapter, then, I will do mainly two things. First, I will present a sketch of Balthasar's treatment of the relationship between finite and infinite freedom. This will give us a concrete glimpse of Balthasar's method, which was presented primarily in chapter three. Then, I will present more fully what we begun in the last chapter, namely, Balthasar's New Testament Christology. Specifically, I will examine Balthasar's treatment of the relationship between the Jesus of the Gospels and the Christ of the early Christian creeds, following his lead that this must be done in terms of Jesus' strong sense of mission. However, since Balthasar's discussion of mission will eventually lead him to a discussion of the nature and person of Christ and the relationship between the economic and immanent Trinity, and since I will be dealing with those matters at length in the next chapter, I will put off giving a full treatment of Balthasar's mission Christology until then. In this chapter, then, I will only deal with this question insofar as it sheds light on the problem of finite and infinite freedom on the other hand, and the relationship between the so-called Jesus of history and Christ of faith on the other.

THE DRAMA OF FINITE AND INFINITE FREEDOM

The reader of Balthasar must be careful not to assume, especially in the light of his critique of Karl Rahner, that Balthasar rejects all "from below" approaches to theology in favor of a "from above" approach. In such a reading, Rahner would have an anthropological starting point while Balthasar would have a Christological one. It might surprise readers of *Theo-Drama*, then, that after an introductory overview of the problem of the relationship between theology and drama, Balthasar proceeds directly into *anthropology*. If we recall for a moment the discussion in Chapter Two surrounding Blondel, the neoscholastics, and the modernists, we will see that Balthasar's approach, like that of Rahner, is actually closer to that of Blondel. The key difference, however, is this: for Balthasar, the anthropological starting point is already undertaken from within a Christological perspective. Or, as he will often put it, it is not, ontologically speaking, first Adam and then Christ, even if it is so from the perspective of time; it is always the case that even Adam is created in and in view of Christ. This "from above" perspective still allows Balthasar to look at things "from below" because the latter is preserved in the former; or, put another way, looking at the human from the perspective of Christ is acceptable not only because the human is preserved in Christ, it is also seen for the first time as it really is precisely from this perspective: for the first time we see human nature as it was intended.

One way of demonstrating this, without simply asserting it, is to show that, even when looked at from a natural or philosophical vantage point, human nature presents a series of *aporiae* which cannot be solved from within the natural vantage point. At this point we would do well to recall the Thomistic paradox that human beings are the only creatures whose end exceeds their natural capacities. In other words, human nature (freedom) *naturally* points to (strives for) an end that it is naturally incapable of attaining.[4] As Balthasar says,

> But because the *"motus"* of freedom is inseparable from the *"causa sui"*, because there is thus in the will a natural longing (*disederium naturale*) for complete, exhaustive self-possession, which would have to coincide with the "possession" of Being as such, we arrive at the Thomist paradox . . . man strives to fulfill himself in an Absolute and yet, although he is *"causa sui"*, he is unable to achieve this by his own power or by attaining any finite thing or finite good.[5]

If it turns out that Christ reveals the meaning of that end while at the same time providing the means for attaining it, then it is no longer the case that God's self-revelation in Christ is simply "extrinsic" to anthropological concerns. In the *Theo-Drama* II, Balthasar sets out to demonstrate this by looking at a series of problems within anthropology which have proved notoriously difficult to resolve. In what follows I will look, in particular, at Balthasar's treatment of human freedom.

On the face of it, modern philosophy has become secular in a way that is not only not true of the philosophy of the Middle Ages, it is also not true of the philosophy of the pre-Christian ancients. Their philosophy was always worked out in contradistinction to the world-view of mythology; but it was, furthermore, always concerned rather naturally with the so-called God question. Theology was always, that is, an aspect of their metaphysics. The attempt to do a purely secular philosophy by the moderns, then, is not only novel, it also involves a rather egregious slight of hand, for the philosophical questions with which these allegedly secular philosophers—and quite frankly, most of them were not even allegedly that secular—were intent to deal were handed over to them only after they had been radically transformed in the light of Christian thought. Robert Sokolowski has demonstrated this very admirably in his *The God of Faith and Reason*,[6] but it is nowhere more obvious than in the modern treatment of such things as freedom, the person, rights, and the like. Put briefly, the attempt to deal with these questions "within the bounds of reason alone," after they, in fact, only became clarified in the context of thoroughly Christological kinds of discussions is not only futile, it is in fact not even honest.[7] That is, modern discussions of these things only succeeded in eliminating one aspect of the context in which they were originally worked out, and this did not make such discussions so much secular as it made them half Christian or heretical.

This not only helps to explain why there is no satisfactory treatment of freedom in Enlightenment philosophy, it also helps to set up Balthasar's treatment of this topic in *Theo-Drama*. The pre-Christian treatment of freedom began—at least in the West—in mythology. Here, because the gods were not truly infinite, but were, rather, human beings writ large, there was an inevitable competition between their wills and those of mere mortals. The will of the gods could only be competitively related to that of their mortal subjects leaving one of two possibilities: either there would be no genuine human freedom, but only the control of the gods, or a hero would arise who would steal his freedom from the gods. In either case, there could only be a competition between divine and human freedom.[8]

When such mythological thinking undergoes purification at the hands of the ancient philosophers, the concept of nature emerges and, with Aristotle especially, the concept of "end" or "*telos.*" If non-rational animals act necessarily towards their "ends," human beings can either act in accordance with the "end" of human nature or not. Aristotle's treatment of virtue and of the various types of human actors in the *Nicomachean Ethics* is interesting in this regard. The virtuous person, for instance, is one who knows the good—which is inseparable, for Aristotle from the proper human *telos*—and who has acted in accordance with it so often that is done without thinking, that is, habitually. The weak person, on the other hand, is one who knows the good, but who, on account of a lack of virtuous habits, has a great deal of difficulty achieving it, has a great deal of difficulty, specifically, of not choosing some lesser and more easily attainable good. In the ancient philosophers, then, we find Balthasar's first type of freedom: namely, freedom of consent. Human freedom, in this view, is always situated within the fact that human beings cannot help but act towards a perceived good, and that such goods always and invariably imply some ultimate good.[9]

But in Aristotle's notion of freedom of consent is also lurking the notion of freedom as self-movement, or what Balthasar calls "freedom as autonomous motion;" for precisely in maintaining the fact that some use their freedom to develop virtues in accordance with their good, one is stating the case for freedom as self-motion. In other words, my ability consciously to move towards the good implies my ability to move myself and thus to be held accountable for my actions on some level. The problem for ancient thought, however, is that it cannot really give a satisfactory account of either of these dimensions of freedom, for implicit in both of them is the relationship between finite and infinite freedom. To say that human freedom necessarily moves towards what it at least perceives to be good—and the "necessarily" here helps to get at the paradox which human freedom is, that it is both free and yet "determined" in some sense—is to say that human freedom is oriented towards infinite freedom. As Socrates puts it in the *Symposium*, "Love desires to possess *the* good *forever*" (emphasis mine). But here ancient thought reaches an impasse. As Balthasar puts it:

> However, this cannot be done by a mere *idea* of infinite goodness: finite freedom might never cease aspiring toward it, but, by its very nature, it could never reach it. Nor can it be done by a *real* infinite good, which, if it be infinite, must be thought of as divorced from all finitude: such, for instance, is Aristotle's "thought thinking itself" . . .[10]

The point that Balthasar is making here is that finite freedom, in the pagan philosophical view, appears to be oriented towards an infinitude that is indifferent to it. Such an infinite freedom would never be able to *give* finite freedom. Or, if finite freedom were able to attain it, it would only be through its own dissolution, as in Buddhism.

It is in Christian thought that Balthasar finds a resolution of these tensions. First, like pagan philosophy, Christian thought begins with a purified conception of God, and not with the mythical gods in competition with finite freedom. In the God of Christianity—and here Balthasar agrees with Plotinus when the latter states that in God, nature and freedom are one—we have a God who deliberately creates the finite world and who, simultaneously, offers it the gift of finite freedom. Next, to go back to our previous definition of God as the *pure-act-of-to-be-itself*, God is wholly other than that which he creates. And, as we have shown before, it is precisely as wholly other that God can simultaneously be the non-other. This is simply to say that it is by virtue of the fact that God is the act of being itself that he is deemed wholly other to the world—the world has its being only as a gift, and is therefore absolutely distinct from the Giver of this gift—and at the same time that he is deemed wholly immanent in the world—that the world has its very being as gift implies that God is present to it, as Giver to gift, and that it has its being only *in* God. This, then, both allows for the existence of finite freedom, for it is grounded in the very fact of a distinct existence on the part of creation, and for the simultaneous situation of this freedom within infinite freedom.

We can simplify this somewhat by going back to our discussion of the two types of freedom. With the Christian doctrine of creation—a creation freely willed out of love by a free creator—comes the notion that human freedom is a gift. Even in the natural reflections of the philosopher, for instance, we have seen that this freedom is oriented towards the good; that is to say, it is *conditioned by* its orientation towards the good. Once we say that this good is both personal and loving, we can say that finite freedom is given by and longs for infinite freedom. But what happens to freedom as autonomous motion in such a setting? For the Church Fathers it is precisely freedom as autonomous motion that explains humanity's seemingly contradictory ability to walk away from its source. Since God was conceived as the origin and end of human freedom, those who abandon their relationship with God—e.g. Adam or the Prodigal Son—actually walk away from freedom and into slavery. In Augustine, for instance, it is within the power of human freedom to do this very thing, to walk away from freedom and into the slavery of sin. It should further be noted that even if the gift of grace is required to reorient freedom to its natural end, that it is precisely to its *natural end* that it is reorienting it.

Notice, also, that the tension between the two freedoms, freedom as consent and freedom as autonomous motion, does not only not go away under Christian auspices, but is actually intensified. Indeed, Balthasar would say that it is intensified into a drama. In such a drama the desire for complete autonomy, the desire which in Christianity is called sin, can only mean the undoing of freedom. Paradoxically, then, the willingness to consent to the infinite will is in fact the beginning of real freedom. But this is not just Christian hocus-pocus. It is rooted in the very nature of freedom itself, insofar as already within finite freedom there is a something akin to the indifference that will be praised by the Christian mystical tradition.

Certainly finite freedom, the openness to all Being, can only strive for something it perceives to be good (having a value)—even if in fact it is evil; but it is equally certain that the knowledge of the good *as good* (*bonum honestum*) removes the element of *interest* from such striving, so that the element of *indifference*—where the one who strives in the clear light of Being has in principle superseded all finite "oppositions"—*turns out to be a new and deeper indifference in which he is able to let the Good "be", whether it be a finite or an infinite Good, simply for the sake of its goodness,* without trying to gain it for himself.[11]

To summarize, already in the classical Greek notion of freedom, we find two important characteristics, both of which remain unresolved. First, there is the tension between freedom as consent and freedom as autonomous motion, with the former tending to swallow up the latter. Next, there is the orientation of finite freedom to infinite freedom, but in such a way that the former would simply have to lose itself in order to attain the latter; the latter remains indifferent towards it and "outside" of it. In the Christian context, the tension between the two freedoms is heightened in a paradoxical way. Consent now becomes consent to an infinite but personal freedom. And since that infinite personal freedom has willed the existence of finite freedom—and not out of any sort of necessity or need—then finite freedom has its insurance precisely in infinite freedom, insofar as it has received itself as a gift from it. Finally, this means that freedom as autonomous motion is paradoxically preserved precisely when it submits itself to infinite freedom. It contrast to the tendency of Platonism and Buddhism, it does not lose itself in order to become "one with the One," but it loses itself in order truly to find itself.

Before proceeding more specifically to the problem of infinite freedom, there are two further aspects of Balthasar's treatment of finite freedom that should be mentioned. First, implicit in Balthasar's treatment is a critique of the modern notion of freedom, which focuses almost exclusively on freedom as autonomous motion. Indeed, the choice between this sort of freedom and the one that Balthasar recommends is rather stark:

Thus a man may decide that, for the purposes of self-realization, the whole area must remain completely open (so that, if there were a preexistent and fully realized absolute freedom, the path of finite freedom would only be distorted and its course frustrated); conversely he may see that finite freedom, if it remains alone and is posited as absolute, is bound to become the hellish torment of a Tantalus if it is not permitted to attain full development in the self-warranting realm of absolute freedom. We shall see why we are bound to choose this second solution.[12]

Secondly, and also in contradistinction to the modern notion of freedom, Balthasar reminds us of the fact that the freedom of the individual only ever makes sense in the context of other freedoms. As Aidan Nichols so aptly summarizes this:

> As an 'I' person, I am by that very fact ready to acknowledge that being is possessed by innumerable others who have just the same uniqueness or incommunicability that I do. Thus for Balthasar we should not say, 'I seem to be unique, but ultimately I am only one individual among millions'. Rather should we say, 'I am unique, but only by making room for countless others to be unique.' This is how finite personal being can be said to echo the being of the tri-personal God, for whom the incommunicability of hypostasis is one with the unity of essence in each divine person.[13]

These two aspects serve to remind especially the modern reader that human freedom is always constituted—if there is to be such a thing as freedom at all—by its relationship to its origin and end and well as by its relatedness to countless other finite freedoms. As we will soon see, modernity is marked in this matter, as in so many others, by a forgetfulness of love.

We are now in a better position to speak more specifically to the issue of infinite freedom. First, and this is simply to reiterate what was said above in the name of Plotinus, the early Christians accepted the Greek notion that in "the One" freedom and nature are one. There is no separation in God between what God is and what God wills to be. As Plotinus puts it, "It [the One] is in harmony with itself, wills to be what it is and is what it wills to be; its will and itself are one and the same."[14] But the creating and redeeming God of Christianity requires that we say more than this about divine freedom. Indeed, so strangely involved does the God of Christianity seem to be, first, in his act of creation, but then even more so in his act of redemption, that there is a perennial temptation after Christianity either to make God dependent in some sense upon the world—the Hegelian temptation—or to divorce God's freedom from his nature—the Ock-hamist/Lutheran temptation. But if Balthasar wants to say more than Plotinus, he does not wish to go in one or other of these latter directions either. And, as is usual with Balthasar, the proper balance can be maintained only if we keep our eyes squarely on infinite freedom as it appeared in the world in Jesus Christ.

First, the Christian doctrine of creation (freely and out of love) helps to answer a question that the classical philosophical approach never could: Why is the finite world here in the first place? Pagan philosophy tends to treat the world as a sort of necessary emanation from the One, on the one hand, and then as necessarily dissolving in order to be reabsorbed back into the One, on the other. Here infinite freedom simply cannot make room for finite freedom. Secondly, and now with regard to the doctrine of redemption, Jesus Christ reveals to us the meaning of infinite freedom, and he reveals it precisely in his *lowliness* vis-à-vis the Father.

> In concrete terms, infinite freedom appears on stage in the form of Jesus Christ's "lowliness" and "obedience unto death". Thus he can call to himself the "weary and heavy laden" and summon even the clumsy and hesitant to be his disciples. We need to keep ever before our eyes the way in which infinite freedom was pleased to appear in the midst of finitude, if we are not to be drawn aside into abstract (and hence falsely posed) speculative problems.[15]

Now, it may seem that this simply reveals to us something about the nature of finite freedom vis-à-vis infinite freedom: namely, that it must sacrifice itself to the former. But what if Jesus' attitude of self-sacrificing love reveals to us also something about the nature of God? Must we not say, if we affirm that Jesus is truly divine, that the Father bestowed his entire divinity upon the Son? The point is this—and this takes us back to the end of the last chapter—that the lowliness of Christ reveals not only the proper attitude of finite freedom before infinite freedom, but, at the same time, something about the very nature of infinite freedom. Once again, we should give Balthasar the final word on this matter.

> In generating the Son, the Father does not "lose" himself to someone else in order thereby to "regain" himself; for he *is always*

himself by giving himself. The Son, too, is always himself by allowing himself to be generated and by allowing the Father to do with him as he pleases. The Spirit is always himself by understanding his "I" as the "We" of the Father and the Son, by being "expropriated" for the sake of what is most proper to them . . . From the point of view of finitude, one might suppose that the infinite self-possession of infinite reality would be bound to be the ultimate satisfaction and blessedness. But in God's self-proclamation in Jesus Christ the more blessed mystery is revealed, namely, that love—self-surrender—is part of this bliss of absolute freedom.[16]

Much more could be said, not only about the relationship between finite and infinite freedom, but also about this glimpse into Balthasar's theology of the Trinity, but this should suffice to provide the foundational treatment of freedom which we need in order to justice to Balthasar's Christology. The key point to be made now, and this will be developed more closely below and in the next chapter, is that by revealing the Trinity, Jesus Christ also reveals to us the proper relationship between finite and infinite freedom, not least by showing us that God has made room within himself for otherness. This is precisely what will provide the necessary safeguard for finite freedom to remain genuinely its own—and here the proper modern concern for autonomy is done justice—without for all of that sinking into the self-contradictory torment of the isolated and self-made freedom of modernity.

This brief sketch of Balthasar's anthropology, through the lens specifically of his treatment of finite and infinite freedom, can be summarized in three conclusions. These conclusions will help us to make the transition to his Theo-dramatic Christology. First, Balthasar shows that even at the level of philosophical anthropology tensions arise which cannot be resolved in an adequate way from within natural reflection alone. I focused on the question of finite and infinite freedom, but the same could be shown—and Balthasar does—with regard to the tensions between male and female, the individual and the community and, finally, between the body and the soul. Again, in each of these cases the philosophical resolutions tend to privilege one aspect at the expense of the other, so that in the ancients, for instance, the individual gets swallowed up into the *polis*, or with the moderns the communal gets sacrificed at the feet of the isolated and alienated individual. Next, these irresolvable tensions point beyond themselves in such a way that the question of infinite freedom, far from being heteronomous to the question of finite freedom, is actually inherent in it. And this would go even for those modern philosophers who are pretending to do pure philosophy. And, third, the resolutions to these tensions which one finds in the person of Jesus Christ can be shown in hindsight to be those most fitting to the question, even as it arises from the side of philosophy. This is not to say that philosophical wonder in the face human nature can anticipate Christology; it is to say, however, that the questions which arise naturally within the philosophical endeavor can be seen to have been answered in a rationally satisfactory way once they have been revealed in Jesus Christ.

THEO-DRAMATIC CHRISTOLOGY

Preliminary Considerations

The approach to finite and infinite freedom sketched above will go along way in preparing the reader for the Christology contained in Balthasar's *Theo-Drama*. Before proceeding, first, to Balthasar's treatment of the problem of the "Jesus of history" and the "Christ of faith," I shall lay out a few preliminary, methodological points which will help to connect this section to the last.

First, a great deal of criticism has been heaped upon the Fathers of the Church for their "essentialist" Christologies which focus so much attention on the question of Christ's nature that they are forgetful of his activity. Not only is this criticism not fair,[17] in Balthasar's view it also misses the necessary connection between nature and act, person and mission. I cannot understand why chimpanzees do not do Calculus unless I understand what sort of creatures chimpanzees are. On the other hand, I cannot determine a chimpanzee's nature without observing a great deal of chimpanzee behavior. The first either-or which Balthasar will reject in his *Theo-Drama* is the essentialist versus act-centered approach to Christology. This rejection can be used against those who would wish to reduce Christology to soteriology, as much as it can against those who wish to separate the latter into an entirely separate treatise.[18]

The next either-or which Balthasar refuses to accept is one which suggests that Christologies must either proceed strictly from above or from below. Classically liberal and rationalist Christologies tend to proceed "from below," either by way of discovering the real Jesus of history behind the Christ of faith or by beginning with anthropology and seeing Jesus Christ as the culmination of human nature, as human nature achieving what it most deeply is. More traditional approaches will insist upon the necessary gulf which separates Jesus Christ, as God's *only* and *begotten* Son from the rest of God's creatures as *made* in God's image. The "begotten not made" of the creed, in this view, forces us to place our Christological focus clearly on the "from above" side of the either-or. But the discussion about finite and infinite freedom above and Balthasar's de Lubacian approach to the problem of nature and grace lead him to a rejection of this either-or as well. First, human beings are not created, finally, in Adam, but in Christ. And while this does not mean that all human beings will inevitably accept their respective vocations in Christ, it does mean that Christ reveals to them the depths of their true natures. Next, the tensions that Christ resolves—e.g. the tension between finite and infinite freedom or the tension between the individual and the community—are tensions that arise from within the anthropological perspective. In this sense, beginning with anthropological discussions can at least help to show that what is revealed to us in Christ is not extrinsic to questions of a universally human nature. Third, however, Balthasar will show that it is only if Christ is truly the one from above that he can resolve the tensions that naturally arise from below. It would be, then, not only bad Christology to proceed strictly from below, but also bad anthropology. The liberal approach can only artificially humanize Christ if it is artificially divinizing human beings at the same time.[19] This becomes most obvious in its evasion of the question of death. If love really does, to go back to the Socrates of Plato's *Symposium*, desire to possess the good forever, such desire alone is not equal to the immortality that it seeks. In short, for Balthasar, in Jesus Christ we have the simultaneity of from above and from below.

Finally, Balthasar rejects a false division between the Jesus of history and the Christ of faith. Again, we will see that in some ways both sides of the rationalist-romanticist/existentialist divide accept this division, only to reach opposite conclusions in its regard. But it is precisely to that division that we must now turn.

The New Testament and Christology

The Jesus of History and the Christ of Faith

Since the methodological foundations for this discussion were laid out in the last chapter, I will focus only on the questions directly at hand. As Balthasar himself succinctly states the problem:

> There can be no doubt that the faith of the first Christians applied ideas, concepts, titles, in varying degrees, to the phenomenon of Jesus in order to communicate it to themselves and others. The decisive question, therefore, is: Has this process articulated an original "form", identified its significance and revealed its true outlines—or has it taken what was originally a relatively form-less core and clothed it in successive garments, which ultimately yield a plausible "form"?[20]

This question should remind the reader of two things from the last chapter which will have to be kept in mind in what follows. First, notice that the second option here—the notion that the Evangelists gave a Christological form to a historical Jesus who was essentially formless—mirrors in biblical methodology the very epistemological prejudices of modernity that Balthasar's theological aesthetics were intent upon calling into question. Second, notice that the problem addressed at the end of Chapter Four—as to how the early church became fixated on a man who was clearly not fixated on himself—is contained in this question as well. The point is this: Balthasar's critique of the modern epistemology which assumes the mechanistic nature of the external world on the one hand and the alienation of the subject from the object on the other, must always be kept in mind when he rejects either Strauss's or Schleiermacher's solution to the above question. This requires some explanation.

For Strauss, as for all Liberal Protestantism of the rationalist as opposed to romanticist variety, form (as in *Gestalt* or "figure") takes the form of myth. Myth, in this view, is the attempt to give expression to an idea that cannot yet be immediately perceived. In the case of Christianity, the idea that cannot be immediately perceived at the time of Christ is the general divinity of humanity and the "incarnation of God from all eternity."[21] Once we are ready to comprehend the idea, in Strauss's view, we can discard the myth and come face to face with the mere humanity of the historical Jesus. The myth of the divine messiah is, in short, only necessary until we can grasp the idea of the divinity of humankind as a whole. What is interesting in Balthasar's discussion of Strauss is the idea that in this seminal thinker is contained both of the options which would mark subsequent Protestant thought on this matter. Either the *historical Jesus* will be sought out in the interest of finding a humanitarian and transtemporal message that is still relevant in a scientific age (Reimarus, Lessing), or the *message about Christ* (the "kerygma") will be singled out for its unique ability to speak in a timeless way to a timeless human nature (Schleiermacher, Bultmann). But notice that in either case the connection between the Jesus of history and the Christ of faith is either denied as false or disclaimed as irrelevant.

If Balthasar is going to maintain his insistence that in the person of Jesus Christ we have a simultaneity of from above and from below, then this *either* mere regard for the historical Jesus, behind the canonical Gospels, *or* disregard of the historical Jesus, in favor of the proclamation of faith, will have to be rejected from the ground up. Balthasar, then, will be more like the third questers (Käsemann, et al.) who insist upon a continuity between the two. Building especially on the New Testament exegesis of Martin Hengel and Heinz Schürmann, he will make three main points in order to bolster his claim for continuity (within the discontinuity made necessary by the events of Easter). First, the proclamation *about* Jesus Christ and his saving significance, far from being a late addition to the simple humanitarian message of the historical Jesus, is already present in the earliest writings of Paul. Here Balthasar repeats Hengel's assertion that,

> between the death of Jesus and the fully developed Christology we meet in the earliest Christian documents, the Pauline letters . . . [there is] an intervening period of time that must be regarded as astonishingly short, considering the scale of the development that took place within it.[22]

This surprisingly early, "high" Christology, furthermore, relies on formulae (e.g. "Christ died for our sins") that are pre-Pauline.

Secondly, an honest exegete must come to terms with the vast array of Old Testament texts that are applied to Jesus in such a short period of time. This has led some—Balthasar mentions Gerhard Delling in particular—to conclude that, unless we are radically to exaggerate the exegetical and theological savvy of the New Testament writers, Jesus must have applied at least some of these texts to himself.[23] Finally, and this time building explicitly on the work of Heinz Schurmann, Balthasar suggests that the post-Easter preaching of the disciples is rooted in certain pre-Easter *logia*, based on the notion that, when Jesus sent his disciples out to preach, he would surely have given them something to say.

> Our suggestion—a bold one, it may be—is that Jesus consciously fashioned his *logia* and gave them to this disciples as a resource for their own preaching activity . . . It was absolutely essential for these uneducated and untutored men of the people to have a store of authoritative words by heart.[24]

This final point suggests that within the preaching of the historical Jesus was an incipient Christology that was not merely discontinuous with the one that developed after Easter. This is especially plausible in the light of such things as the authority with which Jesus taught and his close association of the coming of the kingdom with his own person.[25]

But Balthasar will push the matter even farther than this. If the two points of particular embarrassment for modern exegesis, the two points which gave rise to the separation between the real Jesus of history and the mythical Christ of faith in the first place, were Jesus' apocalyptic preoccupations on the one hand, and the notion that Jesus' death had a universal, salvific significance on the other, then it is precisely these two issues which Balthasar will tackle head on. The question is this: What are we to make of Jesus' imminent expectation of the in-breaking of God's kingdom and the subsequent attribution of saving significance to his death? Is it the case that with regard to the former, that the historical Jesus (at least as recorded in the Gospels) was simply wrong and that with regard to the latter the disciples were guilty of mythologization? A positive answer to either of these two questions will not suffice as far as Balthasar is concerned. They will not suffice, that is, unless we are willing to sever the Christian message from the actual facts of Jesus' life and thereby sever the connection between dogmatics and exegesis. Balthasar cannot proceed to his treatment of the person of Christ, then, until he has satisfactorily dealt with these two questions.

Jesus' Imminent Expectation of the End

With regard to the question of apocalyptic, it cannot be denied that Jesus had an imminent expectation of the in-breaking of the kingdom. "Truly, I say to you, there are some standing here who will not taste death before they see the kingdom of God come with power," Jesus says in Mark 9.1. And then in Mark 13.30, "Truly, I say to you, this generation will not pass away before all these things [e.g. decisive eschatological events] take place." This has led many scholars to assume that Jesus had the same sort of apocalyptic expectations as, for instance, John the Baptist, or, perhaps, the Essenes. Bultmann, who is by no means exceptional in this regard, has simply stated that, "[t]here can be no doubt that Jesus was mistaken in expecting the imminent end of the world."[26]

In the face of this problem, Balthasar offers five points for consideration. First, assertions about the imminent coming of the kingdom are not strictly futurist in Jesus' usage and are, furthermore, not to be separated from his predictions of his own imminent "hour." In other words, in Jesus' expectation of the end, the end of the world and his own end in death were closely linked. Second, this close link helps to explain Jesus' reference to the fact that some of his own disciples would witness that end.[27] Third:

> In contrast to the preaching of the Baptist and that of the primitive Church (which is different from the former's), Jesus' preaching consists in announcing the unique presence of a kingdom that is bound up with his person and his existence in the world.[28]

In other words, in Jesus' own preaching there is an inseparable connection between the in-breaking of the kingdom and his own coming into the world, a connection which makes his particular apocalyptic approach unique. Fourth, Balthasar builds on what seems to be an objection: namely, that Jesus seems to have made little temporal division between his death, resurrection and the parousia, or, that he seems to have thought that they would occur in short succession. Here, Balthasar insists, we must follow the Gospel of John on two counts: first, that the death and resurrection of Christ are seen as inseparable parts of a single "exaltation"; second, that there is a mutual inter-penetration in Jesus' preaching between realized and futurist eschatology. This is the famous "already" and "not yet" that must always be kept together if we are properly to understand Jesus' use of apocalyptic. Finally, Balthasar reverses the naturally human tendency to place Jesus' time *within* that of world time. Conversely, Jesus seems intent upon placing world time within his own time. In this sense, the end of the world really is anticipated in his death and resurrection and is therefore inaugurated therein. The interim, then, between Christ's resurrection and his second coming is not of supreme importance insofar as the latter has already been anticipated in the former. The end really has already begun. This does not mean that world time is of no significance; it is simply that it must be placed *within* the time of Christ. From the perspective of world time, things still have to be played out, whereas from the perspective of Christ's time, the end has dawned. "From this point of view, there is nothing against assuming that what was fulfilled and had reached its goal as far as Jesus was concerned was still moving toward that fulfillment in the terms of world-time."[29]

Pro Nobis

So much for the problem of Jesus' imminent eschatological expectations. What are we to make, however, of the claim that Jesus' death was somehow for the salvation of the world? Surely this is not a claim that can be traced to the historical Jesus. Surely we have here a classic case of subsequent mythologization. Yet Balthasar's treatment of Jesus' apocalypticism above might just provide a key to answering this objection as well. For it is precisely the embarrassment concerning the former that has obscured the centrality of the latter. And it is precisely by salvaging the former that Balthasar can recentralize the cross and its significance in the drama between finite and infinite freedom. The following quote helps to make this connection clear.

However, the awareness that his life is moving toward a "baptism", toward that "cup" he will have to drink . . . means that his life cannot proceed along "wisdom" lines but must follow an "apocalyptic" rhythm. His life is running toward an *akme* that, as man, he will only be able to survive by surrendering control of his own actions and being determined totally by the Father's will (Lk 22.42 par). For this surrendering of control to the Father is essential if, in this hour, the single, indivisible event that dogmatics requires is to take place: he must bear the totality of the world's sin (Jn 1.29), being "made to be sin" (2 Cor 5.21), becoming "a curse" (Gal. 3.13) by the all-disposing will of the Father. If we can define the core of apocalyptic as the imminent expectation of God's final judgment of the old world, and therefore the change of aeon to a new world, we can say that this apocalyptic dimension—if Jesus lives within this horizon of expectation—is most definitely concentrated in him, his person, his span of life (including his death), his destiny. He has to deal with the world and its time on the basis of his unique, temporally circumscribed, human existence: his final "hour" contains the entirety of world-time, whether or not the latter continues to run, chronologically, "after" his death.[30]

Notice that the eschatological expectations of Jesus are unique—in comparison, say, with those of John the Baptist—precisely in the connection between *the* end and his own end. To try to find some general philosophical truth behind the event of Christ's death, then, would be precisely to miss this central point. There is, in short, something unique and necessary in Christ's death that will mark the in-breaking of God's kingdom.

This takes us back to the previous section's discussion of infinite and finite freedom. Because the Christian drama truly entails an interaction of *two* freedoms—and this goes back to the fact that when God gave the gift of human freedom, he truly gave it—there must be a genuine eschatological/apocalyptic dimension to the drama insofar as one of the covenant partners is eternal/infinite. A purely this-worldly reading of the cross and its significance—a reading which would, for instance, reduce it to Jesus' solidarity with the outcast and despised—would miss this crucial dimension. On the other hand, a purely one-sided act from God that did not at the same time involve genuine human freedom, and therefore a genuine human response, would not do justice to the role of finite freedom and would result in something less than a genuine drama.

This latter temptation, namely, to see the cross as a sign that God is always and already reconciled to the world, fails to take sufficient account of the seriousness of God's wrath concerning sin on the one hand and God's demand that his covenant partner respond to his loving initiative on the other. And this means that Anselm's approach to this problem, which has fallen on hard times in recent theology, has got to be retrieved, at least in part. What Balthasar admires about

Anselm's approach is the latter's insistence on taking both sides of the drama between God and his creation with the absolute seriousness demanded by the biblical text. Again, we have to keep two things in mind simultaneously: first, the gracious initiative of God, in both the Old and New Covenants, and, second, the necessary cooperation of the human partner in making amends for sin. If we go back to Augustine's view of freedom, mentioned briefly above, which maintains that sin has damaged finite freedom's ability to response sufficiently to the divine initiative, then we begin to understand the dilemma to which the cross is the solution.

It is here that Balthasar will invoke the classic doctrine of representation, a doctrine that has fallen out of favor, especially within Catholic circles. He will also remind us, at this point, of the four dimensions of this doctrine in the New Testament: the cultic, that Jesus is the Passover lamb who takes the sins of the people onto himself; the legal, that Jesus is the "Suffering Servant" who offers himself for the sins of the many; the ontological, that Jesus enters into the condition of the slave in order to liberate those who are enslaved to sin; and the moral, that the obedience of Jesus outweighs the disobedience of the human race. But of course none of this makes sense unless Jesus is unique, unless, that is, there is something about him that renders him capable of representing the two sides of the covenant mentioned above: God's loving initiative and the sinner's expiatory response. In other words, we cannot ultimately bracket off questions of a Christological nature in order to get to the real Jesus of history without seriously distorting a central aspect of the very Jesus of history that we are trying to understand. Must Jesus not, in other words, have had some sense of his uniqueness in order to account for his equation of his own hour (the particular) with the in-breaking of God's kingdom (the universal)?

Balthasar makes two brief suggestions in response to this question. First, Balthasar believes that Jesus' use of the title "Son of Man" in the Gospels can and should be traced to the historical Jesus. This would go hand in hand with his statement to his disciples, "Where I am going, you cannot follow me now; but you shall follow afterward" (Mk. 13.36). Second, it is not uninteresting that Jesus' disciples did not look for another after his death, but almost immediately made the connection between Jesus and the "Son of Man." And here Balthasar quotes Kümmel accordingly, "There can be no doubt that the evangelists equated Jesus and the Son of Man."[31] It is only this equation that can account for that fact that they, unlike the disciples of John the Baptist, did not look for another to initiate God's kingdom.

We are now in a position to make some necessary connections. It is precisely on account of Jesus' uniqueness, a uniqueness that can no longer be seen simply as a mythological or Hellenistic invention of the early church, that he can represent the clash between and the reconciliation of finite and infinite freedom on the cross. This latter cannot be seen simply in terms of a cathartic moment for the human race in the face of killing a perfectly innocent man, insofar as it is the Father who gives the Son over to death on the one hand and the Son who freely gives himself over to his killers on the other. Again, the divine side of the divine-human drama is not to be gainsaid.

> Whom did they nail to the Cross? Undoubtedly both the One whom God had given up into the hands of sinners and the man who expressed his solidarity with them. Thus the dramatic dimension is regained here not only with regard to God himself (in his inner conflict between wrath and love) but also with regard to the Covenant, the relationship between God and man.[32]

This all too brief treatment of Balthasar's retrieval of the doctrine of representation—a doctrine that will not be given its full treatment until *Theo-Drama* IV—will have to suffice for our present purposes.[33] However, we will have to take it up again in the next chapter when we consider not only how this is an event between finite and infinite freedom but also within the very Triune life of God. In short, we will have to examine further how this drama *between* God and the world can take place only on the basis of a drama *within* the Godhead. For now, we have only to unpack the implications of the above for finite freedom after the Christ event.

What has been said about the uniqueness of Christ and his hour now causes Balthasar to worry aloud: "An abyss seems to be opening between the destiny of Jesus and that of his disciples."[34] This worry leads Balthasar to raise four important problems/questions about the role of the other players in the drama between God and the world. First, "[i]f Jesus' 'hour' is absolutely unique, it is hard to see what role it can have in the life of his followers." Second, "[i]f it is eschatological in the strict sense . . . what 'time' will the post-Easter Church have to live in?" Third, "[i]f Jesus' whole life is lived with a view to his 'hour' . . . how will the post-Easter community portray him?" And here Balthasar wonders whether or not it might be necessary to interpret the temporal life of Jesus in the light of the supratemporal dimension that is introduced by the "mid-point" of the cross. And, fourth, "the unique person of Jesus is transcendent, pointing in the direction of the 'timeless' and eternal 'hour'; thus it cannot be held fast by the laws of temporal historiography."[35]

It is not my purpose here to go into the details of Balthasar's treatment of each of these problems. But before we will be in a position in the next chapter to examine Balthasar's explicit treatment of the person and mission of Christ, a few final comments must be made in their regard. First, the above problems signal the fact that Balthasar's doctrine of representation moves beyond the sometimes narrow Protestant one that treats Christ's death strictly in terms of "in our stead." While Balthasar will admit that Christ dies for us and does so "while we were yet sinners," he will also emphasize the fact that Christ's death really does mark a new beginning for finite freedom. In other words, Christ's death does not simply cover over human sinfulness, it opens up a new condition for human freedom which makes it both possible and necessary for human beings to respond to God's gracious initiative. We could say the same thing by saying that it is not so much that Christ dies instead of us as that he dies so that we can also die and be genuinely reborn to new life. Discipleship, then, is not simply an external following of Christ, but is the living out of a new life on the basis of an inner transformation. Balthasar will remind us, in this regard, of the importance of the Eastern notion of divinization.[36] In short, the redemptive role of Christ, and therefore his "hour," is unique, but it is unique in order to be inclusive. On the cross Christ blazes a trail that he alone can blaze, but it is a trail that makes possible even as it comes to insist upon the following of his disciples.

Next, the Church's time is marked precisely by the already and not yet of Jesus' time. In other words, the death and resurrection of Christ really does mark the beginning of a new age, and, from God's perspective, the victory has been won. Still, the Church must live between the dawning of this new age and its consummation. It lives out this time with a vivid sense that God's kingdom has been inaugurated and yet with a full realization that it must still carry out the mission of the Son until that kingdom has been consummated. As such, it will be given the gift of the Holy Spirit so as to participate in the uniqueness of the Son's work of reconciliation. The Church will be "ministers" in fact of this very reconciliation. This helps to explain its ability to teach with his authority, to cast out demons with his power, and even to proclaim the forgiveness of sins in his name. It, furthermore, only stands to reason that, since the Church understands that the kingdom has already dawned in the person of Christ, it will live in the "in between" time only with a constant view towards the consummation of a kingdom in which it is already participating. Its expectation, that is, like that of the earthly Jesus, will be an imminent one.

Finally, when the Church retells the story of Jesus, it cannot and indeed should not do so without the hindsight vision that makes sense of that story. Nor is this the extrinsic imposition of a foreign, eschatological perspective on a purely this-worldly life. For Jesus' temporal existence was always, already moving towards an hour that transcended the purely temporal. It only stands to reason, then, that it was not until the resurrection and the gift of the Holy Spirit that Jesus' disciples were in a position fully to comprehend the meaning of that life, even in terms of its temporal activity. Again, and this goes back to a point made in the previous chapter, the "eyes of faith" that were given to the disciples in the gift of the Holy Spirit, not only gave them a supernatural perspective by which to understand the "Christ of faith," it also enabled them to understand aright the "Jesus of history." Put differently, the life of the Jesus of history was itself oriented towards an end that could not be grasped by the temporal, historical perspective alone and therefore cannot be grasped by the methods of historical science. The method simply is not proportionate to its object. This allows Balthasar to conclude accordingly,

> In view of all this, the thematic transpositions undertaken by the post-Easter Church will seem less momentous than is usually thought. Things that are implicit in the consciousness of Jesus are duly made explicit by the fact of the Resurrection, and hence . . . by Jesus himself.[37]

PRELIMINARY CONCLUSIONS

If we were to continue to follow Balthasar on his course, from the Jesus of history, to the Christ of faith, to the Triune God who is revealed therein, we would be going over territory that I intend to treat at length in the next chapter. So, I will leave the difficult questions about the person and nature of Jesus Christ and the relationship between the economic and immanent Trinity until then. Still, in order to round out this sketch of the relationship between finite and infinite freedom, and thereby to conclude the present chapter, I shall anticipate, very briefly, what is to come. As the foregoing should have shown, Balthasar's Theo-dramatic approach to the question of finite and infinite freedom cuts in two directions. Against a tendency that is sometimes found in the Fathers and Scholastics, Balthasar insists that our starting point to the question of infinite freedom must begin squarely with the revelation of that freedom in the person of Jesus Christ. Against the recurrent theological tendency to see in Jesus of Nazareth merely a revelation of the proper human disposition towards infinite freedom, or to relegate certain events and dispositions simply to the humanity of Jesus, Balthasar will insist that in Jesus Christ we have a revelation, not just of finite freedom, but also of infinite freedom, that in the very lowliness and obedience of Jesus Christ we see something of the nature of the eternal God.

On the other hand, and this time against the moderns, Balthasar refuses to separate the Jesus of history from the Christ of faith, so that one would have to opt for a purely human faith based on the real Jesus of history, on the one hand, or for a trans-temporal faith, inspired by the message of Jesus' disciples on the other. For in this case too—and here the moderns are closer to the Fathers of the Church than they would care to admit—who God is, is kept safely above and behind the question of who Jesus is/was. In either case, that is, Jesus ceases to be a genuine revelation of the Triune God, in the one case in order to protect the immutable God from the vicissitudes of history and the negative effects of human freedom, and in the other, to do justice to the Jesus of the Gospels in opposition to the Christ of the creeds.

By beginning with the question of Jesus' mission, however, and this will give us a glimpse of where we will be going in the next chapter, Balthasar is convinced that he has found a way to keep all of these things together. As Angleo Scola has so succinctly put it, "in concrete terms, [we have] to take the path which leads from Jesus, the man Jesus, to the Father, and thus to the Son, and from Jesus to the Spirit."[38] And this means seeing in Jesus' very humanity a revelation of the Trinity, thereby taking us back to the old Thomistic assertion that, "The Son of God came and he caused the hidden rivers to gush forth, making known the name of the Trinity."[39] This, then, is precisely what the next chapter, which will also take us into the third part of Balthasar's trilogy, will endeavor to present.

But before we can turn our attention to the question of the relationship between the mission of Jesus and the Trinitarian processions, we should not forget that Jesus really does reveal the meaning of finite freedom as well. That is, besides giving us a glimpse into the nature of the Triune God, Jesus also shows us what it means to be free, and that is what we have spent to bulk of this chapter trying to show. It will be left to the rest of *Theo-Drama* to make this clear, and if we were to give an adequate introduction to the second part of the trilogy, we would have to say a lot more about Mary, the Church, soteriology and eschatology. I only hope that I have given a sufficient enough glimpse of Balthasar's treatment of the problem of finite and infinite freedom, that the reader will be in a better position to tackle these issues as well.

CHAPTER SIX

"THE TRINITY AND THE CROSS"

We cannot entertain any form of "process theology" that identifies the world process . . . with the eternal and timeless "procession" of the Hypostases in God. Accordingly, there is only one way to approach the Trinitarian life in God: on the basis of what is manifest in God's kenosis in the theology of the covenant—and thence in the theology of the Cross—we must feel our way back into the mystery of the absolute . . . To think in such a way is to walk on a knife edge: it avoids all fashionable talk of "the pain of God" and yet is bound to say that something happens in God that not only justifies the possibility and actual occurrence of all suffering in the world but also justifies God's sharing in the latter, in which he goes to the length of vicariously taking on man's God-lessness.[1]

God the Father can give his divinity away in such a manner that it is not merely "lent" to the Son: the Son's possession of it is "equally substantial". This implies such an incomprehensible and unique "separation" of God from himself that it includes and grounds every other separation—be it never so dark and bitter . . . "Love is as strong as hell" (". . . as death" AV, RSV): no, it is stronger, for hell is only possible given the absolute and real separation of Father and Son.[2]

Numerous questions have arisen in the foregoing chapters that have had to wait for some resolution until this chapter. This is fitting, for Balthasar himself ties a variety of loose ends together when he arrives at his Trinitarian discussions, whether at the end of *Theo-Drama* or in the final two volumes of the trilogy in *Theo-Logic*. It could be said, in fact, that if Christ is the *center* of Balthasar's theological method, the Trinity is its *telos*. In short, my decision to end with the Trinity is not just an attempt to save the best for last, but is, rather, necessary in order to round out the many issues that have been raised to this point. I will now try to make this more concrete.

In Chapters Two and Three we looked at Balthasar's method in the light of his reading of the history of theology. There, Balthasar cautions against a tendency to work out the relationship between God and the world within the context of a Plotinian or Aristotelian concept of God, a perennial temptation in the infamous *de Deo Uno/ de Deo Trino* approach. In such a context it is difficult not to disparage all difference, multiplicity, matter, history, relationality, and, yes, all receptivity, for being on the wrong side of the God/world divide. I hinted in Chapter Three above that Balthasar's final solution to this problem would come in his discussion of the Trinity. In this chapter, then, I will return to that suggestion.

Another problem, however, which has persisted in the foregoing chapters is modern in origin: namely, how can an individual man, born 2000 years ago, provide the key to universal meaning. On further investigation, however, we find that these two problems are not so different after all, for it is still a question of the relationship between the particular or individual on the one hand the universal or simple on the other. The question, that is, still concerns the relationship between unity and multiplicity. The modern solution will either tend, like the Platonist one before it, to dissolve all difference in order to attain some abstract unity—and this will, of course, mean the dissolution of the individual person or the "mythological" aspects of the faith—or it will claim that difference is all there is—and thereby destroy all genuine unity. Again, as we shall see, such problems require a Trinitarian resolution.

Finally, in Chapters Four and Five, the first two parts of the trilogy were introduced in the context, first, in terms of the theology of the old and new covenants, and, second, in terms of the relationship between finite and infinite freedom—a problem which arises from the side of nature, but which is resolved only in Jesus Christ. In both chapters the questions were, at their core, Christological ones, but, as we shall see, the farther Balthasar goes into his study of Jesus Christ the less he can avoid talking about the Trinity. In this chapter, then, I will proceed in three major sections. First, in the introduction, I will make a clearer connection between the fundamental-theological questions which were raised in Chapters Two and Three above and

Balthasar's Trinitarian theology contained below. Second, I will resume the Christological questions from the last chapter, but now in the context of more explicitly Trinitarian questions. These questions concern the person, mission and nature of Christ. Third, I will offer a brief overview of Balthasar's doctrine of the Trinity, especially in the light of his suggestion that the Triune God is revealed most clearly in the event of the cross. Since I have focused on the Aesthetics and Dramatics in Chapters Four and Five, I will also try to give *Theo-Logic* its due in what follows. It should be mentioned, however, that the questions raised in *Theo-Logic* have been with us since Chapter Two.

INTRODUCTION: BRINGING IT ALL BACK HOME

Let us recall once more Balthasar's misgivings concerning a certain style of "cosmocentric" theology which relies too heavily upon the *exitus-reditus* schema of the neo-Platonists. In such a schema, the multiplicity, relationality and materiality of the world can only be conceived as a fall from the "really real" world of unity, self-sufficiency and immateriality. Think here of Aristotle's "self-thinking thought" or Plotinus's One who resides even above Being. Of course the Fathers, with their doctrines of creation *ex nihilo*, the incarnation, and the resurrection of the body, went a long way in correcting this neo-platonic approach, especially in their condemnations of Arianism. Still, the tendency lurks to see the world as a fall and to see the "true God" as residing somewhere safely, not only outside of and apart from the world and its multiplicity, but also "behind" either the incarnation or the Trinitarian processions.[3] Here Balthasar will often excoriate a one-sided reading of Palamas's distinction between God's essence and his energies, as if the incarnation and the Trinitarian processions could lie on the "energies" side of this divide and therefore not truly reveal God as his is "in himself."[4] Taken to its extreme, this would mean a pronounced separation between God's activity in Jesus Christ, through the Holy Spirit—the so-called economic Trinity—and God in himself—the immanent Trinity. If we add to this two other sometime Patristic-Scholastic moves, we will begin to see the Balthasarian concern in all its clarity. First, there are Augustine's and Aquinas's reservations concerning any sort of inter-personal analogies for the Trinity, preferring psychological or intra-mental ones—as if, Balthasar would point out, these do not have limitations of their own.[5] Next, there is—as alluded to in Chapter Three above—Aquinas's refusal to admit a real relation between God and the world, this latter resulting in an inability to see "receptivity" in any terms other than the fateful "potentiality" that can only exist for things that are not God.[6]

All of this, according to Balthasar, if left unchecked, leads to difficulties in accounting not only for the genuine goodness precisely *in otherness* of creation, but, even more so, of God's ability to deal with this creation once it chooses against Him. And this leads Balthasar to a series of moves in *Theo-Logic*, which are meant to serve as correctives to the above tendencies. First, although Balthasar has serious reservations about the psychological analogy of the Trinity—how does one account, for instance, for the scene in the Garden of Gethsemene in terms of this analogy?—he is by no means intent upon abandoning all such attempts to find analogies for the Trinity from below. He would only caution that such analogies will never be adequate on account of the "ever greater dissimilarity" between God and the world. This means that the psychological analogies are at least as fraught with inadequacy as the inter-personal ones. He will also insist that the relational nature of inter-worldly beings, culminating in the human person, and this culminating in the fruitful union between a man and a woman, ought to have received more attention from the tradition than it did. Here Balthasar refers positively to the work of Richard of Saint Victor, but, more recently, to the nineteenth century theologian Matthias Scheeben.[7] Again, we should recall here that, for Balthasar, knowledge finds its highest earthly expression in the encounter between two persons and couple this with the fact that the husband-wife-child triad is the best evidence we have for the Trinitarian structure of worldly logic.

Next, we should keep in mind the principle that was articulated in Chapter Three above that no excellence can be found at the level of worldly Being that does not have its source in God. Certainly the ability to give *and receive* that is found at the human level of worldly Being should be understood as higher than the relatively non-relatedness of, say, rocks. It would be strange, in short, if God were more like a rock in its inability to receive than the human person in its ability to do so. This will become clearer in the discussion of personhood below, but it also invokes the discussion in Chapter Three of the simultanaeity of wealth and poverty in Being. In Balthasar's discussion of the fourfold distinction, non-subsistent Being is at once the

fullness of Being (wealth) and yet also dependent upon actually existing things for its subsistence (poverty). In *Theo-Logic* II, Balthasar is
going to trace such simultanaeity of wealth and poverty back to God
himself. Again, this will be spelled out at great length below.

Finally, we must remember the principle articulated in terms of the
nature-grace relationship touched on in various ways in the first four
chapters. For this relationship to be conceived in a fully Catholic
fashion, we must be able to account *both* for the newness of what
occurs in Christ—"lest the cross be emptied of its power"—*and* for
the continuity in God's work of creation and redemption. If the
continuity is overemphasized, we lose the entire theology of grace
and the uniqueness of Christ—insofar as Christ comes simply to
bring more of what, say, Moses brought, but not something *new in
kind*. If, on the other hand, the newness is overemphasized, then we
must deny that Christ really comes to restore the glory of God's
creation, and grace becomes arbitrary and heteronomous to that
which is *human* or *natural*. As we will see later, this delicate balance is
seen at its clearest precisely *in* the person of Jesus Christ. But with
regard to Balthasar's Trinitarian theology it means the following:
that the movement towards God from below, and with it the various
analogies of the Trinity taken from this world, cannot have pro-
gressed so far that there is no room for genuine newness or surprise
when these things are revealed by God from above. In other words,
it is certainly the case that Jesus Christ really fulfills the inclinations
of the created order and, in doing so, reveals the deepest truth of that
order, but unless this revelation is to be conceived in terms of "more
of the same," it must contain a newness that stands as the final
measure for all that went before. In short, none of our Trinitarian
analogies can balk at things that revelation itself does not balk at.

JESUS CHRIST: HIS PERSON, NATURE AND MISSION

Balthasar's Starting Point: The Mission of Jesus

At the end of the last chapter I quoted Angelo Scola regarding Jesus
of Nazareth as the proper starting point for both Christological and
Trinitarian reflections. I must now quote him in full.

A solid Trinitarian doctrine must, consequently, first of all win
access for itself from Jesus to the personal Trinity. For Balthasar

this means, in concrete terms, to take the path which leads from Jesus, the man Jesus, to the Father, and thus to the Son, and from Jesus to the Spirit.[8]

In the light of what has been said to this point, it should not surprise the reader that Balthasar begins his Trinitarian theology with the person of Jesus Christ, nor that he begins his study of Jesus Christ with the man Jesus and his profound sense of mission. Such a concrete starting point presents a problem only if the created order with all of its connection to multiplicity, time (history), and even the flesh, are simply opposed to all things divine. If this were the case, of course, then God really could not reveal himself through these mediums. But because Balthasar insists that everything that exists in this world that is good must find its pre-eminent source in God, he does not shy away from the specificity of Jesus of Nazareth in his attempt to talk about God. This may sound like a trivial point, but in many ways it has proved a stumbling block to both the ancients and the moderns, as was stated above. Furthermore, it is precisely those things in Christ that are most embarrassing to a certain style of philosophical thinking that Balthasar will make the center of his study. Again, beginning with the mission of Jesus Christ would not amount to much if one were either, (a) going to see Christ's obedience to the Father as revealing to us something about the proper disposition of the creature before the Creator, that is, if one were going to relegate such "obedience" to the humanity of Christ; or (b) going to understand Christ as merely a prophet or a sage, as so much modern theology has done. But Balthasar does not opt for either of these alternatives. Rather, he will see in Christ's very lowliness, obedience and deference to the Father a revelation not only of the proper meaning of human freedom—"He who wishes to save his life must lose it"—but at the same time a revelation of the nature of Triune God. God is revealed, to put it simply, precisely *in* Christ's humanity, not "behind" it or in spite of it.

One interesting implication of this can be seen in Balthasar's discussion of the consciousness of Jesus and the question of his self-knowledge. Here too we have a divide between the classical treatment on the one hand, which, in its battle with Arianism, wanted to insist on the total omniscience of Jesus from his conception (*visio immediate*), and the modern treatment on the other hand, which limits Jesus' knowledge to that of a, perhaps, very special prophet or sage.

As far as the *knowledge* of Christ is concerned, we have already seen that the Church Fathers' and Scholastics' intensive preoccupation with constructing a doctrine of Christ's omniscience . . . had a certain biblical foundation, particularly in John . . . who deliberately portrays each *status* of Jesus mirroring the other. It was hardly noticed, however, that John emphasizes Jesus' obedience just as strongly as his supermundane knowledge, nor that the greater good of this obedience required that the Son's intrinsically "fitting" and "direct" knowledge should be "laid up" with the Father for reasons of the "economy". The questions posed by the Fathers and Scholastics proceeded from a static view of the "dignity" of Jesus, a dignity that was his . . . right from the beginning of his Incarnation.[9]

This, of course, does not imply the modern view that Jesus had no knowledge concerning his true nature, but it does imply that God's choice to reveal himself in a *human being* entails that any knowledge that Jesus had regarding his own identity would be appropriate to such a medium. In other words, Balthasar need not shy away from the fact that the Son of God really did take on a human nature—something that, of course, the Fathers knew—and that even the limitations of that nature became the vehicles through which he was able to reveal both the true meaning of God and the true meaning of the human person.

Balthasar points out several implications of this, but I will mention two in particular. First, if Jesus does not possess knowledge of his mission all at once, his dependence upon Mary becomes easier to explain. Here would be a good place to recall Balthasar's numerous positive references to the spirit of childhood in keeping with Jesus' famous exhortation, "Unless you become as this child . . ." Again, if it is the case that whatever is to be commended about the spirit of childhood must have its ultimate source in God, then Jesus' state of dependence on his mother cannot be a cause for embarrassment. Indeed, it too is revelatory. Jesus himself possesses the very spirit that he is encouraging in others.

Without this spiritual handing on, which takes place simultaneously with the bodily gift of mother's milk and motherly care, God's Word would not have really become flesh. For being in-the-flesh always means receiving from others. Even if the One who receives the word of tradition is himself "the Word from the beginning", from whom all genuine tradition takes its origin, he must accept this earth-grown "wisdom" as a form—in the terms of the world—of his Father's will and providence. So we see that the Incarnation of the Word that brings the promised fulfillment, of the "new and eternal Covenant", has an inherent need of an antecedent history that we call the "Old Covenant"; in Mary, the (Abrahamic) faith that characterized this Covenant becomes a contributory element in the Incarnation.[10]

Second, Balthasar's starting point in the mission of Jesus allows him to pay greater attention to the role of the Spirit in Jesus' ministry than is typical of some traditional Christologies. Here too Balthasar will speak of a certain "laying up" of certain privileges on the part of the Son so that he can genuinely enter into the human condition. At times Balthasar will speak of this in terms of "Trinitarian Inversion,"[11] and at other times in terms of "Spirit Christology."[12] In terms of the former, the "inversion" comes about insofar as the standard Catholic understanding of the processions—the Spirit proceeding from the Father and the Son (who also proceeds from the Father alone)—has become, in the order of the economy, the Spirit being given to the Son by the Father in order to equip him for his mission. The first point to be made with regard to the present discussion is that the Spirit's role in the life of Jesus is another way of emphasizing the fact that the Son really did take on human nature and that, as such, his mission had to be mediated to him, step by step, as it were, rather than all at once. But another important point to be made in this regard concerns the obedience of Jesus *to* the Father *through* the mediation of the Spirit. This obedience, which might normally seem to imply a merely human Jesus, becomes in Balthasar also revelatory of the Trinity. If we accept the filioque, that the Spirit proceeds from the Father and the Son (and Balthasar does), then we must say that the condition under which the Son is under the leading of the Spirit is only possible on the basis of a prior decision, on the part of the Trinity, and upon a prior "obedience" on the part of the eternal Son, to the incarnation.

This not-grasping, which is primary, governs the entire attitude of the Son in becoming man: in the obedience that has Incarnation as its goal, he *allows* himself to be transported into the womb of the Virgin; accordingly, the One who transports him there cannot be himself but only the Spirit.[13]

Here we catch a glimpse, both of Balthasar's reading of the role of Spirit in Christology, but also of his particular take on the question of kenosis. This is a point to which we shall have to return, but already it must be said that the kenosis of the Son in the incarnation refers back ultimately to what can only be called a Trinitarian kenosis.[14]

A final point about Balthasar's mission starting point will help us to make a connection with the last chapter. By focusing on the historical Jesus' orientation towards his "hour," Balthasar was able to make a natural link between the so-called humanitarian and "timeless" aspect of Jesus' teaching and his apparently "time-bound" obsession with the end of the world. As such, Balthasar was able to take Albert Schweitzer's re-emphasis on the centrality of apocalyptic to the message of the historical Jesus and use it for entirely different ends. Now, by beginning with the profound sense of mission of the historical Jesus—which entails Jesus' constant deference to the will of his "Father"—Balthasar is able to unite two other things which have been severed in Christologies of a Liberal stripe: namely, the mission of the historical Jesus and the Church's doctrine of the Trinity. This move also allows Balthasar to counter at the same time the sometime classical tendency to separate questions of the Immanent Trinity from questions of the economy.

The Person and Nature of Jesus in the Light of His Mission

In his famous study of Karl Barth, Balthasar commends the former for his insistence on reconnecting all theological problems to their Christological center. In fact, Barth's famous condemnation of the analogy of Being had to do with Catholicism's alleged attempt to establish a relationship between God and the world prior to God's definitive self-revelation in Jesus Christ. In Barth's view, the philosophical concept of "Being" was being applied indiscriminately to both God and the world, bringing God under the control of human reason. This could be nothing less, for Barth, than idolatry, the attempt to construct a notion of God outside of God's self-revelation. Another example of Barth's Christocentrism can be seen in his critique of the individualistic doctrine of predestination in Protestant scholasticism. Here, again, the question of individual salvation is dealt with while bracketing the question of Christ's predestination, and the question that all human beings are included, in some way, in the destiny of Jesus Christ. In both of these areas we encounter a Christocentric approach that Balthasar finds worthy of commendation to his fellow Catholics. And, yet, towards the end of the Barth study Balthasar voices some serious reservations, reservations that have nothing to do with Barth's Christocentric approach, but, rather, with what Balthasar refers to as Barth's "Christomonism." In short, it was not that Barth was too Christocentric, in Balthasar's view, it is that he was not Christocentric enough. A genuinely Christocentric approach, that is, must make more room for that which is not God insofar as the Son does not destroy human nature when he assumes it in the incarnation.

When Balthasar gets into his discussion of the problems surrounding Christ's person and nature in the *Theo-Drama*, this critique of Barth must be kept in mind, especially when Balthasar refers to Jesus Christ as the concrete analogy of Being. In order better to understand this, and in order better to understand the relationship between this question and the question of mission that we have been discussing to this point, we will have to look at two final issues in Balthasar's Christology. First, what is a person, and what light does this question shed on the question of the identity of Jesus Christ? Second, what does Balthasar mean by calling Jesus Christ the analogy of Being in person?

It is important to point out that in the background of Balthasar's discussion of these issues lies the perennial Christological problem of how a single person can possess two natures at the same time without compromising either of these natures. Since Balthasar will eventually describe his own thought as walking "the knife-edge between Nestorianism and Monophysitism,"[15] it might be helpful to remind the reader of the central issues involved here. These controversies centered upon the question of relationship between the divine and the human in the single person of Jesus Christ. Monothelitism—the heresy that received its refutation at the capable hands of Maximus the Confessor—is not terribly far from Monophysitism insofar as both entail a denial of the full humanity of Christ by replacing his human will—Monothelitism—or his human nature—Monophysitism—with a divine will or nature. Soteriologically this would present a problem because it would entail that *human nature* cannot be redeemed without being replaced by the divine nature. In his writings Maximus

wanted to do justice to the "fully human" of the Chalcedonian decision, without in any way, of course, denying his full divinity. It should
be clear what would happen to the question of finite and infinite
freedom if Monothelitism were maintained: namely, finite freedom
would have to be swallowed up by infinite freedom, and we would be
back to a position too close to that of Platonism and Buddhism.

If the Monophysites, as we have just seen, tended to confuse the
two natures of Christ to such a degree that he ended up with only
a divine nature, the Nestorians wanted to so separate the natures
that we could attribute now this action to Jesus as man and now that
action to Jesus as God. Here we lose the fact that Jesus Christ was
a single person. This is why Nestorius could refuse to call Mary the
mother of God; Mary, he insisted, had only given birth to the human
Jesus. In either case, however, we have an embarrassment, typical of
hellenistic thought, of the fact that God really took on human nature
without that nature ceasing to be human and without, for all of that,
God ceasing to be God.

So, how does the question of personhood fit into all of this? And
what does Balthasar's unique reflection on this question add to the
post-Chalcedonian debates? Balthasar begins by reminding us of the
fundamental problem of the human person: I am at once a member
of a species of countless other human beings who possess the same
nature that I possess; and yet I possess this nature in an absolutely
unique and incommunicable way. Of course I can draw a sketch of
those things which set me apart from others—physical characteristics, family tree, race, language, class, and the like—but even here
I would only be giving an external description without really getting
to the inner reality of what makes me a unique person. I could then
take the more recent approach of philosophical personalism and
emphasize the fact that I only come to a realization of my "I" when
I am addressed by an other. I might, in fact, only ever come to realize
my uniqueness when I come to see how much I matter to my mother
or father or children or spouse. But even here, Balthasar suggests, we
can still do without the concept of "personhood." We are still only at
the level of individuality. There is yet "no guarantee of *who* the individual is."[16]

Such a guarantee . . . can be provided neither by the nonpersonal,
empirical world nor by our fellow men . . . It can only be given by
the absolute Subject, God. It is when God addresses a conscious

subject, tells him who he is and what he means to the eternal God of truth and shows him the purpose of his existence—that is, imparts a distinctive and divinely authorized mission—that we can say of a conscious subject that he is a "person."[17]

But what does all of this have to do with the question of the nature of Jesus Christ? It should be pointed out that it is really only in the Christological and Trinitarian controversies that the concept of personhood was given serious attention. The ancients were not particularly interested in the question, which helps to explain why the individual was usually swallowed up into the *polis* or some other whole. And even when they were taken up in the early church the conversation was often short-circuited by the terms of the debate or by the position which was being refuted. For instance, the whole connection between person (*prosopon*) and "mask" had to be downplayed in the face of Sabellius' notion that the Father, Son and Spirit were merely modes of the single God's existence. Balthasar suggests that there were really two tasks that had to be carried out in the context of these discussions. First, "[w]hat was needed . . . was an adequate means of expressing the fundamental mystery of Christology, namely, that a perfect man, endowed with reason and even possessing a free will . . . can be God."[18] The early Church largely succeeded in this first task, especially in Maximus' critique of Monothelitism, wherein the genuinely human will of Jesus Christ was defended. We can also see this success in the Church's insistence that "One of the Trinity has suffered," against the notion that Jesus only suffered in the flesh. As John Meyendorf reminds us: "Only *Someone* can die, not something, not a nature or flesh."[19]

But there was a second task which, Balthasar laments, "remained unfulfilled": "there was no progress beyond the tension between genus and individual." In other words, there was no real settling of the question of personhood. And, so, Balthasar concludes this section with the following, crucial, point:

All the empirical approximations we use to try to describe the characteristics of the conscious subject within a species (man) are inadequate. Only God can define and designate such a subject in his qualitative uniqueness. And in the one, sole, archetypal instance, it is God who defines who this Subject is and why he is there; it is he who sets forth the meaning, the task, the vocation.

In Jesus, the two are identical: this is what distinguishes him from other subjects . . . Jesus acts accordingly; he does not communicate a divine plan but speaks as the personal Word of God.[20]

If we combine the foregoing with a final insight, the relevance of this discussion of personhood will become clearer. It is not only that we attain no real foundation for the personhood of the person outside of God's creative act and call, it is also the case that it is only in the context of Christian revelation that we come to appreciate fully the irreducibly relational aspect implied in the very term. Consider, for instance, Boethius's standard definition, "A person is an individual substance of a rational nature." Again, we really do not move beyond individuality in this definition. Furthermore, Balthasar will emphasize the etymological roots of "substance," from *substantia*, or "standing-in-itself." In other words, not only does Boethius's definition not really get beyond the basic notion of the individual—and therefore does not really need the concept of the person—it cannot account for the utterly relational nature of the person, especially as this arises out of the Trinitarian and Christological disputes of the early church. "Doesn't this definition, dominant in the Middle Ages, [make] it extremely difficult . . . to apply the term to God?"[21] In other words, far from "standing in themselves," the persons of the Trinity are what they are precisely in their relations with each other. If we tie this into what has gone before, the utter deference to the Father on the part of the man Jesus reveals to us something of the utter deference to the Father on the part of the eternal Son—insofar as the Father holds back absolutely nothing of himself in the generation of the Son. The person of the Son, then, consists precisely in his utter gift of himself to the Father, and vice-versa.

We are now in a better position to comment briefly on the question of the Balthasar's assertion that Jesus Christ is the concrete analogy of Being. The following two programmatic quotes should be kept in mind in what follows.

Quite simply, this means that the person of the Logos in whom the hypostatic union takes place cannot function, in any way, as the ("higher") union between God and man; this person, as such, is God. Since the person of the Logos is the ultimate union of divine and created being, it must constitute the final proportion [*Mass*] between the two and hence must be the "concrete *analogia entis*" itself.[22]

And, then, this:

> For Christology . . . gives an account of an event that cannot be made subject to any universal law but that subjects all other laws (regulating the relationship between God and the creature, that is) to its own uniqueness. This insight is the only basis on which we can speak theologically of analogy. This rules out any attempt to devise philosophical laws beforehand and then apply them as prescriptions to Christology.[23]

We are now in the midst of the thorniest area of Balthasar's theology. It is crucial that we keep the two principles above in mind. First, the analogy established between the Creator and creature in the incarnation does not do away with the always present, greater dissimilarity between the two. And within this principle the converse must always be kept in mind: namely, that there must still be a genuine analogy. Second, no philosophical understanding of analogy (analogies from below) can be allowed to constrict what we learn about the relationship on the basis of the person of Jesus Christ (analogies from above).

This is not the place to try to deal with all of the complexities associated with Balthasar's treatment of the hypostatic union, but we must at least be aware of the following points. First, Balthasar locates the difference between God and the world *within* the difference between the Trinitarian processions. Otherwise it is difficult to see how this difference will not be construed in a purely negative manner, and, therefore, have to be obliterated in the reconciliation between God and creation. Second, as the concrete analogy of Being, Christ simultaneously reveals the true nature of the Triune God and the true nature of the meaning of the creature. The fact that the humanity of Christ is not only not destroyed, but is not even taken over by the divine will, means maintaining the goodness of creation in all its difference from God. Again, this implies that the difference of worldly Being must be rooted in the difference within divine Being. But the other side of the equation must be kept in mind as well: Christ does not only reveal the true nature of humanity, he also reveals the true nature of what it means to be God. If there were not something analogous between worldly and divine Being, this would be impossible. Specifically, if creaturely Being were simply the opposite of divine Being, then Christ would not have been able to use it to make God known.

Third, we must keep in mind that Balthasar's approach to analogy always includes within it the "ever greater dissimilarity." Balthasar maintains the goodness of the world even in its distinction from God by insisting upon an analogy between the procession of Christ from the Father and the creation of the world from the Father. Indeed, as was stated in the first point above, he situates the latter in the former. It is this that helps to explain why when Christ comes into the world he finds language ready to hand in order to make known the Triune God. But Balthasar is careful to insist that the analogy can never become an identity. In other words, the hypostatic union of the two natures in the one person of Jesus Christ never amounts to a merging of the two into one. The mistake of Hegel and even Eckhardt was to blur the distinction between begetting and creating into an identity.

In the light of the foregoing we can say the following. Because there is a real analogy between the creation of the world in its difference from God and the procession of the Son in his difference from the Father—indeed, because the former can only arise from within and on account of the latter—then Jesus precisely need not step outside of his place in God in order to come into the world, even when this entails entering into this world's alienation from the Father on account of sin. This last point allows Balthasar to make two further moves. First, he can take more seriously than some in the tradition Paul's insistence that Jesus "became sin" in order to reconcile humanity to the Father. The distance which separates the sinner from the Father can never be greater than the positive distance which separates the Son from the Father, if for no other reason than that the latter distance is what accounts for the distance of the created freedom which makes sin possible in the first place. And this means, secondly, that there is no reason to relegate Jesus' suffering for sin to his humanity in what could only be a quasi-Nestorian fashion. Indeed, the cross should be seen as the highest revelation of Father's "pathe" in the face of human sinfulness, even as it also reveals the "diastasis" between the persons of the Trinity. These final points will become clearer in what follows, but we should give Balthasar the final word on both of these points.

We can even say that, in the cry of dereliction on the Cross, Jesus reveals how God is forsaken by sinners. Jesus' whole existence, including the aspect that the Greeks found so difficult, his *pathe*, is in the service of his proclamation of God. But he does this in a fully human conscious subject who simultaneously brings to light the full truth of man, and—since he primarily reveals the truth of God—the truth of man as God sees him.[24]

And then:

> Yet this "infinite distance", which recapitulates the sinner's mode of alienation from God, will remain forever the highest revelation known to the world of the diastasis (within the eternal being of God) between the Father and Son in the Holy Spirit.[25]

Some Preliminary Conclusions: The Implications of the Word

In the light of the foregoing we are in a position to return to the critique of Barth mentioned above, namely, that Barth's Christocentrism amounted, at times, to a Christomonism on account of his tendency to swallow all activity into the activity of Christ. In terms of *Theo-Drama*, this would result in the inability of other roles once Christ has come onto the stage; in terms of *Theo-Logic*, such a view could not account for Christ's ability to make use of human language—"ready to hand"[26]—in order truly to make God known. But we must remember also to keep the opposite tendency in mind, and this goes back to the other modern theological method mentioned in Chapter Three above, that of Karl Rahner. If Barth tended to reduce all activity to that of Christ, Rahner tended to see Christ as the simple playing out of tendencies already latent within anthropology. In this latter case, the analogy between Christ's being begotten and our being created threatens to slide over into an identity, even as in the case of Barth the two sides were often seen in simple opposition.

If we look at this a little closer, we will be able to bring together in a preliminary way all that we have said about Jesus Christ in this section. Part of Barth's rejection of the Catholic doctrine of analogy had to do with Barth's rejection of the so-called "Catholic and": faith and works, Christ and Mary/saints, bible and tradition/church, grace and cooperation, etc. One is tempted to include here: Jesus, God *and* man. Balthasar's approach to analogy, contrary to the version which Barth feared, is not premised on a neutral idea established outside of God's self-revelation in Christ. Indeed, the human movement towards God is always and already undertaken, for

Balthasar, within God's prior movement, in Christ, towards human beings. Even the act of creation, for Balthasar, occurs in Christ. But Balthasar's Christocentrism never leads to the disparagement of the genuine otherness of the created order, because such otherness is offered a place within the positive otherness of the Trinitarian processions. What we catch a glimpse of in the mission of Christ, then, is the real meaning of personhood—difference in relation. Of course we are not "other" to the Father in the same way the Son is other to the Father; he is begotten and we are made. The Incarnation does nothing to reverse that fundamental distinction. But neither is our otherness from the Father totally unlike the Son's. And this means that when he took on human nature, he really could show us what human nature, in all of its otherness from the Father, should look like. It shows us that the true freedom and difference of the person is not attained in grasping after autonomy. This was the move, after all, of Adam and Eve. Rather, the true meaning of freedom and personhood is revealed precisely in Christ's obedience, lowliness and the sacrifice.

Of course this would be terrifying if it not were two final things also mentioned above. First, we see that in Jesus such an attitude really does result in the gaining of one's self. Jesus did not just command the saving of one's life by losing it; he lived it. But, second, this law of self-surrender has its source in the Trinity: for Jesus does not come primarily to reveal the Son, but the Father. In Jesus' surrender of himself on the cross, then, we catch a glimpse of the Father's eternal surrender of himself to the Son. In other words, the God of Jesus Christ is not a threat to us in all our otherness precisely because our otherness is his gift to us. This takes us back to Barth's dreaded "Catholic and": the fact that Jesus could make use of human nature to reveal to us both the meaning of God and ourselves, means that human nature has this capacity for God. And so the Catholic "and" has its origins, already, in Christ. And this can be illustrated rather easily by looking—very briefly—at Balthasar's treatment of Mary. It is not Christ *and* Mary, as if Mary is some independent principle outside of Christ to be added in order to make salvation possible. It is, rather, that Mary represents what all human beings were intended to be precisely *in* Christ. Mary's "yes," the Church has always insisted, takes place only within the gambit of the grace made available by her Son. It is just that when that grace was given, it really was Mary who said "yes." The ultimate source of the Catholic "and," then, is the

Trinitarian "and." And it is precisely to some final comments on Balthasar's Trinitarian theology that we must now turn.

THE TRINITY AND THE CROSS

If Balthasar's starting point into Trinitarian theology is Christology and his starting point into Christology is the mission of Christ, then the origin and end of that mission must be of singular importance. Balthasar repeatedly refers to Thomas's notion that the mission of Christ into the world is rooted in his procession from the Father, and this is a point that the former makes more central to his Trinitarian thought than the latter. But it is not only the origin of the mission that is important to Balthasar, it is also the fact that that mission culminates in the crucifixion and resurrection. If we combine this with the Johannine notion that the cross is a revelation of God's glory, we are forced to ask the driving question of Balthasar's Trinitarian theology: What does the cross reveal to us about God? We also find out that this answer can and has been answered in two extremes which serve as the Scylla and Charybdis for Balthasar's own answer. The first of these extremes would deny God's immutability by saying that God only becomes God by entering into and taking on the sins of the world. Such an answer would result in a reversion to myth and therefore be subject to the legitimate criticisms of the ancient philosophers: for instance that both God and world would be subject to a higher principle, such as, in this case, fate. At the opposite extreme stands the temptation to see the true God as residing somehow, somewhere safely above the events of the Incarnation and crucifixion. The suffering of Jesus on the cross would therefore be attributed only to Christ's humanity or the "lower parts" of his soul and the divinity would be safely protected from any negative effects. It is hard to see how this latter position can either do full justice to John's notion, mentioned above, that it is precisely in the cross that we are witnesses to God's glory, or how it avoids some sort of Nestorianism.

It is in answering this question without going in either of these directions that we arrive at the heart of Balthasar's Trinitarian theology. I mentioned at the beginning of this chapter that Balthasar regrets the fact that the mainstream of the tradition did not pay greater attention to the Nuptial analogy for the Trinitarian relations. Again, it is not so much that Balthasar simply rejects the psychological analogy, nor that he rejects the use of such analogies in general; it is, rather, that he insists that any analogy used must account for what is actually revealed to us in the person of Jesus Christ and his mission. And it is precisely the sort of self-sacrificial love that we witness in the love between and husband, a wife and their child that we get a glimpse of what Balthasar has repeatedly referred to as the "Trinitarian law of self-surrender." In speaking of the creation of Eve out of the side of Adam, therefore, Balthasar can say,

> The removal of the rib was for Adam an infinitely ennobling grace: the grace of being allowed to participate in the mystery of the Father's self-giving to the Son, by which the Father empties himself of his own Godhead in order to bestow it on the Son who is eternally of the same nature as he is. It was a wound of love that God inflicted on Adam in order to initiate him into the mystery, the lavish self-prodigality, of divine love.[27]

Balthasar will go so far as to say that when Adam and Eve renounce their independence and come together, they follow "a deep-seated law of self-giving, which, through the loss of what seemed to be oneness, finds this oneness with and in the other."[28]

Several important points follow from these quotes that should not only help us to better understand Balthasar's Trinitarian thought, but also tie this in with what was said before in the context of mission and person. By bringing mission and person together, Christ shows us the true meaning of personhood: finding oneself only in making a gift of oneself to another. Elsewhere, for instance, Balthasar says that true love always takes the form of a vow, or, that it is always sacrificial. But what Christ reveals in his absolute obedience to the Father is not just something about what all human beings should offer to the Father; it is, at the same time, a revelation that love, even in God, has the nature of sacrifice. In Christ's self-offering to the Father—whether we are speaking of his mission in general which meant always having to be about his "Father's business," or the culmination of the mission in the self-offering on the cross—we even get a glimpse of the eternal self-sacrifice that the Father has made in giving his divinity to the Son, without holding anything back. In other words, the self-offering of the Son traces itself all the way back to the self-offering of the Father so that there is no use trying to locate the essence of God anywhere "behind" such self-offering.

Thought's incapacity to exhaust God is one with its incapacity to exhaust the mystery of the Father, who was never a self-enclosed, all-knowing, and all-powerful person, but one whose identity, from all eternity, was to dispossess himself in favor of the Son and, that not being enough, to give himself over yet again, this time with and through the Son, to the Spirit.[29]

These sorts of assertions about God "in himself" only make sense if kept together with the analysis of analogy offered above. Since Balthasar places the relationship between God and the world in an analogical relationship with the relations in God between Father, Son and Spirit, he need not fear the analogies from below that entail genuine otherness, dependence, temporality and even bodiliness. For instance, there is little doubt that one of the reasons—spoken or otherwise—for the sometime rejection of the Spousal analogies for the Trinity stemmed from a fear of the sexual/bodily duality of the male and female. In the context of the general Hellenistic contempt for the body, and perhaps especially for the female body, all such analogies could certainly seem to entail a compromise of the transcendence of God. But, Balthasar asks, what if the duality of the sexes and even the creation of matter and the body are goods? What if they are to be, as of course they are, included in God's pronouncement of the "very good" at the end of the creation narrative? And of course the Fathers and Scholastics knew this to be the case and even defended it against Gnostics and Manicheans of all stripes. The question is whether or not the full implications of the goodness of such things were always taken sufficiently in to account, especially in terms of the goodness of all things having its origins in God. While it is certainly the case that God is not embodied or sexual or temporal, it must still be maintained that the *origin* of all of these things must be in God. If there is some basis in God, for instance, for the duality of the sexes, then using such duality as an analogy cannot be all bad.[30]

If we now go back to Nick Healy's gentle criticism—in Chapter Three above—of Kenneth Schmitz's distinction between God in himself and God "as a lover," we can now see that the origins of that critique lie in Balthasar's unwillingness to allow God to be anything less than love all the way down. This is the very point of an important section in the second volume of *Theo-Logic* entitled,

"Love Cannot Be Anticipated by Thought." In his footnote to this section, translator Adrian Walker explains the meaning of this difficult-to-translate German phrase (*Die Unvordenklichkeit der Liebe*) accordingly:

> It suggests, first, that God the Father has, so to say, already loved the Son before there is any chance of reflective deliberation about whether he wants to or not. It also suggests that God's love is the context in which his intellect, and all other faculties and proper- ties, take shape. Finally, it suggests that no human thought can get behind God's love, which is thus the source of God mysterious- ness for us.[31]

It is important to note, however, that Balthasar's (and Walker's) point here is not that, therefore, God is somehow irrational or beyond or "without" Being; it is rather, that in God, who God is and the fact that he is love are inseparable, so that all of the attributes of his Being are going to be conditioned by love, again, all the way down.[32]

Now is the time to go back to the two extremes mentioned at the beginning of this section. For Hegel or even for Moltmann, in order to be able to account for the co-existence of God and that which is not God—and this would include the otherness of sin—God must become something he was not. For Hegel this means a blurring of the distinction between God and the world—as was said before, a blurring of the distinction between the begetting of the Son and the creating of the world—in order to end up with something like a worldly God or a divinized world. For Moltmann it means that in order to take sin seriously and seriously deal with its effects, God must allow himself to become affected by it, become something after it, so to speak, that he was not before it. It is not uninteresting to note that both of their systems are thoroughly Trinitarian. But it is also important to note that both approaches involve a rejection of God's immutability. Of course the problem here is that it is hard to see how a God who is also subject to the fate of the world and its sin should be expected to be its solution, its Savior. This goes back to the Patris- tic insistence that if Jesus is not divine then he cannot *save* us.

On the other hand lies the tendency to see God's immutable essence as lying behind the events of the cross. To go back to Palamas's distinction, in the cross we would get a glimpse of God's energies, but not his essence. Or to recall another classic (but not universally classic) move, in the cross it is the humanity of Christ that is touched by sin, not the divinity. But here we seem to have failed the other side of the Patristic insistence: what has not been assumed has not been saved. Here it is not Jesus' ability to save that is called into question, it is his ability to save *us*, insofar as only his humanity touches our sinfulness.

But what if, again, God is always and already self-giving and even self-sacrificing love in his very essence? It is in the light of this rhetorical question that Balthasar will make his famous reference— alluded to in Chapter Four above—to Bulgakov's notion of a *kenosis* within the life of the Trinity which makes possible the *kenosis* of the Son in his mission. He must be quoted here in full:

> For this reason, the immemorial priority of the self-surrender or self-expropriation thanks to which the Father *is* Father cannot be ascribed to knowledge but only to groundless love, which proves the identity of love as the "transcendental par excellence." We can understand this only if we dare to speak, with Bulgakov, of a first, intratrinitarian *kenosis*, which is none other than God's positive "self-expropriation" in the act of handing over the entire divine being in the processions, or, with Ferdinand Ulrich, of the unity of "poverty" and "wealth" in absolute being itself—which unity, once again, can be exhibited concretely in the child. Love can therefore thus be considered the supreme mode, and therein the "truth", of being, without for all of that, having to be transported beyond truth and being.[33]

A God, then, who has allowed himself to be wounded by the self-sacrificial nature of all love, from all eternity, is not a God who is either taken by surprise or changed when he has to make a sacrifice for the sins of the world, which he also, we should not forget, loves. This need not be in opposition to the immutability of God—an attribute which Balthasar defends—provided that our notion of immutability is neither simplistic nor absolved from the "ever greater dissimilarity" of all of the other attributes. In the fifth volume of *Theo-Drama*, Balthasar, in the context of quoting François Varillon, asks whether the immutability of God who is life and love can be a simple lack of motion. Is it not rather the case that in God "becoming is a perfection of being, motion a perfection of rest, and change a perfection of mutability"? "Can we consider life without move-ment to be life," Varillon asks.[34] Balthasar then makes a direct connection between this question and the question of whether only Christ's humanity is affected on the cross. We shall therefore follow Balthasar in giving the last word on this question to Heinz Schürmann:

> In Jesus' God-forsakeness it is not only that he drinks the 'loss of God', the 'failure of God' to the last drop. The 'death of God' actually takes place in him in the *kenosis* and *tapeinosis* of the love of God . . . Jesus' death does not leave God unscathed, for when we say 'love', we must remember that, out of love for the world, God did not spare his own Son . . . The ontic possibility for God's self-emptying in the Incarnation and death of Jesus lies in God's eternal self-emptying in the mutual self-surrender of the Persons of the Trinity. Ultimately, the death of Jesus can be understood as a saving event only in the contexts of events within the Trinity.[35]

CONCLUSION

In Chapter Two, I mentioned the fact that, when Balthasar attempted to situation himself in a "school of thought," he did not simply place himself with the *ressourcement* school. On the one hand, I do not want to invest this single quote with so much weight that it undermines the enormous indebtedness to and collaboration with the various figures of this school. On the other hand, by placing himself in the company of Heinz Schürmann, Louis Bouyer and Heinrich Schleier, I would like to suggest that Balthasar was trying to say something. This something also helps to explain why Balthasar refused to allow his own thought to be separated from that of Adrienne von Speyr. All of the Protestant outcries against Catholic theology that are worthy of attention begin with a vivid sense of the centrality of the cross. Luther's earliest disputations (against the various forms of late medieval scholastic theology) contain the seeds of his famous *theologia crucis*. And, more recently, it is Karl Barth who has raised his outcry against any version of the analogy of Being which would gainsay what we know to be the case in the light of the cross. And, of course, in both cases it should be pointed out that Balthasar saw a legitimate insight that was sometimes taken to such an extreme that an important aspect of the Church's teaching was either jettisoned or ignored. Still, I would like to suggest that no Catholic theologian of the twentieth century took these criticisms more to heart than has Hans Urs von Balthasar. And in doing so, he has bequeathed to the Church a fully robust and at the same time a fully Catholic theology of the cross that has within it all that Luther and Barth attempted to offer, without for all of that falling into their occasional—or, perhaps in the case of Luther, not so occasional—one-sidedness.

It is precisely this attempt—at a fully Catholic and yet fully robust theology of the cross—that has made Balthasar the sometime *theologian non grata* of both the so-called "conservative" and "liberal" wings within the Catholic Church. For the former he has shown too much sympathy for the concerns of Luther and Barth and has sometimes even opted for them against the likes of Thomas Aquinas. For the latter, who have long since relegated any sort of Anselmian reading of the cross to the mythological at best and the sadistic at worst, it is precisely Balthasar's (heavily qualified) revival of Anselm's view that verifies his place in the dustbin of dead, European males, oblivious of the real issues of social, gender and racial injustice. For these the cross is merely evidence that Jesus was indeed on the side of radical, political reform and that it is this that got him in trouble with the Romans (and *only* the Romans), or else it is a sign that God stands in solidarity with all outcasts, downcasts, criminals and sinners. Making the cross central, then, is certainly one of the things that makes Balthasar's theology "perplexing" to readers of various theological stripes. It is for this reason that I made it the subject of the end of this last, substantive chapter. In the chapter which follows, therefore, I will offer a summary and suggestions concerning the future of Balthasar's role in the theology of the twenty-first century. This will entail also offering some suggestions for further reading.

CHAPTER SEVEN

BALTHASAR'S ONGOING ROLE IN THEOLOGY

Unless we are much mistaken the standpoint which we have chosen should be more classical than the classicism which has grown sterile but also more modern than many superficial modernisms in Church and theology and more ecumenical than many hastily conceived attempts to bridge the gap between confessions which claim that title.[1]

SUMMARY AND CONCLUSION

In the foregoing I have made no effort to provide a topical overview of Balthasar's theology. Instead, in keeping with the title of this series, "Guides for the Perplexed," I have tried to get to the heart of Balthasar's project. At the heart of this project lies the person of Jesus Christ, but the *telos* is always the Trinity. If there is anything that Balthasar does not do, it is to set up a purely philosophical or scientific method to which he could then append a Christology or a theology of the Trinity. Instead, since all things are created by the Father, in Christ, through the Holy Spirit, all natural endeavors of thought are always and already undertaken within the one creative and redemptive order. This is not to deny philosophy or natural reason its proper place and role, but it is to deny a purely natural or neutral reason which could work out the rules of the game before playing it. Think here of Hegel's quip that Kant is the kind of philosopher who feels that he has to learn how to swim before ever getting into the water.

This approach has definitely made Balthasar's theology perplexing to many insofar as it does not fit well into either the typically modern approach to theology predominate in American and European universities, or the typically traditionalist approach which still too often subscribes to neo-scholastic habits of thought. As was shown in the early chapters with reference to de Lubac and Gadamer, the modern, purely academic approach would fail at two levels in Balthasar's view. First, it would reproduce the old neo-scholastic dualism, but this time by trying to bracket the influence of grace or the supernatural until it has found out the facts of the matter. Second, and in keeping with the first move, it would pattern its approach to its object on the model of the hard sciences. It makes very little sense, furthermore, to refer to Balthasar's rejection of this approach as being "conservative," especially since its origins go all the way back to Goethe, Herder and Hamann, continue at the turn of the century in thinkers like Kierkegaard, Nietzsche and Soloviev, and is maintained, more recently, by the likes of Polanyi, Gadamer, MacIntyre and others.

On the other hand, traditionalists find Balthasar no less perplexing, or perhaps frustrating, than their academic foes. Here, too, Balthasar's apparent blurring of the lines between nature and grace, faith and reason seems a betrayal of neat, Thomistic divisions. From this side, Balthasar appears to have given too much to the modernists and to Blondel's "method of immanence." Indeed, his account of truth in the first volume of *Theo-Logic* seems, from a certain perspective, to be overly relativistic and historicist. Furthermore, Balthasar grants things to philosophy—say, the nuptial nature of reason or the self-sacrificial (kenotic) nature of Being—that belong more properly to theology; or, to put it differently, his theology extends its influence too far back into his philosophy. On the other hand, his philosophy does not seem to do enough: e.g. prove the existence of God on the basis of purely rational arguments or establish a purely natural law ethic, agreeable to all people of good will regardless of their theological or metaphysical presuppositions. Here, the charge of "progressive" would make as little sense to Balthasar as the charge of conservative, insofar as he would point out that his more integrated approach is actually the more traditional one. He would here point out a whole list of people to defend his cause: Irenaeus, Augustine, Dionysius the Aereopagite, Maximus the Confessor, Aquinas, Bonaventure, Nicholas of Cusa, Pascal, and so on.

After presenting a brief biographical sketch in Chapter One, I offered an overview of Balthasar's theological method, both in terms of its relationship to the history of Western thought and in terms of the method itself in Chapters Two and Three. These chapters are important because they show that superficial attempts to define his theology as either liberal or conservative, progressive or traditional are bound to fail, just as they do for all great thinkers. The very fact that Balthasar centers his theological masterpiece around the transcendental properties of Being should be evidence enough that he is anything but a theological modern, just as his treatment of the Trinity, the cross and the possibility of an empty hell should allay any charge that he is a reactionary or obscurantist. The purpose of these two chapters, then, was to show how Balthasar's theology involves a robust retrieval of the fullness of the Catholic tradition without in any way subscribing to an obscurantist version of traditionalism. I will now need to make this a little more specific.

In his programmatic little book, *Love Alone is Credible,* Balthasar presents the "cosmological" approach of the Fathers and Scholastics and the "anthropological" turn of the moderns, only then to offer his own "third way" of "love alone." It is not hard to imagine that Balthasar would have had Martin Luther's various "alones" (*solas*) in mind when he wrote this. But in any case, already in this book we get a glimpse of Balthasar's hermeneutical principal in retrieving the thought of the past. It is an abiding theme of his thought that one must always break through to the "distinctively Christian;" and what did Christianity offer to the world if not the notion that God not only loves, but that God *is* love? In his reading of the great tradition, then, Balthasar's method of retrieval is to allow the center of Christian thought—that God is a Trinity of loving persons—to serve as a corrective to any aspects of the periphery that are not sufficiently reflective of this. The basis of his critique of the Platonist tendencies in the cosmological approach is not some anti-philosophical bias; nor is it a crypto-Protestant attempt to get to the "pure Gospel" or, in the case of liberal Protestantism, the "pure humanitarianism," beneath just so much Hellenistic overlay. It is, rather, the attempt to make sure that the philosophy that is used—and Balthasar is insistent that some philosophy will be used—has allowed itself to be sufficiently taken into the service of a God who *is* love. As Balthasar demonstrates in the *Theo-Logic,* all of the attributes of God, including the fact that he is truth, are conditioned from the ground up by the fact that he is love.

Balthasar's slight modification of Aquinas's real distinction between God and the world, then, to which he is favorably disposed in general, consists of its placement in a relational context. This is where the central role of meta-anthropology comes into play. It is not that Balthasar now wishes to replace metaphysics with anthropology; it is rather that Balthasar offers metaphysical analysis at that point where Being has reached its inner-worldly highpoint: in the encounter between free persons. To recall just one implication of this: notice what happens to the act of knowing when it is investigated in terms of two persons coming to know each other. Notice, that is, how this helps to get past the false opposition of subjectivism and objectivism. Another person is never merely the "object" of my knowledge, as if I stand over and against some neutral thing which is naturally unrelated to me but which must now become the object of my knowledge. This false objectivism is just the other side of a false subjectivism which understands all knowledge as an act of the subject upon a purely passive object. The model of knowledge for so much modern philosophy is the encounter between a knower and a machine, or at least a machine-like thing.

But there are two other aspects of Balthasar's turn to meta-anthropology which were highlighted in these early chapters. First, because Balthasar follows de Lubac's reading of the relationship between nature and grace, he has no need to defend a notion of pure reason. Although Balthasar defends the proper autonomy of reason and its genuine independence vis-à-vis theology and revelation, he insists that reason is never the truncated sort of thing that modern philosophy insists that it is. Reason in Balthasar, as it is in Plato for that matter, is dynamic, erotic, tending of itself towards that which transcends reason. It is open, in theory and in practice, to a word from the other side, so to speak. There is no reason simply to dismiss Plato's references to oracles, Diotima's and the like. In the case of Balthasar, because reason is not closed in on itself but is open to that which transcends the finite world, there is no reason that it should go on unaffected if the Infinite should choose to appear. In other words, Balthasar, following Guardini, is willing to allow the light of revelation to fall back on those things which are the proper concern naturally speaking of philosophy. It is just that once these questions are pursued, now in the light of revelation, they take on a new light. It is important to note, however, that they do not now simply become theology; they are *philosophical* concerns which are now being undertaken in the light of revelation.

We see the greatest implications of this approach in Balthasar's treatment of the relationship between God, *esse* and *essentia* in the dim light cast backwards by the doctrine of the Trinity. What strikes Balthasar in his metaphysical wanderings is the fact that relationships of mutual dependence seem to extend all the way down to the lowest levels of Being. Of course he begins with the experience of the child and its absolute relationship of dependence upon its parents. But eventually the child will come to realize that its parents are in just such a state of dependence upon their parents, and so on. If this is pursued we come to realize that all beings are dependent on or come to find their place only in Being in general (*esse*). But then we get to the really interesting point. Being itself does not subsist apart from the things which actually exist. It is at once the fullness of wealth and is yet dependent upon actually existing things for its subsistence. Eventually, as we came to see in the later chapters, Balthasar will trace this simultaneity of wealth and poverty back to its source in the Triune God.

Alongside of Balthasar's unique treatment of the real distinction lies his approach to the analogy of Being. Building once more on the philosophy of Thomas Aquinas, Balthasar reiterates the principle that no excellence can be found at the level of creation that does not have its preeminent source in God. Of course neither Thomas nor Balthasar allow this principle to override the fact of the always greater dissimilarity between God—in whom to be and to be God are simply one; or in whom Being and existence are one—and the creature—who exists only ever as this or that thing. As Thomas puts it,

> Everything which comes after the first being, since it is not its own *esse*, has an *esse* which is received in something by which the *esse* is limited; and thus in every creature the nature of the thing which participates in *esse* is one thing, and the participated *esse* is something else.[2]

Far from putting God and his creation on the same level or under the same umbrella—the fear of Barth—analogy properly understood emphasizes the absolute otherness of God even as it establishes that in another sense he is precisely not-other. Perhaps we can say that God is non-other precisely because he is wholly other. But here too we caught a glimpse of the distinctiveness of Balthasar's approach. With the help of certain Thomists who have noted that receptivity seems to be one of the perfections of love, and combining this with the notion that no excellence can be found in the created order that does not have its pre-eminent source in God, Balthasar is able to insist that even receptivity must have its source in God. In order to do this, of course, we had to remove any notion of potentiality from the notion of receptivity. This is yet another area of Balthasar's metaphysics which does not become fully clear until he unveils his doctrine of the Trinity.

In Chapters Three through Six, then, I turned to Balthasar's theology proper, first, by looking at his approach to Scripture, with a view towards his theological aesthetics; then, by offering an overview of the relationship between finite and infinite freedom, especially in the light of *Theo-Drama*; and, finally, by examining Balthasar's theology of the Trinity in the light of the cross. In each case we saw that Balthasar approaches these issues through the person and mission of Jesus Christ. With regard to Balthasar's approach to biblical exegesis, for instance, while he is open to the use of the modern, historical method, he is deeply suspicious of any attempt to bracket faith in order to get to the simple facts. Retrieving the past is never merely a matter of getting to the facts. What is lost in so much modern biblical scholarship, in Balthasar's view, is a vision for wholeness. A mere video recording of everything that Jesus said and did would not amount to a gospel for the simple reason that it would provide no framework for understanding either Jesus' identity—"Who do you say that I am?"—or significance. For Balthasar, even the person who has allegedly put aside all faith in order to get to who Jesus was, must approach the subject matter from some vantage point. For instance, why should we even care in the first place? Or, why these particular texts? The point is simply this: some vision of the whole will necessarily be in place when one treats the parts, and this will become evident by the way one treats the parts.

With regard to the question of finite and infinite freedom, I noted the interesting fact that Balthasar begins his *Theo-Drama* with a study of finite freedom (anthropology) before proceeding, in the third volume, to Christology. This alone should help to correct a sometime stereotype of Balthasar's approach that it is "from above" *rather than* "from below." It is actually the case that Balthasar refuses to see these two things in opposition to each other. The "from below" is always and already situated within God's movement "from above" to create all things in Christ. But this does not mean that there is not a genuine from below. When God gives the gift of freedom to his creatures, he really gives it. And this freedom helps to explain the natural religiosity of human beings. But two things in particular have to be pointed out in this context. First, the movement of human beings towards the infinite is never a neutral one which, then, may or may not end up in a relationship with the God of Jesus Christ. In such an approach, the various religions would be the product of humanity's search for God, and God would somehow reside above and beyond the various leaders of each of these religious quests: e.g. Mohammed, the Buddha, Moses, Jesus Christ, etc. Each of these leaders would then be a way to God. For Balthasar, on the other hand, there is no God besides the God of Jesus Christ and there are no human beings who are not created precisely in Christ. In short, the movement of human beings towards God is always undertaken within God's movement towards human beings in Jesus Christ. But, second, finite freedom is by definition of the determinate kind. There is no absolutely unconditioned freedom at the level of the finite, by definition. Human beings cannot help but seek the good. Of course they may mistake some lesser good for *the* good, but this would certainly not grant them greater freedom. It is this that helps to explain the paradoxical nature of Christian freedom, seen fully in Jesus Christ, which insists that finite freedom is only free when it finds its place within infinite freedom. Lurking in the background here is the notion that one will end up being obedient to someone or something and that that might as well be the God who gave freedom in the first place.

This discussion led, of its own steam, to more properly Christological discussions, which lead, in Balthasar's theology, to the doctrine of the Trinity. It is axiomatic for Balthasar that there is no way to the Immanent Trinity apart from the Economic Trinity, but this has become somewhat commonplace. What makes Balthasar's approach distinct is his refusal on the one hand simply to identify the Economic with the Immanent Trinity, but then his insistence on the other hand that we really do come to know something about the latter on the basis of the former. The key here is, once more, the doctrine of analogy. There are two aspects of the final two chapters, then, that we would do well to reiterate, for they are of central importance to Balthasar's theological endeavors.

First, there is the notion that Jesus Christ is the concrete analogy of Being. There is much that can be said about this, but I will limit myself to a few points. While Balthasar does in no way deny the importance of philosophical theology, nor its endeavor to ascend to God from below through the way of negation, he does want to qualify this approach in important ways. To go back to what was just said, it must first be understood that this movement towards God is always undertaken on the basis of God's movement towards us. But, next, it is also important not to get so caught up in negative theology that we forget that the God of Christianity, at any rate, created the world on purpose and declared it "very good." In other words, for the God of Christianity at least, there is something positive to be said about the world in all of difference from God and this positive difference cannot simply be seen in opposition to God.

Now, all of this gets clarified in a singular way when God becomes a man in Jesus Christ. The important point that Balthasar makes in this regard is that the union of the human and divine natures in the person of Jesus Christ does in no way undermine the absolute distinction between what is God and what is not. In other words, the Incarnation does not amount to an identity between the divine and human natures. Still, on account of the principle that any goodness that is found at the level of created Being must have its source in God, God can make use of the human nature of Jesus in order to reveal himself to the world. And this is because there is a genuine analogy between the procession of the Son from the Father and the creation of human beings in God's image. This enables Jesus Christ to do two things at once: first, he is able to reveal the nature of God in and through his human nature—for instance, his human obedience can become a picture of the obedience of the eternal Son to the Father; second, he is able to reveal the genuine meaning of the human person as a "capacity for God." In other words, human beings were created from the outset in order to be taken into a loving relationship with the Father, through the Son. Jesus, therefore, can represent both sides of the covenant: the gracious initiative of the Father towards the world, and the Spirit-filled response of the creature to this initiative.

The second major point in the final two chapters concerns the Trinity and the cross. As we just saw in the last chapter, there have been two tendencies: either to relegate the suffering of Jesus on the cross to Jesus' humanity, so as to keep the divinity safely above the effects of sin; or, to come right out and say that God in his essence is affected by sin, as in, becomes something after the Incarnation that he was not prior to it. For Balthasar, these two extremes represent a failure properly to integrate the notion of God's immutability with the notion that God is a Trinity of persons in an irreducible relationship of love. Love, for Balthasar, is always seen at its highpoint in the sacrifice of the self for the sake of the other. Obviously, on the cross Jesus sacrifices his own life for the sake of sinful humanity. But Balthasar follows John in his insistence that this event, which on the face of it seems to reveal only defeat and failure, is actually a revelation of God's glory. If this is the case, then there must be something in God's nature that provides the basis for the revelatory nature of this event: that something, Balthasar insists, is the sacrificial nature of the love of the Trinitarian persons. In the kenosis of Jesus, in his willingness to enter into the human condition in order to win it back for the Father, we see a picture of the *ur*-kenosis in the Trinity, by which the Father from all eternity has made a gift of himself to the Son, so that the two of them could make a further gift to the Spirit, who is that gift of love in person.

In short, in the foregoing I have tried to trace Balthasar's theology from its foundations to its culmination in a God who loved the world so much that he was willing to die for it on a cross. The only question which remains, a question to which we can only offer a few brief suggestions, is the place of Balthasar in the current theological setting.

BALTHASAR'S PLACE IN THEOLOGY TODAY

When I was a graduate student in the 1990s, Balthasar's theology was still fairly unchartered territory. And when I wrote my dissertation, the most pressing concern was to try to get Balthasar a hearing in Catholic circles where the methodologies of Rahner, Lonergan and the various Liberation Theologies were still very much dominant. After the rise in popularity, however, of the post-modern and post-liberal critiques of Enlightenment reason, this is no longer the case. If in the 1980s and even 1990s Balthasar was still being dismissed as a conservative or even a fideist, since the rise in influence of the so-called Yale School and Radical Orthodoxy, Balthasar is increasingly being seen as having been ahead of his time. But the rise of this new turn in theological thinking has brought in its wake several other interesting turns. If the progressivist reading of the Second Vatican Council showed promise up through the decade of the 1980s, the younger generation of theologians now seem to be marked by a yearning for much that was tossed out. Indeed, we are beginning to see a resurgence of interest, for instance, not only in the thought of Thomas Aquinas, especially his theology, but even in the (at least partial) rehabilitation of neo-scholasticism.[3] In what follows I would like to look at three movements in particular that might help us better to understand Balthasar's place in the theology of our day.

Balthasar and Post-liberalism

In his helpful essay on post-liberal theology,[4] George Hunsinger has warned against an over-hasty use of the title, "Yale School." While he admits that George Lindbeck and Hans Frei (and even Brevard Childs) turned out a fair number of students (Stanley Hauerwas, William Placher, Ronald Thiemann, etc.) who share certain, common theological themes, the differences, first between the teachers (Lindbeck and Frei), but then even more so between their students, turn out to be too significant to form a single school of thought. Still, he does acknowledge some common themes under the broader category, "post-liberal." Two common influences stand out which are of particular interest for our current concerns: Karl Barth and Ludwig Wittgenstein. First, with regard to Barth, there is a thoroughgoing critique of "foundationalism," the view that before we can proceed to any theology based on faith and revelation, we must first lay a philosophical or scientific foundation upon which to build. Post-liberalism is, in other words, opposed to trying to find some sort of pre-theological method which would be suitable to people of various confessional stripes and which would facilitate the later-to-come theological work. In response to this, post-liberals respond that there is no purely pre-theological, pre-confessional set of rules that everyone can agree to because the very rules of the game will always, already betray certain at least quasi-theological presuppositions.

Here we can also see the influence of Wittgenstein and his theory of language games. For Wittgenstein there is no pre-linguistic, pre-cultural rationality that one could use to get underneath or behind the various cultural and linguistic interpretations of reality. Reason is itself, in this view, linguistic all the way down. But this is precisely where the differences between the various adherents to post-liberalism begin. George Lindbeck's favored way of speaking of God's self-revelation is precisely in these cultural-linguistic terms, and this gives his theology a pragmatic coloring that prefers practices to abstract doctrines and propositions. Jesus, in such a view, does not come primarily with a set of abstract teachings, but begins a concrete community whom he expects to engage in a set of concrete practices. The truth of what Jesus is saying can only be discovered in the practices in which he is engaged. Foundationalism, then, would be the attempt to try to get at the truth about Jesus prior to following him, and this, Lindbeck would suggest, is precisely impossible. If we couple this with the fact that one is always, already, in a cultural-linguistic framework, the problem becomes even more pronounced, for then one would be trying to ascertain the truth about Jesus not only from some imaginary, neutral perspective, but even from within a possibly foreign one.

So far, perhaps, so good, but there is a tendency in Lindbeck to pit this cultural-linguistic approach against a propositional approach, as if it were merely a matter of practice and not also of truth, or, sometimes, as if people are so locked into their respective cultural-linguistic communities that they are incapable of communicating with those on the outside. As such, we can end up with the same sort of relativization of doctrinal truth that is the trademark of the very liberal Protestantism that Lindbeck is supposed to be "post." As George Hunsinger puts it,

> For Lindbeck as for modern liberal theology, both "doctrine" and "truth" are so defined as to make them significantly non-cognitive. Any conceivable propositional content in theological language is relativized. Although the strategies of relativization are different, the modern liberal aversion to propositional content is much the same.[5]

This has led some in the post-liberal camp, such as Hunsinger, to commend the more analogical understanding of truth that we have seen in Balthasar. Again, here is Hunsinger:

> With respect to language about God, by opting for analogical modes of reference, post-liberalism merely retrieves patristic and medieval insights that were often eclipsed during modernity by the polarized clash between liberalism and fundamentalism . . . Whether post-liberalism thinks this matter through with someone like Barth in terms of the actualism of grace, or with someone like von Balthasar in terms of the Roman Catholic understanding of the *sacramentum mundi*, the false polarizations of modernity are overcome. Instead of divine availability at the expense of irreducible transcendence (literalism), or divine transcendence at the expense of real availability (expressivism), post-liberal critical

realism recovers the historic ecumenical conviction of divine availability to true predication in the midst of transcendent ineffability.[6]

In short, Balthasar can be an ally in the attempt to keep post-liberalism from simply subscribing to a new form of doctrinal indifference. Analogy preserves at once the ability of our language to say true things about God, while at the same time emphasizing the fact that God is always and ever greater than that which we can say about him. This is why Balthasar is so fond of quoting Augustine when the latter says, "If you have understood it, it is not God."

But I would like to recommend one other area in which Balthasar might have something to offer the post-liberal school, and that is his retrieval of the ancient metaphysical tradition. There is a danger in the post-liberal school and its strong critique of foundationalism that it underestimates the so-called natural religiosity of human beings and the erotic nature of the human intellect. To go back to the differences between Balthasar and Barth alluded to above, if God's descending revelation is simply the opposite of all human religious longing, then it is hard to explain how Jesus could find language ready at hand when he came to reveal the Father. It seems, rather, that Jesus presupposes the natural religiosity of his listeners, even if he challenged that religiosity in significant ways. We are back to the themes of continuity and newness, but a potential danger of the post-liberal approach is that it denies all continuity. This has two practical side effects which Balthasar's understanding of the Christological analogy of Being might help to fix. First, Balthasar's approach allows for a renewed interest in philosophy and natural reason without in any way wanting to establish the proper relationship between God and the world outside of God's self-revelation in Christ. This is because, for Balthasar, reason finds its proper autonomy precisely *in* Christ.

I shall only allude to the second implication. There is a danger in a hyper-Wittgenstinian approach that nature is totally swallowed up into culture. This would mean that there is literally no remainder, so to speak, once one has stripped away cultural-linguistic factors, such as, for instance, human nature created in God's image. If this is taken too far, it would be difficult to account for the classical Christian notion that when God became man he transformed universal human nature on an ontological level. We can see this in the sometime post-liberal treatment of inter-religious dialogue. Here, the various religions are so thoroughly different that the only purpose of inter-religious dialogue is to listen to the other and come to respect the other in all of his/her otherness. But as then Joseph Ratzinger has shown in *Truth and Tolerance*, this is not, in fact, the way religions have interacted in history. The mythological religions, say, of the ancient Near East, did not do well in their confrontation with what Ratzinger calls the philosophical enlightenment. They either developed in the light of reason or they died.[7] It is not uninteresting to note that the early Christians sided with the Greek philosophers in their critique of pagan mythology. In a passage somewhere, Balthasar refers to the tradition of Asian interpreters of Mozart's music. He sees this as evidence of the fact that the human runs deeper than the cultural or ethnic, without in any way suggesting that these latter things are simply trivial. The point to be made with regard to religious diversity is this: the relationship between the various religions and Christianity as sketched in *Nostra Aetate* needs precisely some sort of Balthasarian defense of nature in order to work. This would be an interesting area for further dialogue between Balthasar and at least some strains within post-liberalism. One could begin by comparing the more Balthasarian approach of Joseph Ratzinger noted above with that of George Lindbeck in, *The Nature of Doctrine: Religion and Theology in a Post-liberal Age*.

Balthasar and Radical Orthodoxy

Everything that was said above about the "Yale School" would have to be reiterated about the school of Radical Orthodoxy. A friend of mine who contributed to the original volume entitled *Radical Orthodoxy: A New Theology*, informed me that he did not know even know that there was a "radical orthodoxy" before he was asked to contribute, and that he is still not sure what it entails. At any rate, there do seem to be some common themes. First, there is a critique of secular reason[8] in particular and of the secular in general. The opening line of the first chapter of John Milbank's first major work reads, "Once there was no secular."[9] The point here is that secular reason is in no way "pure reason," but is itself a particular form of belief, derived in part from Christian thought but also in part from the faulty notions of reason, the person, freedom, science, etc. that came with modernity. The notion, for instance, that there is a purely secular form of politics within which people of different faiths can live side by side in neutral sublimity is a laughable one in Milbank's view. It would not be enough, therefore, simply to choose a more conservative form of liberal politics, one which, for instance, made more room for traditional Christian values (such as not killing our children); rather, the entire project of liberal politics of either the conservative or liberal variety needs to be called into question in the light of perennial Christian beliefs. Liberalism, and the secular realm which it allegedly creates, is understood here as a parody of Christian ecclesiology.

A second common theme, connected to the first, is the radicalization of de Lubac's nature-grace thesis, discussed in the pages above.[10] I say it is connected to the first for the simple reason that, if nature is radically oriented to grace, then there can obviously be no neutral reason or politics either to which one would add subsequent Christian content or within which Christians could live as good citizens provided they make public arguments on a *purely natural* law basis. This leads, once more, to the notion that there is no purely secular politics, or, put positively, to the notion that politics will always entail an underlying theological view of the whole. Milbank, therefore, seems to suggest that the only politics to which a Christian could give support would be explicitly Christian in nature, such as, say, Christian Socialism. *Theology and Social Theory* is dedicated to "Alison and the Remnant of 'Christendom'."

A final theme follows from the first two: namely the tendency to absorb metaphysics into theology. Here, in the interest of space, I will simply refer the reader to John Milbank's essay, "Only Theology Overcomes Metaphysics," in *The Word Made Strange: Theology, Language, Culture.*

There is no way that I can do justice in a work of this nature either to this movement or to its relationship with Balthasar. This is even more the case given the complexity, nuance and range of thought even in the thought of John Milbank. Any suggestions I make, then, ought to be taken merely as provocations to further reflection and discussion. With regard to all three of the above themes, I would like to suggest that in each case Balthasar's position is more cautious, although I realize that Milbank would simply say that Balthasar has not taken the de Lubacian revolution to its logical conclusion. While Balthasar would agree, for instance, that there is no purely secular reason—in the sense of a reason totally autonomous from the influence of God or even grace—he would argue that the God of Christianity respects the proper autonomy of the created order *within* the supernatural order, or, what Balthasar sometimes calls God's single order of creation and redemption. In other words, to radicalize de Lubac's thesis on nature and grace so that nature is supernaturalized, the secular is sacralized, or philosophy is theologized, would be precisely to jeopardize the knife-edge that must be walked in the light of the Christological analogy of Being.

The notion that is sometimes implied in Milbank's writings, that if some de Lubac is good, more must be better, fails to recognize that de Lubac's position is precisely intent upon holding two ends of a paradox together. And part of the paradox of the analogy of Being when examined in the light of Christology is that the human—and therefore reason and therefore nature—becomes more authentically itself the more it is given over to the divine. To point out just one implication of this: a philosophy which allows itself to be influenced by the light of grace does not now becomes less philosophical and more theological; instead, in a paradoxical way, it becomes more genuinely philosophical. Thomas Aquinas's interest in Aristotle's philosophy, then, would not merely be a matter of trying to turn it into theology, even if after its brush with Thomas, Aristotle's philosophy does, in fact, look quite different. But I think Balthasar would say that Aristotle's philosophy becomes better philosophy as a result of the encounter. In this latter regard, I suspect that Balthasar would suspect Milbank of granting too much to Heidegger's critique of onto-theology. In order to sort all of this out, however, the reader would have to look, in general, into the relationship in Balthasar between reason and love,[11] and, more specifically at Balthasar's treatment of Heidegger in the fifth volume of *The Glory of the Lord.*[12]

Balthasar and the Resurgence of Traditional Catholicism

Once more, I intend in this short space only to raise questions for further discussion; I make no pretence at settling them. I stated earlier that when I began work on my dissertation in the mid-1990s, the main issue in Balthasar studies was to get Balthasar a hearing in a context still dominated by Rahner, Lonergan and Liberation Theology. Of course things were already changing. Milbank's *Theology and Social Theory* had already come out in 1990 and Fergus Kerr's *Theology after Wittgenstein* had come out even before that. I mention these as just two examples of the growing dissatisfaction over an academic approach to theology that was still under the sway of Enlightenment patterns of thought. But once the modern has been put in its place, room is made not only for the post-modern (post-liberal, radically orthodox, etc.), but also, in the case of some, for the pre-modern. In our own day, for instance, we are beginning to witness a new interest in the thought of Thomas Aquinas, not simply as a philosopher, and not simply out of historical curiosity, but as a theologian to be reckoned with.

Indeed, some of the more interesting criticism of Balthasar is no longer coming out of the *Concilium* wing of American Catholicism, but from the Thomistic or traditionalist wing. Thomas Weinandy, for instance, in numerous articles and books has mounted a sustained and intelligent defense of the classical understanding of divine immutability, and with it, a defense of the notion that on the cross it is only the humanity of Christ that suffers.[13] A yet more traditionalist, Thomistic approach can be found in Guy Mansini and Matthew Levering,[14] who focus on the same questions of divine immutability and the Trinity. And finally, a more radical, less nuanced denouncement of Balthasar's approach to these questions, which centers, finally, on the question of the descent into hell, can be found in a recent book by Alyssa Pitstick, *Light in Darkness: Hans Urs von Balthasar and the Catholic Doctrine of Christ's Descent into Hell.*[15] I do not intend to situate all of these critiques into a single "camp": Weinandy's defense of immutability is not as strictly wedded to Thomas as, say, that of Levering or Mansini; and none of these former have the "edge" that Pitstick's book has, which basically considers Balthasar's theology to be heretical. Still, there is a common concern that Balthasar has abandoned the traditional doctrine of the Trinity, the traditional notion of the non-confusion of the two natures in Christ, and the classic understanding of God's immutability. I should say at least something about this critique.

First, one of the reasons that I began this study the way I did was to show just how wedded in many ways Balthasar's thought is to that of Thomas Aquinas. I repeat, for instance, that the entire first volume of *Theo-Logic* reads like an extended commentary on Aquinas's *On Truth.* Furthermore, in spite of the fact that Thomas does not make Balthasar's famous list of clerical styles that makes up the second volume of *The Glory of the Lord*, he is more than compensated by playing the pivotal role in the two volumes on metaphysics which come later. As I stated in Chapter Two, Aquinas marks a *kairos* for Balthasar between the Fathers' tendency to swallow philosophy into theology and the moderns' tendency either to separate the two entirely, or to absorb theology into philosophy. Balthasar, therefore, commends in large part Aquinas's understanding of the relationship between philosophy and theology. This leads to a further point: it is not so much a question of whether Balthasar is faithful to Thomas as it is a question of which Thomas we are talking about. For Balthasar, Thomas is decidedly *not* the Thomas of the neo-scholastics. Balthasar's reading of Thomas is much closer to that of Etienne Gilson, Henri de Lubac, Gustav Siewerth, Erich Przywara, and Ferdinand Ulrich, to name just a few. Indeed, even today Balthasar has his Thomistic defenders such as Norris Clarke and Kenneth Schmitz. Clarke even suggests that Thomists need to do a better job of explaining how God's immutability should be understood both in the light of Scriptures and the fact that Thomas defines God as "pure act."[16]

But the larger question in the background here concerns Balthasar's fidelity to the tradition. To refer once more to Chapter Two, I tried to offer a series of rules which Balthasar applies for retrieving past thought. Obviously fidelity to the past cannot mean slavish repetition, if for no other reason than that there are tensions in the tradition. It is interesting to note, for instance, that Alyssa Pitstick's book makes almost no reference to models of the Trinity except the psychological one preferred by Thomas and Augustine. Bonaventure is mentioned once in her book, and here she is quoting Balthasar. Neither Richard of St. Victor nor Matthias Scheeben are even mentioned. Any time Balthasar is trying to work through a difficult issue, for instance, which analogies from below work best for the Trinity, he examines an amazing array of authors from all sorts of time periods, from the East and the West, major thinkers and minor ones. This is part of his act of discernment. No single author in the Church's past is right all of the time. Thomas was wrong, for instance, about the immaculate conception and about the torture of heretics. Augustine was at least partially wrong about predestination and, we can hope, the *massa damnata*. It could be argued that in examining such a wide variety of thinkers and teasing out the position which is most faithful to God's self-revelation in Jesus Christ, Balthasar is actually more traditional, in some ways, than some of his traditionalist critics. This is an issue that deserves more attention in the coming years.

Still, the criticism of Balthasar from this more Thomistic side could be seen as prompting what I think is the next, promising phase in Balthasar scholarship. In the early years, since the major foil for Balthasar was likely Karl Rahner and the so-called "mediating" school of theology, the emphasis was placed on Balthasar the non-rationalist. In the discussions that swirled around the Yale *versus* Chicago schools, Balthasar was almost always placed in the Yale camp. It was all but admitted that Rahner and Lonergan were the philosophers and fundamental theologians while Balthasar was the better intra-Catholic, doctrinal theologian. It was sometimes suggested that while Rahner and Lonergan followed Thomas and were therefore more philosophical, Balthasar followed Bonaventure and was more fideistic. But recently, partly on account of increasing interest in the thought of Gustav Siewerth and Ferdinand Ulrich and partly on account of the Thomistic critique mentioned above, more attention is being paid to Balthasar's philosophy and his defense of reason and metaphysics.

In closing this final chapter, then, I would like to mention three young thinkers, all associated with the American edition of *Communio*, who are doing groundbreaking work in the area of Balthasar's philosophy: Adrian Walker, Nicholas J. Healy, and David C. Schindler. The latter two have written important books on Balthasar's philosophy which will appear in the "suggested readings" below; the former has written numerous articles in the American edition of *Communio* on Balthasar's philosophy, especially on the relationship between Being, truth and love. It is my conviction that these three names will figure heavily in the future of Balthasar studies.

NOTES

1. BALTHASAR: THE MAN AND HIS PLACE IN TWENTIETH-CENTURY THOUGHT

1 Cornelia Capol, quoted in Maximilian Greiner, "The Community of St. John: A Conversation with Cornelia Capol and Martha Gisi," *Hans Urs von Balthasar: His Life and Work*, ed. David L. Schindler (San Francisco: Ignatius Press, 1991).

2 The following biographical sketch is taken primarily from Peter Henrici's fuller sketch, "A Sketch of von Balthasar's Life," in Schindler (1991) (subsequently, Henrici), and Hans Urs von Balthasar, *Our Task*.

3 Henrici, 8.

4 Quoted in Ibid., 9.

5 *Our Task*, 37.

6 GL IV.

7 Henrici, 11.

8 Henrici, 14.

9 Henrici, 15.

10 Hans-Georg Gadamer, *Truth and Method*, trans. Joel Weinsheimer and Donald G. Marshall (New York: Crossroad, 1991). As Gadamer puts it: "Thus, for example, historicizing presentations—e.g. of music played on old instruments—are not as faithful as they seem. Rather, they are an imitation of an imitation and are thus in danger 'of standing at a third remove from the truth' (Plato)" (119–20). The point is not, of course, that serious historical and linguistic work is not necessary to interpretation, it is that human culture transcends such things and is therefore able to speak beyond the confines of the time and place. For Balthasar, as for Gadamer, faithfulness to the past is never a matter, then, of mere repetition, which would, at any rate, be impossible, but, rather, of retrieval and discernment.

11 For a helpful overview of the issues here, see: the introduction by Medard Kehl to *The von Balthasar Reader*, eds Medard Kehl and Werner Loser (New York: Crossroad, 1982), 17–22; Edward T. Oakes, *Pattern of Redemption: The Theology of Hans Urs von Balthasar* (New York: Continuum, 1994), 15–44; and Nicholas J. Healy (2005).

12 *Our Task*, 38.
13 In a word, Christology presupposes a real similarity along with the "ever greater dissimilarity." Balthasar came to worry that Przywara pitted the Being of God and the being of the creature against one another. See, especially, TL II, 94, n. 16.
14 Henrici, 20–1.
15 *Our Task*, 35–45.
16 For what follows see, Hans Urs von Balthasar, *The Theology of Henri de Lubac* (1991).
17 *The Theology of Henri de Lubac*, 39.
18 Ibid., 39.
19 Ibid., 41.
20 For an excellent treatment of the historical background of this dispute, see the introduction by Alexander Dru and Illtyd Trethowan to Maurice Blondel, *The Letter on Apologetics & History and Dogma,* Trans. Alexander Dru and Illtyd Trethowan (Grand Rapids: Eerdmans, 1964).
21 Alexander Dru and Illtyd Trethowan (1964), 55.
22 George Tyrrell, "Revelation as Experience," cited in Allesandro Maggioliolini, "From Modernism to Vatican II," *Communio: International Catholic Review* (Summer, 1996), 231.
23 For an excellent introduction to the nature-grace controversy and de Lubac's role in it, see David L. Schindler's introduction to *The Mystery of the Supernatural* (New York: Crossroad, 1998).
24 For a helpful account of de Lubac's treatment of this, both historical and theological, see Balthasar (1991), 61–89 and Bruno Forte, "Nature and grace in Henri de Lubac: from *Surnaturel* to *Le Mystère du surnaturel,*" *Communio: International Catholic Review* (Winter 1996), 725–37.
25 Forte, "Nature and grace," 726.
26 Henri de Lubac, *The Mystery of the Supernatural*, (1998), 82, cited in Balthasar (1991), 62–3, in the original French, *Le Mystère du surnaturel* (1965), 114.
27 Balthasar (1991), 71. See also the important article by Marc Ouellet, "Paradox and/or Supernatural Existential," *Communio: International Catholic Review* (Summer, 1991).
28 de Lubac, (1998), xxix.
29 Ibid., xxx.
30 For a manageable introduction to de Lubac's vast literature in this field, see the three essays in *Theological Fragments* (San Francisco: Ignatius Press, 1989), under the section, "History of Exegesis."
31 As de Lubac puts it: "Does this mean that we would propose returning to it as a guide for today's exegesis and theology? No one would seriously dream of that . . . Preserving or rediscovering its spirit is not the same thing as literally reestablishing it" ("Doctrine of the 'Fourfold Sense' in Scripture," de Lubac (1989), 124.
32 *Our Task*, 13.
33 For the details of her young life and their eventual collaboration, see *Our Task,* 21–95.
34 Ibid., 65.

35 Ibid., 47.
36 Ibid., 56.
37 Ibid., 19, 80.
38 Schindler (1991), 22.
39 See especially Kevin Mongrain, *The Systematic Thought of Hans Urs von Balthasar: an Irenaean Retrieval* (New York: Herder and Herder, 2002) for the most boldly stated version of this position. After stating the degree to which Balthasar claims that his work is inseparable from Adrienne's, Mongrain says the following: "These are extremely dubious claims whose lack of self-evidence troubled even Balthasar himself. As a general rule, interpreters should defer to the explicit opinions of authors when they comment on their own writings . . . In the case of von Balthasar's odd claims about von Speyr's influence on his theology, however, this rule should be suspended. The assumption guiding my reading of von Balthasar is that von Speyr's influence on his is deforming rather than constructive, derived rather than original; von Speyr is essential for psychologically understanding von Balthasar but completely dispensable for theologically understanding him." Not only is this latter claim exceedingly arrogant and condescending, it betrays a superficiality which is hard to imagine from anybody who has given serious thought to this issue.
40 *Our Task*, 94.
41 Ibid., 60.
42 Hans Urs von Balthasar to Henri de Lubac (July 1950), from the Appendix to Henri de Lubac, *Theology in History*, trans. Anne Englund Nash (San Francisco: Ignatius Press, 1996), 597.
43 *Our Task*, 17–18.

2. BALTHASAR'S METHOD: BACKGROUND AND HISTORY

1 TL II, 107.a.
2 Balthasar says this repeatedly, but it is most fully developed in GL, I.
3 De Lubac (1988), xxxv.
4 In the beginning of the *Epilogue* to his entire trilogy, and in the context precisely of the question of method, Balthasar himself refers to Karl Barth on the one hand and his tendency towards fideism (false particularism) and Karl Rahner and his tendency towards rationalism (false generalism). *Epilogue*, 17.
5 David Tracy, foreword to *God Without Being*, trans. Thomas A. Carson (Chicago: University of Chicago Press, 1991), ix–x.
6 For a succinct overview of Rahner's method, see J. J. Mueler, S. J., *What Are They Saying About Theological Method?* (New York: Paulist Press, 1984), 5–13.
7 "Current Trends in Catholic Theology," 80.
8 See, for instance, the difference between Werner Löser's classic treatment in *Im Geiste des Origenes: Hans Urs von Balthasar als Interpret der*

Kirchenväter, (Frankfurt: Josef Knecht, 1976) and Edward T. Oakes, *Pattern of Redemption: The Theology of Hans Urs von Balthasar* (New York: Continuum, 1994). It should be noted that Oakes realizes the differences of emphasis between his and Löser's approach and notes that his chapter, "Balthasar and the Church Fathers" serves as a balance.

9 These rules come from the important essay, originally written in 1939, discussed further below, "The Fathers, the Scholastics, and Ourselves," *Communio: International Catholic Review* (Summer, 1997), 366–70.

10 Ibid., 370.

11 Joseph Cardinal Ratzinger, *Truth and Tolerance* (San Francisco: Ignatius Press, 2004), 21–2.

12 For a helpful account of the world-transcending aspect of Plato's thought see Josef Pieper's important little book, *Divine Madness* (San Francisco: Ignatius Press, 1995).

13 GL IV, 181.

14 Ibid., 156.

15 For what follows see especially, "The Fathers, the Scholastics, and Ourselves." The early date of this essay should not concern the reader, for the basic criticisms of Patristic and Scholastic thought contained in this essay, and the genealogy of modernity contained therein, are repeated in their basic contours throughout Balthasar's later works as well. For instance, the notion that Thomas Aquinas should be seen as a pivotal figure, between the Patristic tendency to swallow philosophy into theology (and vice versa) and the modern tendency absolutely to separate the two, is repeated in the volume on metaphysics in *The Glory of the Lord*, written in 1967. Furthermore, the rather negative tone of the piece is not simply replaced by a more positive tone in later and more specific pieces; it is rather the case that, for Balthasar, the very thing which makes the Fathers great is that which is sometimes their biggest liability. In short, the positive and negative assessment which he makes of the Church Fathers must always be held together. As Balthasar puts it, "For ironically enough, it was precisely the very certainty of victory with which the Fathers contemplated all the truths that they encountered, it was their very confidence that these truths were already Christian and which they therefore claimed for their own, using them to pour the truth of the Gospel into the language of their time, the thought forms of late Hellenism (above all, of neo-Platonism), that hid the danger of an unconscious alienation of the original deposit of revelation" ("The Fathers, the Scholastics, and Ourselves," 372).

16 Ibid., 374.

17 Ibid.

18 *Love Alone* is Credible, 18.

19 Ibid., 384.

20 For the secondary literature in what follows see especially, GL IV, 393–412; Etienne Gilson, *History of Christian Philosophy in the Middle Ages* (New York: Random House, 1955), 361–83; Josef Pieper, *Guide to Thomas Aquinas*, trans. Richard and Clara Winston (Notre Dame, IN: University of Notre Dame Press, 1987), 33–161; Nicholas J. Healy,

The Eschatology of Hans Urs von Balthasar: Being as Communion (New York: Oxford University Press, 2005), 19–90.

21 *De spiritualibus creatures*, a. I., cited in Healy, 2005, 44.
22 *Questiones quodlibetales*, III, q. 8, a. 20., cited in Ibid., 45.
23 GL IV, 403.
24 From GL IV, 393. This new understanding of God's transcendence derives from the God of Jewish-Christian revelation. As Yehezkel Kaufmann points out, "all of these embodiments involve one idea which is the distinguishing mark of pagan thought: the idea that there exists a realm of being prior to the gods and above them, upon which the gods depend, and whose decrees they must obey. Deity belongs to, and is derived from, a primordial realm . . . This is to say that in the pagan view, the gods are not the source of all that is, nor do they transcend the universe." Cited in Oakes, 1994, 28–9.
25 These four principles are presented in GL IV, 393–5.
26 GL IV, 403–4.
27 "Avicenna and Thomas had seen knowledge of God as being mediated by the act of being as such; to Scotus this seems to be a theological *a priori*; in the fact of a God who, if he is to be really known, can only disclose himself, our cognitive ability is insufficient . . . henceforth, therefore, the philosophical endeavor will have to content itself with empiricism, whereas theology will be the contingent recapitulation, mediated by free revelation, of that *a priori* absolute knowledge that God has of himself" (TD II, 245–6).
28 For the details of this, see Gilson (1955), 181–225 (on Arabian philosophy), and 431–520 (from Scotus to Nominalism). See also, GL V, 9–47.
29 Cited in GL IV, 403.
30 Gilson, 1955, 491.
31 Kant, Streit der Fakultäten I: Allgemeine Anmerkung; von Religious sekten (Prussian edn, 7:58f.), cited in *Love Alone*, 34.
32 *Love Alone*, 43.
33 Ibid., 10.

3. BALTHASAR'S THEOLOGICAL STYLE

1 *My Work* in Retrospect (MW), 118–19.
2 MW, 114.
3 Healy (2005), 52.
4 "A biological and evolutionary sequence of stages—if there ever could be such a thing as a self-sufficient system—would at best be able to allow the ascent of the individual essential form, say that of a bird, from its pre-formations in an earlier form, say that of the fish, but it would never be able to derive the inherent necessity of a single perfected essential form in which—in a wholly anti-Kantian manner—*pulchritudo* and *perfectio* evidently coincide, from the ends of a total evolution of the whole of life or the whole of Being in movement towards itself. The entities, precisely the sub-intellectual art works of the *prakriti*, of creative Nature, bear the

mark of an unconditionally original imaginative power to which one must be blind if one—I do not say classifies their forms within the evolutionary process, but explains them entirely on the grounds of their position with this process. To this degree the realm of forms of subhuman Nature remains a singularly illuminating touchstone for the value of a metaphysics: anyone like Descartes and the Materialists, who explains animals in a purely mechanical way has already lost, but so too have those who, like Schelling and Hegel, interpret the forms of Nature as the ways and stages of the Absolute Spirit which explicates Itself. The first approach cannot interpret the *glorious* freedom of the essential forms, indeed not even the necessity of such forms, while the second does not explain how the Spirit which is still only in search of Itself achieves such perfection which presupposes, not only a luminous intelligence . . . but a superior and playful freedom beyond all the constraints of Nature" (GL V, 620–1).

5 *Epilogue*, 23: "The consequences of this restriction [of reason to the empirical] are tragic: we get precisely the opposite of what we bargained for: slavery, not freedom. For technology does not liberate but actually enslaves man on every level."

6 See *The God Question and Modern Man*, 24; Epilogue, 20.

7 It is interesting to note that Martin Bieler finds some foundation for a meta-anthropological starting point even in Aquinas insofar as the latter says, *"esse autem simpliciter est superius ad esse hominem* [to be man is to be absolutely]" in ST III, 16, 9 ad 2. Cited in Martin Bieler, "Meta-anthropology and Christology: On the Philosophy of Hans Urs von Balthasar," in *Communio: International Catholic Review* 20 (Spring, 1993), 139.

8 GL V, 615.

9 "[Thomas] is a kairos in the even stronger sense that he sees man, to whom it has been given to reflect on being, in a peculiar state of suspension between nature and supernature: he is disposed by nature for the revelation of God in grace; and although he can make no claim to grace, without it he can never be fulfilled or complete" (TD IV, 396). This is just one of the innumerable places in which Balthasar refers to this central paradox.

10 See the two important essays in ET I, "God Speaks as Man," and "Implications of the Word".

11 In numerous places Balthasar will juxtapose a purely masculine notion of knowledge, which is marked by a sort of grasping that is not properly "receptive" of the object of knowledge, with a more feminine or childlike notion which is marked by a sort of "indifference" in the face of the object to be known. In TL I, 48, Balthasar articulates this accordingly, "From the side of potency, the cognitive capacity gets its perfect readiness for, and indifference toward, every occasion for knowledge, whose specification is reserved exclusively to the object. Every anticipation of truth's self-presentation in the form of innate ideas, schemata, or categories would hinder this pure readiness . . . At bottom, one would be finished with what the other was going to say before he even had a chance

to open his mouth ... Innate ideas would prevent any true dialogue, wound courtesy, and make love impossible."

12 For an excellent discussion of this change at the beginnings of modernity, see Joseph Cardinal Ratzinger, *Introduction to Christianity* (San Francisco: Ignatius Press, 1990), 32–7.

13 TL II, 96.

14 Romano Guardini, *Welt und Person* (Würzburg: Werkbund, 1952), 67. Cited in ibid., 96.

15 *The God Question and Modern Man*, 12.

16 TL I, 30: "Of course, insofar as it works in a relative abstraction, prescinding from creaturely nature's embedding in the supernatural, philosophy can indeed highlight certain fundamental natural structures of the world and knowledge, because this embedding does not do away with, or even alter the essential core of, such structures."

17 TL I, 30: "The world, considered as an object of knowledge, is always already embedded in this supernatural sphere, and in the same way man's cognitive powers operate either under the positive sign of faith or under the negative sign of unbelief."

18 TL I, 31.

19 TL I, 31.

20 TL I, 31.

21 GL V, 621.

22 Ibid.

23 GL V, 624.

24 GL V, 625.

25 *Summa theologiae* I, q. 45, a. 3. This is not the place to go into what, precisely, Aquinas means by this. For a helpful discussion, see Kenneth Schmitz, *The Gift: Creation* (Milwaukee: Marquette University Press, 1982), 94–7.

26 *Summa theologiae* I, q. 13, a. 7.

27 See, for instance, Schmitz (1982), W. Norris Clark, *Person and Being* (Milwaukee: Marquette University Press, 1993) and "Person, Being and St. Thomas," *Communio: International Catholic Review*, 19 (1992): 601–18. For an engagement between W. Norris Clarke and David L. Schindler on this very question, see *Communio: International Catholic Review*, 20 (1993) and 21 (1994). For an overview of the entire question of Balthasar's and Thomas's positions on the question of Being, God and relationality in the context of the Schindler–Clarke exchange, see Healy (2005), 72–81.

28 Schmitz (1982), 93.

29 Healy (2005), 78.

30 GL V, 626-7.

31 Healy (2005), 81.

32 "Theology and Sanctity," in ET I, 194–5.

33 TD III, 221–2.

34 TL II, 67–8.

35 See the entire section on "Negative Theology," in TL II, 87–122.

36 TL II, 17.

37 *I Sent.*, Prologue, cited in Scola (1995), 53.
38 See, for instance, the conclusion to Balthasar's sketch of "Christocentrism" in his important study of Karl Barth. KB, 362–3.
39 For the best overview of the transcendentals and their role in the trilogy, see *Epilogue*, 43–86.
40 *Epilogue*, 59.
41 Ibid., 59.
42 For an excellent overview of the aesthetics, see Ibid., 59–67.
43 The God Question and Modern Man, 32.
44 TL I, 17: "Of course, the ultimate ground of the mysterious character inherent in the knowable is disclosed only when we recognize that every possible object of knowledge is creaturely, in other words, that its ultimate truth lies hidden in the mind of the Creator, who alone can speak the eternal name of things."
45 See the important section on the scientific notion of the "given" in Schmitz (1982).
46 "Whatever is born fits in with every other being; and this is the soul, which in a certain way *is* everything," De veritate, I, I, cited by Balthasar in *Epilogue*, 77.
47 *Epilogue*, 86.

4. JESUS CHRIST AND THE MEANING OF SCRIPTURE

1 ET I, 149.
2 See especially Robert Wilken, *The Christians as the Romans Saw Them* (New Haven: Yale University Press, 2003), for an account of the sorts of criticisms raised against Christianity by the educated class in Rome. Typical is Celsus's incredulity that a man who lived in flesh and blood in time could be identified with God: "If Christians taught that 'God is father of all and that we really ought to worship him alone' there would be no quarrel. But Christians make Jesus almost equal to God, 'not because they are paying very great reverence to God but because they are exalting Jesus excessively" (105–6). As Wilken shows throughout the book, however, it was not just the exaltation of this man to the status of God or godlikeness that offended Roman sensibilities, it was also the notion that Jesus was in some sense a unique representative of God and that, therefore, Christianity was uniquely true. The Romans, therefore, made repeated attempts to incorporate Christianity into a broader religious pluralism, making it one path to God among many, a move also typical of modern thought. See especially the chapter on Porphyry.
3 Even the modern, critical study of the Bible is not totally without precedent in the ancient Roman critique. Demythologization, for instance, was a Roman move even with regard to the texts of Homer, and thinkers like Porphyry submitted the Christian Scriptures to close, philosophical scrutiny, criticizing both the so-called argument from the prophets and the consistency of the Gospel narratives. See Wilken (2003), 126–63.
4 See David L. Schindler's introduction to de Lubac (1998), xxix–xxx.

5 Ibid., xxx.

6 TL I, 11–12.

7 See, for instance, *Short Primer for Unsettled Laymen*, where Balthasar says the following: "Closely connected to the plurality of biblical ways of access to the mystery of revelation stands the contribution made by exegesis to its understanding. Since, taken abstractly in itself, it is a neutral philological science, it can be practiced by a believing or an unbelieving scholar, but of course in a very different spirit. Jesus demands a radical Yes or No to his person and claim. What is 'neither hot nor cold' is spat out. Someone who wants to 'bracket' this claim 'methodologically,' even if he does so only provisionally, in order to wait and see if this claim had really been made and, if so, if it was made rightly, exposes himself to the danger of a neutrality which is forbidden by the object and falsifies it" (47).

8 See, especially, TL I, 96.

9 I do not find W. T. Dickens' approach to Balthasar's exegesis sufficiently clear on this point. Specifically, Dickens seems to imply that Balthasar's criticisms are often too harsh and reactionary and that his "synchronic" (aesthetic, Christ-centered) approach to Scripture has to allow more room for a "diachronic" (historical, critical) approach. But the impression is given that this can be done by finding a place somewhere between (as in compromise) the approach of the Fathers or Balthasar and that of modern exegetes. For Balthasar, on the other hand, there can be no compromise whatsoever with a method that insists that the whole is no more than the sum of its parts, or that insists that faith can (and must) be *de facto* bracketed in order to get to the truth of things. Balthasar will, and does, allow for any biblical science that allows itself to be taken up into a larger approach. It is not so much, then, a question of compromise as it is a question of cart and horse. See, W. T. Dickens, "Balthasar's biblical hermeneutics," in *The Cambridge Companion to Hans Urs von Balthasar*, eds Edward T. Oakes, S.J. and David Moss (Cambridge: Cambridge University Press, 2004).

10 Josef Pieper, *Living the Truth* (San Francisco: Ignatius Press, 1989), 19. Pieper is quoting here from Kant's *Critique of Pure Reason*. For the full quote see, Immanuel Kant, *Critique of Pure Reason*, trans. Norman Kemp Smith (New York: St. Martin's Press, 1929), 118.

11 *The God Question and Modern Man*, 34.

12 For an excellent discussion of just this difference see Oakes (1994), 185–7.

13 "Certainly the present time is one where love is absent, where things are deprived of the splendor reflected from eternity. Even for Christians it is extremely difficult to avoid the contagion and not to fall into a kind of eschatological spiritualism which abandons the world to the 'powers', which views all that pertains to it in a positivist and neutral light . . ." ("Revelation and the Beautiful," ET I, 110).

14 The God Question and Modern Man, 4.

15 GL VII, 97: "Thousands of rivulets of meaning followed their separated course, until they flowed into one another, thousands of paths crossed one another and seemed to part from each other again, until they united

definitively to form one highway; the historical-critical method, with its patient unraveling of the material backwards to the origins, gives us some glimpses of strata where material that was later to be united lies as yet without any coordinating unity. Nevertheless, these glimpses are not decisively important, because the thread of Ariadne—love as the solution of all intellectual questions—leads unambiguously forwards to the unifying of the different points of view."

16 "A purely secular view of history is quite impossible. Historical science may attempt to be neutral as regards the philosophy of history but it cannot controvert the fact that its subject—man and his acts and sufferings—conducts himself, in small things and in great, according to his basic idea of ultimate meaning, that is to say, as a philosopher" ("The Word and History," ET I, 27).

17 For the connection between aesthetics and the Eros–Agape relationship, see "Revelation and the Beautiful," ET I, 102–4.

18 Of course even a photograph is never merely a photo-reproduction, but is always taken from a certain angle under certain kinds of lighting, etc. And this is why even photography can be an art form.

19 The reader would do well to re-read the entire introduction to GL I at this point, but here is a sample of quotes to bear out the point that I am making. "Works of art can die as a result of being looked at by too many dull eyes, and even the radiance of holiness can, in a way, become blunted when it encounters nothing but hollow indifference" (23). "One must possess a spiritual eye capable of perceiving (*wahrnehmen*) the forms of existence with awe" (24). Balthasar points out here that the original (in German) meaning of perception is "seeing truly," but has come, in modern philosophy, to mean just the opposite. "It is more difficult because our eyes lose their acumen for form and we become accustomed to read things by starting from the bottom and working our way up, rather than by working from the whole to the parts . . . [We] no longer have a vision for wholeness" (25). "Does it not make one suspicious when Biblical philology's first move in its search for an 'understanding' of its texts is to dissect their form into sources, psychological motivations, and the sociological effects of milieu, even before the form has been really contemplated and read for its meaning *as form*? For we can be sure of one thing: we can never again recapture the living totality of form once it has been dissected and sawed into pieces . . . " (31).

20 "Two Say Why," 20, cited in Oakes, 1994, 190. See also "Revelation and the Beautiful," where Balthasar applies this aesthetic principle to the fact that no one could have predicted the form of Christ simply from the fragments which led up to him from the Old Covenant (117–18).

21 Oakes, 1994, 190.

22 GL VI, 403.

23 "It is essential today to insist as strongly as possible that Christianity cannot be understood without the old covenant: every attempt to interpret the form, message and subsequent impact of Christ in the world necessarily fails unless it is able to assess it all precisely in its closeness to and its distance from the old covenant. It has become impossible today simply

to discard the innumerable references to the Old Testament in the New as time-conditioned proofs from Scripture . . . " (GL VI, 403).

24 GL VI, 403–4.

25 GL VI, 406, n. 7.

26 GL VI, 406.

27 GL VI, 409–11. This is not the place to go into Balthasar's entire theology of Israel and its relationship to Christianity. It may seem patently anti-Semitic to suggest that Jesus really is the fulfillment of Israel's faith and that, therefore, the Church is the New Israel. But in a paradoxical way, those more Liberal approaches to this question, which downplay the promise-fulfillment approach of the tradition, end up also downplaying any relationship at all between Synagogue and Church. One need only consider the utterly non-Jewish Jesus of the Jesus Seminar or the disdain for religious particulars in classical Liberal Protestantism to see this fact. For a defense of the notion that the Church is true Israel is in fact the best way to preserve Christianity's closeness and indebtedness to as well as respect for the faith of Israel, see George Lindbeck, "The Church as Israel: Ecclesiology and Ecumenism," in *Jews and Christians: People of God*, eds Carl Braaten and Robert Jenson (Grand Rapids, MI: Eerdmans, 2003). For Balthasar's treatment of question, see TD III, 361–401 along with Oakes, 1994, 201–8.

28 GL VI, 404.

29 GL VI, 405.

30 GL VI, 407.

31 Marianne Meye Thompson, "Jesus and his God," in *The Cambridge Companion to Jesus*, ed. Markus Bockmuehl (Cambridge: Cambridge University Press, 2001), 41.

32 It should be pointed out that Balthasar, aside from the fact that he rejects the approach to history that makes such claims seem plausible, also thinks that this is bad reasoning even at the level of the historical-critical. "The words of the Gospels point concentrically to his peerless sense of mission, and if anyone were to suggest that these words had been amplified and inflated in the course of decades until they came to be written down by the faith of the primitive Church, such a suspicion is countered by the early Pauline Christology, which, with regard to the person of Jesus, affirms no less than the strongest words of Jesus himself . . . Whether explicitly or implicitly, Jesus must have acted as if he were the Archimedean point of the religious history of the world, otherwise it would have been impossible for a theology like the pre-Pauline and Pauline to have developed in so short a time" (TD III, 26–7).

33 *Martin Luther's Basic Theological Writings*, ed. Timothy Lull (Minneapolis, MN: Fortress Press, 1989), 32.

34 Ibid., 31.

35 GL VII, 213.

36 Ibid., 213–14.

37 Ibid., 215. The quotes from Barth are taken from *Church Dogmatics* (ET), IV/I, 185ff.

38 Balthasar dedicates an entire chapter to this hiddenness in GL VII, 318–85.

39 For an elaboration of this principle, see especially ET I, "The Word, Scripture and Tradition."

40 On this point, see George Hunsinger's critique of George Lindbeck in *The Cambridge Companion to Post-modern Theology* (Cambridge: Cambridge University Press, 2003). Lindbeck's rightful objections against what he calls the "cognitive-propositional" approach to revelation can be addressed without in any way denying that revelation is both cognitive and propositional. The important thing to note is that it is so *analogously* and not *univocally*. Balthasar will emphasize this very thing.

5. JESUS CHRIST AND THE DRAMA OF FINITE AND INFINITE FREEDOM

1 GL VII, 408–9.

2 TD III, 22.

3 Cited in, Robert Wilken, *The Christians as the Romas Saw Them* (New Haven, CT: Yale University Press, 2003), 104–5.

4 Balthasar refers to this principle repeatedly. In TD II, he puts it accordingly: "But because the '*motus*' of freedom is inseparable from the '*causa sui*', because there is thus in the will a natural longing (*desiderium naturale*) for complete, exhaustive self-possession, which would have to coincide with the 'possession' of being as such, we arrive at the Thomist paradox (which Henri de Lubac has again brought to light): man strives to fulfill himself in an Absolute and yet, although he is '*causa sui*', he is unable to achieve this by his own power or by attaining any finite thing or finite good (225)."

5 TD II, 226-7.

6 Robert Sokolowski, *The God of Faith and Reason: Foundations of Christian Theology* (Notre Dame, IN: University of Notre Dame Press, 1982). See especially Chapters Six and Seven where, in his treatment of natural and theological virtue, he shows that Kant's allegedly secular ethics in fact incorporated all sorts of Christian habits of thought. He does this by contrasting it with that of Aristotle.

7 TD II, 197: "Post-Christian philosophy, even if it claims to be pure philosophy, like Kant's thought on freedom, is directly influenced by Christian revelation."

8 Ibid., 12–20.

9 For a discussion of Aristotle's notion of virtue and freedom, see Sokolowski (1982), 53–67; for Balthasar's discussion of the "freedom of consent," see, TD II, 227–42.

10 TD II, 200.

11 TD II, 211.

12 TD II, 213.

13 Aidan Nichols, *No Bloodless Myth: A Guide Through Balthasar's Dramatics* (Washington, D.C.: The Catholic University of America Press, 2000), 67.

14 *Enneads*, VI, 8, 13, cited in TD II, 244.

15 TD II, 250–1.
16 TD II, 257.
17 In the remarkable little work *The Making of the Creeds* (Philadelphia: Trinity Press International, 1991), Frances Young has shown quite convincingly that the early discussions surrounding Christ's person and nature were neither the result of a false hellenization nor the product of abstract, metaphysical fixations, but were rather intent upon explaining how Christ could be who the Scriptures said he was: namely, the savior of human beings. According to Young, the entire Christological controversies could practically be boiled down to the assertion that only a divine savior could *save* us, while only a human savior could save *us*. The savior of humanity must therefore be fully divine and fully human. The point is that this was not the result of abstract speculation but was, rather, the conclusion to a very practical problem.
18 TD III, "In what follows, therefore, there can be no question of retaining the usual textbook approach, which starts from an essentialist Christology that claims to have prior knowledge of Jesus' essential nature as the Incarnate Word even before the action begins, only subsequently moving over to a dramatic soteriology."
19 See TD III, 65, n. 18.
20 TD III, 64.
21 TD III, 65.
22 TD III, 82, citing Martin Hengel, "Christologie und neutestamentliche Chronologie" in *Neues Testament und Geschichte* (Tubingen: *TVZ*-Mohr, 1972), 45.
23 TD III, 84.
24 TD III, 85, citing Heinz Schürmann, *Traditionsgeschichtliche Untersuchungen zu den synoptischen Evangelien* (Dusseldorf: Patmos, 1968), no page number given.
25 TD III, 86.
26 Quoted in TD III, 88, n. 61.
27 With regard to the cited passage in Mark that some of his own disciple would not taste death before seeing the coming of the kingdom, Balthasar says, "We should bear in mind that this may not necessarily refer to a specific time (e.g. I Cor 15.6); it could signify a choice: some will see, others will not" (TD III, 93, n. 81).
28 TD III, 97.
29 TD III, 99.
30 TD III, 110–11.
31 TD III, 116, n. 48.
32 TD III, 120.
33 For a fuller discussion of Balthasar's theology of redemption, see Rodney Howsare (2005), 62–8; 136–42.
34 TD III, 122.
35 TD III, 122.
36 In the important treatment of redemption in TD IV, Balthasar offers a list of five different aspects of redemption that must be kept together if we are to have a sufficiently biblical view of salvation. The fourth of these

is *theosis* or the gift of the Holy Spirit that must always be kept in mind in addition to the negative liberation from sin that often gets one-sided attention in the West. For the five elements, see TD IV, 240–3.

37 TD III, 141.
38 Scola, 1995, 57.
39 From *I Sent.*, Prologue, cited in Scola, 1995, 53.

6. "TRINITY AND THE CROSS"

1 TD IV, 324.
2 TD IV, 325.
3 See the entire section on "Negative Theology" in TL II (87–123), but especially, 107–8.
4 TL II, 67; TD V, 405–6.
5 TL II, 39–40: "Consequently, Augustine's triadic logic calls for a complementary counter image, which bursts open the narrow confines of the self-enclosed subject, even as it fails to maintain the unity of the divine substance because of its emphasis on interpersonal love."
6 We have to be careful not to oversimplify here. It is not simply the case that Balthasar disagrees with Aquinas's refusal to see a "real" relation between God and the world. First, Balthasar has a deep appreciation for what it is that Aquinas is trying to preserve here. But, second, and more importantly, Balthasar's own willingness to admit such a relation is itself premised on Thomistic principles which Balthasar thinks should allow for a real relation understood in the proper way: namely, as a result of the difference between God and the world being rooted ultimately in the difference between the Trinitarian persons. This will become clearer in what follows. My only point at present is to say that any impression that Balthasar's theology is simply opposed to Thomas's on this matter would be wrong.
7 With regard to the fruitful union of the married couple, Balthasar says the following: "It is a cause for amazement that in discussion of Trinitarian logic in the world the parent-child relationship is always lightly brushed aside" (TL II, 59). And, then, after summarizing Scheeben's contribution, he concludes: "The relationship described here, which is the simple but necessary complement to the dialogic we outlined above, remains, in spite of all the obvious dissimilarities, the most eloquent imago Trinitatis that we find woven into the fabric of the creature. It not only transcends Augustine's self-contained I, but also allows the 'condilectus [co-beloved]' that Richard's model imports from the outside to spring from the intimacy of love itself . . . while avoiding the dangerous tendency of the dialogicians to allow interpersonal encounter to slide into a mere two-way monologue . . . It is the permanent proof of the triadic structure of creaturely logic" (62).
8 Scola, 1995, 57.
9 TD III, 192.
10 TD III, 177.

11 TD III, 183–91.
12 TL III, 33–51.
13 TL III, 49.
14 Balthasar discusses this at greater length in TD V, 223–47.
15 TD III, 221.
16 TD III, 206.
17 TD III, 207.
18 TD III, 215.
19 TD III, 216.
20 TD III, 220.
21 Hans Urs von Balthasar, "On the concept of person," *Communio*: International Catholic Review (Spring, 1986), 22.
22 TD III, 221–2.
23 TL II, 311.
24 TD III, 225.
25 TD III, 228.
26 In TL II, Balthasar sees Jesus' use, in his parables, of common human wisdom and experience as evidence of the fact that God can make use of the created realm in order to make himself known. See especially TL II, 73–83.
27 The Christian State of Life, 228.
28 Ibid., 246.
29 TL II, 137.
30 TL II, 83; TD V, 91–5.
31 TL II, 135 n. 11.
32 In TL II, 135 n. 10, Balthasar's words of caution against Jean-Luc Marion's endeavor to explain the Christian God "without being" should assuage any fears that Balthasar sees love as contrary to either reason or metaphysics. It is not either truth or love; it is truth in love.
33 TL II, 177–8.
34 TD V, 243.
35 TD V, 243–4, citing Heinz Schürmann's *Jesu ureigner Tod* (Herder, 1975), 146.

7. BALTHASAR'S ONGOING ROLE IN THEOLOGY

1 GL IV, 17.
2 See note 21 in Chapter Two above.
3 See, for instance, Russell Reno's essay, "The Paradox of Hans Urs von Balthasar," in *How Balthasar Changed My Mind: 15 Scholars Reflect on the Meaning of Balthasar for Their Own Work,* eds Rodney A. Howsare and Larry S. Chapp, (New York: Herder & Herder, 2008).
4 George Hunsinger, "Post-liberal Theology," in *The Cambridge Companion to Post-modern Theology,* ed. Kevin J. Vanhoozer, (Cambridge: Cambridge University Press, 2003), 42–57.
5 Hunsinger (2003), 44.
6 Hunsinger (2003), 47.

7 Joseph Cardinal Ratzinger, *Truth and Tolerance* (San Francisco: Ignatius Press, 2004), 21–2.

8 See the collection of philosophical essays in post-secular philosophy . . .

9 John Milbank, *Theology & Social Theory: Beyond Secular Reason* (Cambridge, MA: Blackwell Publishers, 1990), 9.

10 See *Milbank's book*, The Suspended Middle: Henri de Lubac and the Debate Concerning the Supernatural (Grand Rapids, MI: Eerdmans, 2005).

11 With regard to secondary literature, one could begin with Adrian Walker's, "Love Alone: Hans Urs von Balthasar as a Master of Theological Renewal," *Communio: International Catholic Review* (Fall, 2005), 517–39.

12 GL V, 429-50. See also David C. Schindler's, "'*Wie kommt der Mensch in die Theologie?*': Heidegger, Hegel, and the Stakes of Onto-Theo-Logy," *Communio: International Catholic Review* (Winter, 2005).

13 See, for instance, Thomas Weinandy, *Does God Change?: The Word's Becoming in the Incarnation* (Still River, MA: St. Bede's Publications, 1985) ; *Does God Suffer?* (Edinburgh: T&T Clark, 2000); and *The Father's Spirit of Sonship: Reconceiving the Trinity* (Edinburgh: T&T Clark, 1995). An article-length statement of the basic argument can be found also in, "Does God Suffer?" *First Things* 117 (November, 2001), 35–41. David Bentley Hart takes a similar position in, "No Shadow of Turning: On Divine Impassibility," *Pro Ecclesia*, Vol. XI, no. 2, 184–206.

14 See especially, Guy Mansini, O.S.B., "Balthasar and the Theodramatic Enrichment of the Trinity," *The Thomist* 64 (2000); Matthew Levering, *Scripture and Metaphysics: Aquinas and the Renewal of Trinitarian Theology*, (Oxford: Blackwell Publishing, 2004).

15 Alyssa Lyra Pitstick, *Light in Darkness: Hans Urs von Balthasar and the Catholic Doctrine of Christ's Descent into Hell* (Grand Rapids, MI: Eerdmans, 2007). See also my review in *The Thomist* (January, 2008).

16 "In the past Thomistic metaphysicians seem to have been content for the most part to assert and defend the absolute immutability of God and to relegate all change and diversity to the side of the creature. But they have not gone on to explain how God can enter into a truly interpersonal dialogue with created persons, how his loving of them and their response to him in the particular contingent ways which are proper to a free exchange between persons can truly make a difference to him, how he is not the completely impassive, indifferent metaphysical iceberg, or at least one-way unreceptive Giver, to whom my loving or not loving, my salvation or damnation, make no difference whatever, as Hartshorne and other process philosophers have objected. It does seem to me that they have a legitimate grievance against the way Thomists have handled, or failed to handle, this problem," (Norris Clarke, *Explorations in Metaphysics: Being, Person and God*, Notre Dame, IN.: University of Notre Dame Press, 1994, 184–5).

BIBLIOGRAPHY

PRIMARY SOURCES

Balthasar, Hans Urs von. *The Christian State of Life*. Trans. Mary Francis McCarthy, San Francisco: Ignatius Press, 1983.

—*Creator Spirit: Explorations in Theology*. Vol. 3. Trans. Brian McNeil, San Francisco: Ignatius Press, 1993.

—"Current Trends in Catholic Theology and the Responsibility of the Christian" (*Communio* 5, Spring 1978), 77–85.

—*Epilogue*. Trans. Edward T. Oakes, San Francisco: Ignatius Press, 2004.

—"The Fathers, Scholastics, and Ourselves." Trans. Edward T. Oakes, *Communio* 24 (1997): 347-396.

—*The Glory of the Lord: A Theological Aesthetics*. Vol. 1, *Seeing the Form*. Trans. Erasmo Leiva-Merikakis, San Francisco: Ignatius Press, 1979.

—*The Glory of the Lord: A Theological Aesthetics*. Vol. 2, *Studies in Clerical Style*. Vol. 3, *Studies in Lay Style*. Trans. Andrew Louth, John Saward, Martin Simon, Rowan Williams, Francis McDonagh and Brian McNeil, San Francisco: Ignatius Press, 1982.

—*The Glory of the Lord*. Vol. 4, *The Realm of Metaphysics in Antiquity*. Trans. Brian McNeil C.R.V., Andrew Louth, John Saward, Rowan Williams, and Oliver Davies, San Francisco: Ignatius Press, 1989.

—*The Glory of the Lord*. Vol. 5, *The Realm of Metaphysics in Modernity*. Trans. Brian McNeil C.R.V., Andrew Louth, John Saward, Rowan Williams, and Oliver Davies, San Francisco: Ignatius Press, 1991.

—*The Glory of the Lord*. Vol. 6, *The Old Covenant*. Trans. Brian McNeil C.R.V. and Erasmo Leiva-Merikakis, San Francisco: Ignatius Press, 1991.

—*The Glory of the Lord*. Vol. 7, *The New Covenant*. Trans. Brian McNeil C.R.V., San Francisco: Ignatius Press, 1989.

—*Love Alone*. Trans. David C. Schindler, San Francisco: Ignatius Press, 2005.

—*Mysterium Paschale: The Mystery of Easter*. Trans. Aidan Nichols, Grand Rapids, Michigan: William B. Eerdmans Publishing Company, 1993.

—*My Work in Retrospect.* Trans. Cornelia Capol, San Francisco: Ignatius Press, 1993.

—*New Elucidations.* Trans. Mary Theresilde Skerry, San Francisco: Ignatius Press, 1986.

—*Our Task: A Report and a Plan.* Trans. John Saward, San Francisco: Ignatius Press, 1994.

—*Spirit and Institution: Explorations in Theology.* Vol. 4. Trans. Edward T. Oakes, S.J., San Francisco: Ignatius Press, 1995.

—*Spouse of the Word: Explorations in Theology.* Vol. 2. Trans. A. V. Littledale and Alexander Dru, San Francisco: Ignatius Press, 1991.

—*Theo-Drama.* Vol. 1, *Prolegomena.* Trans. Graham Harrison, San Francisco: Ignatius Press, 1988.

—*Theo-Drama.* Vol. 2, *The Dramatis Personae: Man in God.* Trans. Graham Harrison, San Francisco: Ignatius Press, 1990.

—*Theo-Drama.* Vol. 3, *Dramatis Personae: Persons in Christ.* Trans. Graham Harrison, San Francisco: Ignatius Press, 1991.

—*Theo-Drama.* Vol. 4, *The Action.* Trans. Graham Harrison, San Francisco: Ignatius Press, 1995.

—*Theo-Drama.* Vol. 5, *The Last Act.* Trans. Graham Harrison, San Francisco: Ignatius Press, 1998.

—*Theo-Logic.* Vol. 1, *Truth of the World.* Trans. Adrian J. Walker, San Francisco: Ignatius Press, 2000.

—*Theo-Logic.* Vol. 2, *Truth of God.* Trans. Adrian J. Walker, San Francisco: Ignatius Press, 2004.

—*Theo-Logic.* Vol. 3, *The Spirit of Truth.* Trans. Graham Harrison, San Francisco: Ignatius Press, 2005.

—*The Theology of Henri de Lubac: An Overview.* Trans. Joseph Fessio and Michael Waldstein, San Francisco: Ignatius Press, 1991.

—*The Theology of Karl Barth: Exposition and Interpretation.* Trans. Edward T. Oakes S.J., San Francisco: Ignatius Press, 1992.

—*The Word Made Flesh: Explorations in Theology.* Vol. 1. Trans. Arthur V. Littledale and Alexander Dru, San Francisco: Ignatius Press, 1989.

OTHER SOURCES

Bieler, M. "Meta-anthropology and Christology: On the Philosophy of Hans Urs von Balthasar." *Communio* 20 (Spring 1993): 129–46.

Blondel, Maurice. *Letter on Apologetics & History and Dogma.* Trans. Alexander Dru and Illtyd Trethowan. Grand Rapids, MI: Eerdmans, 1994.

Carabine, Deirdre. "The Fathers: The Church's Intimate, Youthful Diary." In *The Beauty of Christ: A (sic) Introduction to the Theology of Hans Urs von Balthasar,* 73–91. Ed. Bede McGregor, O.P. and Thomas Norris. Edinburgh: T&T Clark, 1994.

de Lubac, Henri. *Letters of Étienne Gilson to Henri de Lubac.* Trans. Mary Emily Hamilton. San Francisco: Ignatius Press, 1988.

—*The Mystery of the Supernatural.* Trans. Rosemary Sheed. New York: Herder and Herder, 1967.

—"A Witness of Christ in the Church: Hans Urs von Balthasar." In *Hans Urs von Balthasar: His Life and Work*, 271–88. Ed. David L. Schindler. San Francisco: Ignatius Press, 1991.

—*Theological Fragments*. Trans. Rebecca Howell Balinski. San Francisco: Ignatius Press, 1989.

Gadamer, Hans-Georg. *Philosophical Hermeneutics*. Trans. and ed. David E. Linge. Berkeley, California: University of California Press, 1976.

—*Truth and Method*. Trans. Joel Weinsheimer and Donald G. Marshall. New York: Crossroad Publishing Co., 1991.

Gawronski, Raymond. *Word and Silence: Hans Urs von Balthasar and the Spiritual Encounter between East and West*. Edinburg: T&T Clark, 1995.

Gilson, Étienne. *Being and Some Philosophers*. Toronto, Canada: Pontifical Institute of Medieval Studies, 1949.

—*History of Christian Philosophy in the Middle Ages*. New York: Random House, 1955.

—*The Unity of the Philosophical Experience*. New York: Charles Scribner's Sons, 1937.

Healy, Nicholas J. *The Eschatology of Hans Urs von Balthasar: Being as Communion*. Oxford: Oxford University Press, 2005.

Howsare, Rodney. *Hans Urs von Balthasar and Protestantism: The Ecumenical Implications of His Theological Style*. London: T&T Clark, 2005.

Howsare, Rodney and Larry S. Chapp (eds). *How Balthasar Changed My Mind: 15 Scholars Reflect on the Meaning of Balthasar for Their Own Work*. New York: The Crossroad Publishing Company, 2008.

Kant, Immanuel. *Religion Within the Bounds of Reason Alone*. Trans. Theodore M. Greene and Hoyt H. Hudson. New York: Harper Torchbooks, 1960.

—"The Strife of the Faculties." In *German Essays on Religion*, 4–13. Ed. Edward T. Oakes, S.J. New York: Continuum Publishing Co., 1994.

Lindbeck, George. *The Nature of Doctrine: Religion and Theology in a Postliberal Age*. Philadelphia: Westminster Press, 1984.

Marion, Jean-Luc. "Christian Philosophy and Charity." *Communio* 19 (Fall, 1992): 465–73.

—*God Without Being*. Trans. Thomas A. Carson. Chicago: University of Chicago Press, 1991.

Milbank, John. *Theology and Social Theory: Beyond Secular Reason*. Cambridge, MA: Blackwell Publishers, 1990.

—*The Word Made Strange: Theology, Language and Culture*. Cambridge, MA: Blackwell Publishers, 1997.

Mongrain, Kevin. *The Systematic Thought of Hans Urs von Balthasar: An Irenaean Retrieval*. New York: Crossroad Publishing Company, 2002.

Nichols, Aidan. *No Bloodless Myth: A Guide through Balthasar's Dramatics*. Washington, D.C.: Catholic University of America Press, 2000.

—*Say it is Pentecost: A Guide through Balthasar's Logic*. Washington, D.C.: Catholic University of America Press, 2001.

Oakes, Edward. *Pattern of Redemption: The Theology of Hans Urs von Balthasar*. New York: Continuum, 1994.

Ouellet, Marc. "Paradox and/or Supernatural Existential." *Communio* 18 (Summer 1991): 259–80.

Pieper, Joseph. *Guide to Thomas Aquinas.* Trans. Richard and Clara Winston. Notre Dame, IN: University of Notre Dame Press, 1987.

Schindler, David. "Christology and the *Imago Dei*: Interpreting *Gaudium et Spes.*" *Communio* 23 (Spring, 1996): 156–84.

—*Heart of the World, Center of the Church: Communio Ecclesiology, Liberalism, and Liberation.* Grand Rapids, MI: William B. Eerdmans Publishing Company, 1996.

—"On the Catholic Common Ground Project: The christological foundations of dialogue." *Communio* 23 (Winter 1996): 823–51.

Scola, Angelo. *Hans Urs von Balthasar: A Theological Style.* Grand Rapids, MI: William B. Eerdmans Publishing Company, 1995.

Sokolowski, Robert. *Eucharistic Presence: A Study in the Theology of Disclosure.* Washington, D.C.: The Catholic University of America Press, 1994.

—*The God of Faith and Reason: Foundations of Christian Theology.* Notre Dame, IN: University of Notre Dame Press, 1982.

SUGGESTIONS FOR FURTHER READING

I. PRIMARY SOURCES: A SHORT LIST TO START WITH

The student who wishes to know something about the theology of Balthasar can be put off at the early stage by the sheer volume of what he wrote. The trilogy alone makes up a total of 15 fat volumes, with an epilogue. It can also be dense and demanding. It might be best, then, for the student to begin with the shorter works, and only later take on the various volumes within the trilogy. Here is a short list of English translations that would serve as a good starting point, prior to tackling the trilogy.

A. *Love Alone is Credible*, trans. David C. Schindler (San Francisco: Ignatius Press, 2005). This is not an easy book, but it serves as a programmatic and succinct statement of the thesis of the first part of the trilogy, the aesthetics.

B. *Engagment with God: The Drama of Christian Discipleship*, trans. R. J. Halliburton (San Francisco: Ignatius Press, 2008). This book does for the second part of the trilogy (the dramatics), what *Love Alone* does for the first.

C. *Explorations in Theology*, vol. 1, *Word Made Flesh* trans. A. V. Littledale and Alexander Dru (San Francisco: Ignatius Press, 1989). In keeping with my attempt to offer a shorter overview of each part of the trilogy, this collection of essays deals with the questions that will receive fuller treatment in the third part of the trilogy, the logic. I would recommend especially, "God Speaks as Man," and "Implications of the Word."

D. *In the Fullness of Faith: on the Centrality of the Distinctively Catholic*, trans. Graham Harrison (San Francisco: Ignatius Press, 1988). This is a great, little book where Balthasar shows how the so-called "Catholic and" is actually already part of the center of the faith. For instance, a proper understanding of faith entails the importance of works, or a proper understanding of Jesus Christ entails the role of Mary, and so on.

E. *Convergences: To the Source of the Christian*, trans. E. A. Nelson (San Francisco: Ignatius Press, 1984). A short and eminently readable work, this book offers a nice preview of Balthasar's biblical theology, coupled with his notion that, in the face of Protestant doubts, Catholics have to show how the seemingly peripheral elements of the Catholic faith are actually organic outgrowths of its center. This book and the book just listed (*In the Fullness of Faith*) would be a good place for a Protestant to begin reading his theology.

F. *Truth is Symphonic: Aspects of Christian Pluralism*, trans. Graham Harrison (San Francisco: Ignatius Press, 1987). In another readable book, Balthasar lays out his theory of truth while avoiding the extremes of fundamentalistic propositionalism on the one hand (false objectivism) and liberal relativism/agnosticism on the other (false subjectivism).

G. *Explorations in Theology*, vol. 4, *Spirit and Institution*, trans. Edward T. Oakes, S.J. (San Francisco: Ignatius Press, 1995). This volume in the *Explorations* series contains some demanding essays, but in the end serves as something akin to a "Balthasar reader." Here one encounters not only some of the central themes of Balthasar's ecclesiology, but also his eschatology.

II. SELECT SECONDARY SOURCES

A. Oakes, Edward. *Pattern of Redemption: The Theology of Hans Urs von Balthasar*. New York: Continuum, 1994. I think Oakes' book is still the most accessible, best overview of Balthasar's theology on the market. There may be better studies of Balthasar's theology, but they are not as readable nor as comprehensive.

B. Schindler, David ed. *Hans Urs von Balthasar: His Life and Work*. San Francisco: Ignatius Press, 1991. The title just about sums this book up. It remains one of the best collection of essays on Balthasar's thought in the English language.

C. Scola, Angelo. *Hans Urs von Balthsar: A Theological Style*. Grand Rapids, MI: Eerdmans, 1995. A demanding but excellent work that gets to the heart of Balthasar's theology in very few pages.

D. Riches, John. *The Analogy of Beauty: The Theology of Hans Urs von Balthasar*. Edinburgh: T&T Clark, 1986. This is a fine collection of essays dealing with most of the major areas of Balthasar's theology. Rowan Williams' essay on "Balthasar and Rahner" is practically worth the price of the book.

E. O'Hanlon, Gerard F. *The Immutability of God in the Theology of Hans Urs von Balthasar*. New York: Cambridge University Press, 1990. A demanding look at one aspect of Balthasar's thought which really grants entryway into its entirety.

F. Schindler, David C. *The Dramatic Structure of Truth: A Philosophical Investigation*. New York: Fordham University Press, 2004). An excellent and clearly written introduction to Balthasar's philosophy.

G. Healy, Nicholas J. *The Eschatology of Hans Urs von Balthasar: Being as Communion*. Oxford: Oxford University Press, 2005. A demanding and succinct introduction to the thorniest aspects of Balthasar's thought: the analogy of being, Christology, Trinitarian theology and eschatology.

H. Walker, Adrian J. "Love Alone: Hans Urs von Balthasar as a Master of Theological Renewal," *Communio: International Catholic Review*. Vol. 32, no. 3, Fall 2005, 517–39.

I. Of course there are many other fine studies in English on specific aspects of Balthasar's theology, but I have found the above list to be singularly helpful. There are also a number of fine articles to be found in the English language edition of *Communio: An International Catholic Review.*

INDEX